The Great Omission

Resolving Critical Issues for the Ministry of Healing and Deliverance

Forthcoming Publications

The Great Substitution by Dieter Mulitze
Toxic Waste of the Soul by Dieter Mulitze
Into the Heart of Deeper Love by Carsten Pellmann
The Healing Power of Deeper Love by Carsten Pellmann

Deeper Love Ministries Books are written by the Spiritual Directors of Deeper Love Ministries, Winnipeg, Manitoba, to help advance spiritual wholeness, healing, and growth in individuals, based on the model and ministry of Jesus Christ. The ministry Web site is **www.deeperlove.ca**.

DIETER MULITZE

The Great OMISSION

Resolving Critical Issues for the Ministry of Healing and Deliverance

Essence PUBLISHING

Belleville, Ontario, Canada

The Great Omission

Copyright © 2001, Dieter K. Mulitze

All Rights Reserved. No part of this publication may be reproduced, stored in a retrieval system or transmitted in any form or by any means—electronic, mechanical, photocopy, recording or any other— except for brief quotations in printed reviews, without the prior permission of the author.

All Scripture quotations, unless otherwise specified, are from *The Holy Bible, New International Version*. Copyright © 1973, 1978, 1984 International Bible Society. Used by permission of Zondervan Publishing House. All rights reserved.

ISBN: 1-55306-315-5

Essence Publishing is a Christian Book Publisher dedicated to furthering the work of Christ through the written word. For more information, contact: 44 Moira Street West, Belleville, Ontario, Canada K8P 1S3.
Phone: 1-800-238-6376. Fax: (613) 962-3055.
E-mail: info@essencegroup.com
Internet: www.essencegroup.com

Printed in Canada
by
Essence PUBLISHING

*To my wife, Ellen,
and my daughter, Karissa*

Table of Contents

Acknowledgements 9
Foreword 11
Introduction 17

   1. The Ministry of Jesus 27

   2. Compassion Deficit Disorder. 39

   3. Re-Thinking The Great Commission 55

   4. The Ministry of Wholeness In The Church 77

   5. Vanishing Spiritual Gifts?. 115

   6. Unmasking Cessationism. 133

   7. Spiritual Abuse: When Churches Wound 187

   8. Deliverance Ministry: Myth or Mandate? 229

   9. Conclusion 277

Bibliography 281
About the Author. 291

Acknowledgements

Foremost, I wish to acknowledge Ellen, my faithful wife over the years and now a partner in healing prayer. Without Ellen's support and encouragement, this book could not have been written.

Many thanks to Carsten Pellmann for encouragement, friendship, and seemingly countless hours of mutual sword sharpening. To Dietrich Desmarais, another close friend with a strong passion for healing prayer. And, of course, their wives, Linda Pellmann and Edith Desmarais, dear friends and part of the Deeper Love Ministries team.

Special thanks to all the precious brothers and sisters in Christ, who have shared their lives and their pain with me in experiencing the healing presence of Jesus.

The stories of people as recounted in this book have been written to safeguard the identity of the individuals involved. Names have been changed, along with some of the details.

To God be the glory!

 # Foreword

I suppose the first question might be, "Why should an Old Testament scholar be interested in this book?" It is fair to say that little in my tradition or my education prepared me for such an interest, and much would have discouraged such. But that is simply to say where I began.

I was nurtured in a circle that valued the gifting of the Spirit in the Church, but limited that gifting in ways that made the supernatural virtually disappear into the natural. Our prayer meetings often focussed on the sick among us, and we believed in the power of God to heal, but when healing did take place it was unexpected and difficult to explain.

My people were Bible students, and thus knew the prominent role healing had in the ministry of Jesus, together with the so-called "gifts of healing" in the writings of Paul. But although we sought to emulate the New Testament Church in many respects, it didn't occur to us that healing gifts were a part of the primitive Church that should still work our own day. Indeed, although we knew of those who claimed to have a "gift of healing," we associated such people with fringe groups rooted in questionable experience rather than solid biblical exegesis. More to the point, no-one I knew had such a gift, or indeed any gift that required a clear infusion of supernatural power as opposed to natural talent.

When later I undertook theological studies, I learned that our own tradition was called "cessationist" (meaning that these kinds of gifts were intended to be temporary). Although I had been raised in what is known as the Dispensational tradition, my seminary teachers were often solidly Reformed, but there was no argument on the point in question. Both agreed that these so-called "sign gifts" had fulfilled their function in the days of the apostles, or ceased with the completion of Scripture.

As I began teaching the Bible myself, using the methods so painstakingly imparted, it became increasingly clear that the arguments against these gifts seemed inconsistent with the hermeneutical arguments themselves. The more I researched, the more evident it was that the New Testament writers expected life in the Church to reflect the ministry of its Lord. This obviously included "healing," along with preaching and teaching. But we didn't do this, and I found myself asking why?

Over time, I found some answers, initially in the community of biblical scholars who, though generally as remote from healing ministry as I, were almost universally uncomfortable with the exegetical and theological arguments that relegated spiritual gifts to the New Testament era. And since our focus was the faithful exposition of Scripture, it became increasingly difficult to ignore, or write out of the Bible, what was so prominent and even normative within it.

Only later did I begin to experience a different kind of Christianity, one in which spiritual gifting was haltingly, and sometimes even unconvincingly, put into practice. In the midst of what was a struggle to discover a more biblical reality, despite the smoke that sometimes got in our eyes, I recognised the fire of the Holy Spirit, and the presence of Jesus. What had long been an exegetical given was slowly becoming an experiential reality.

However, it was not in the context of this book that I met, and later teamed with, Dieter Mulitze. Dieter was a student in the theological college I led, and in later years that association led us to shared teaching ministry in a mission setting. Even then, little was exchanged about spiritual gifts, or healing as a ministry, though Dieter and his wife, Ellen, shared with my wife and me a number of common concerns for our families and our churches. We knew the Mulitzes as friends with a love for God, a heart of obedience to the gospel, and a passion to build up the people of God. But in those days we didn't speak much about healing. As one of his theological teachers, I had no trouble recognizing in Dieter the work of a meticulous and exacting (even scientific) Bible student. When he spoke about truth, I knew it had been thoroughly researched, as well as lived out. Hence, my interest when Dieter told me he was writing this book and my sense of honor when he asked if I might contribute a few words at the beginning.

Why, then, such a book? Is it really needed? Does it add to the discussion? Will it find an audience, and should it? And why would I recommend it to you, the reader?

The answer is simple, and compelling. The book claims to concern the nature of the gospel itself and what it means to be obedient to it, and thus to the Lord himself. If this is indeed the case, and it is difficult to avoid the conclusion that it is, none of us can be indifferent to what is being said. The author has clearly researched his subject, and concluded that there is a case to be made. It is, however, much more than a theological treatise; Dieter Mulitze has clearly read his textbooks, but he has also seen and heard things in a wide experience of ministry. These are the realities he feels compelled to share.

If Dieter is right in his claim of a widespread failure to understand and live out the gospel in the contemporary Church, the problem needs to be addressed, and addressed urgently. To fail to do so is to sit by while the Church and its witness is seriously impoverished by disobedience. The cry of alarm must be given, and the corrective prescribed. If, as he claims, the Church has committed the "Great Omission" in its failure to emphasize what Jesus taught and modeled, and if the implications of that omission are what he claims them to be, that in itself calls for a serious response. His contention is not that the true gospel is in any way inaccessible; indeed in the work of Christ and his Spirit it is everywhere present. Rather, we, the Church, have debased the coinage to the point where people now go elsewhere desperately seeking reality.

But what does this book contribute to the discussion? Those who know the field will be aware of a vast bibliography on spiritual gifts, the hows and whys, arguments pro and con, and manuals of all sorts. Why another book? Let me give a few answers.

The Great Omission is at once a didactic book (it teaches convincingly what Scripture and experience have shown), a hortatory book (it exhorts us to put into practice the whole counsel of God), and a devotional book (it draws us into a more complete relationship with Jesus, whose heart for the Church burns throughout the book). If ever there were a subject on which we need good teaching, compelling exhortation, and a warming of our cold hearts, this is it. And I was not disappointed.

Finally, let me share some of the qualities that make this book, for me, a "must read." You will see my biases here, but I think they are worth considering.

First, *The Great Omission* is thoroughly biblical. Its appeal is to Scripture, and its author combines a comprehensive grasp of the text with a sure hand in his exegetical skills and theological reading. This, I submit, is where such a book must begin.

Second, the biblical teaching of this book has been tested in the crucible of experience. Mulitze is no armchair theologian. From the opening words to the closing challenge, examples are drawn from the author's extensive work in healing prayer and its results. He knows what happens when theory is taken into the field. He has seen the fruits, and understands the dangers. And his readers are left in little doubt that what he is talking about makes a difference in people's lives.

Third, the book will appeal to those who, like the author, insist on rigorous scientific examination and logical argument. From its opening pages, despite their warm devotional tone, the book spares no effort to build a solid, scholarly, and logical case for the centrality, the importance, and the effectiveness of a biblical healing ministry. The same passion that cries out for the compassion of Jesus in healing is leveled against fuzzy thinking and unresearched conclusions.

Fourth, the book is practical. At the end of the day, Dieter is far less concerned to win an argument than he is to bring the Church into conformity with the gospel as taught and lived out by Jesus. Although the book presents a case for healing ministry rather than the steps to be taken in implementing such, the result is a challenge not only to how we think, but what we do. The gospel must be obeyed, not simply understood (indeed, the Hebrew mind would consider both the same!).

Finally, it must be acknowledged that this is a polemical work on a controversial subject. Much that has been written on the subject has generated more heat than light, and given the issues, this book will raise some temperatures. At times the polemic is sharp, though Dieter's arrows are never poisonous. Few readers will emerge neutral. In fact, the book leaves little room for neutrality, arguing that the issues are far too basic to faith for ambiguity.

I conclude with a word of personal testimony. I am among those who have long been convinced of the rightness in theory of Dieter Mulitze's position on spiritual gifts and healing prayer. But I have struggled with the reality, finding much to question amongst the practitioners and teachers. What has gripped me in reading this book is not simply its arguments; for I have long known that the case could be convincingly made from Scripture. Rather, I am left with a fresh and compelling picture of the heart of Jesus for those who suffer, and long to find the healing touch of the Saviour's hand. Dieter has taken us into the heart of Jesus for his Church, and wants to take the heart of the Church into Jesus. When all the arguments have been concluded, that is what this book is all about.

—Carl E. Armerding, Ph.D.,
Senior Research Fellow, The Oxford Centre for Mission Studies
Oxford, UK;
Director, Schloss Mittersill Study Centre
Mittersill, Austria

 Introduction

Real People with Real Pain

I have ministered healing prayer to many brothers and sisters in Christ, often living with immense and deep pain, both physical and emotional. At a healing prayer conference at a small, rural church, about eighty percent of the women had been sexually abused at least once in their lifetime. Unfortunately, for many long years they had silently carried the pain in their aching hearts. I know of Christians on psychiatric drugs, somewhat thankful for the relief from the drugs, but deep down in their hearts wondering why God is apparently not able to bring a healing and release from the driving force behind their depression, paranoia, phobia, schizophrenia, or whatever the label from psychiatry. Others lead lives of quite desperation in bondage to sexual sin or an addiction, often resigned to their situation after many attempts and strategies to gain release and freedom.

I know of a number of Christian couples who appeared to have lives of joy and commitment to Jesus, even sometimes with effective ministries, yet a sudden separation and divorce left many close friends somewhat stunned. In many of those cases it was later revealed that deep areas of woundedness on the part of one or both spouses had built up over time and finally sabotaged the marriage. I heard of one Christian man completely devastated when his Christian wife abruptly left him and their children, for another woman. Then, there are other Christians who have painful, recurring memories, with no understanding how to seek healing and release from Jesus. I once prayed with a lady at a healing conference who, with many tears, shared how there had been many suicides and accidents in her family. She was truly heartbroken and in desperate need of God. Then, there are whole families or individual Christians with various mental or physical illnesses, with no known cause established by the medical profession. They continue to suffer, still hoping that one day God will respond in a clear, tangible way to their prayers and the cry of their hearts.

Not all believers are enjoying an abundant life in Jesus. In fact, sometimes their situation is made worse by Christians who suggest that they must have sinned or failed, and thus they are burdened with guilt and shame. Churches which claim "victorious" Christian living tend to deny or minimize the real pain of Christians in their midst.

Marla's Story

I met Marla at a healing prayer service. After she had come forward with a friend, I asked her how I could pray for her. Without hesitation, she said that she was coping with suicidal tendencies, intense fears of abandonment, depression for many years, a lot of physical pain, trauma from a car accident, and frequent terror or panic attacks to the point that she could not live by herself any longer and was therefore living with a friend. She was desperate for help and under the care of a psychiatrist. She had received some prayer at her church and other places, and had also seen a Christian counselor who in the end said that she did not know how to help her. After sharing her needs with me, and realizing that the roots of her problems were many and deep, I looked straight at her and said that she had probably been analyzed and diagnosed many times, and what she really needed was the healing presence and power of Jesus brought into her precise places of need, her deepest wounds. She readily agreed, and I could see hope arise in her face. Since many other people had already come into her life, most with professional capabilities, and she was still not substantially helped, what could I offer her other than to bring her into the presence of Jesus, to know more of his healing presence and power? Any analytical cleverness on my part would not help her.

Since there was not enough time to minister effectively to her at the service she agreed to several more in-depth sessions later. At the first session, a prayer team partner and I just listened for about one hour. She bravely shared her life's story, how she had been rejected by her mother and sexually abused by her alcoholic father, an uncle, and a brother. In her journey she saw a massage therapist and counselor who unfortunately practiced a lot of New Age beliefs. This eventually caused a whole other set of problems for her. I was quite concerned for her since she had a gaunt look, with not much life, all the more reason for Jesus to come in his gentleness and power.

I realized that there were many inter-related issues, and sensed the Lord wanted us to pray through the rejection and abuse experiences first. The Lord came and gave relief and healing to her heart and spirit, and began to release her from shame, false guilt, fear, deeply rooted lies, and impurity. As we prayed, the Lord cut the many emotional and relational bondages that had imprisoned her mind and spirit. As the burdens were lifted, she felt lighter, and the countenance of her face began to change, especially after the second and third sessions.

Today Marla is living by herself—a major accomplishment. The terror attacks have ceased, most of her body pain has disappeared, the depression is conquered, and suicidal tendencies are gone. But most important, she experienced more of Jesus' love and healing presence. Some emotional pain remains, but part of the healing will come from constant affirmation and lots of hugs and caring relationships from others in the Body of Christ.

My Story

I, too, have experienced pain. While in my early twenties, less than two years as a Christian, I was diagnosed with cancer. In only two weeks my world changed from that of a university student to a cancer patient. I can vividly remember waking up the morning after the surgery, still feeling groggy from the anesthetic. The surgeon informed me that I had at most a ten percent chance of living. The only way I could begin to cope was to unreservedly put my life in Jesus' hands—whether I would be healed and live, or die, I belonged to Jesus. It was the assurance of eternal life that was the final solid ground for me as I spent the next few days in the hospital. The Lord's presence and reassurance sustained me. The head nurse came in on the second day and asked how I could be so cheerful since I was seriously ill. I replied that the reality of Jesus, my Lord and Savior, and the sure hope of eternal life were sustaining me no matter the outcome. I said that I had a strong sense that I would be healed; yet each day I just continued to trust in Jesus. After some silence, the head nurse left without a word. I prayed for her and the other staff, hoping that my witness would touch their lives. Although I was seriously ill, I fully realized that more serious still is the plight of those who do not know Jesus.

Why did I get cancer? No one really knows. Although I didn't fully realize it at the time, God was helping me to practice the presence of Jesus in the midst of suffering. I was jubilant when the doctors sensed that I was healed from the first spread of cancer. But my faith was tested even more when the cancer spread into my lungs. I can still vividly remember the oncologist showing me the X-ray, and pointing out how each of the many lesions would become a tumor. I know firsthand about struggling with cancer and sharing my faith with other patients in a cancer ward. In those days, I was unaware of healing prayer, much less of any church where this was practiced. Not being closely connected to a church and thus not having a pastor, I relied on my InterVarsity Christian Fellowship friends who were praying for me while I underwent two years of chemotherapy plus radiation treatment. In the end, Jesus healed me through medical means and intercessory prayer.

I have my own version of a "Damascus road" experience. While living in Syria on a post-doctoral appointment at an international agricultural research center, I was invited to interview for an assistant professorship position with the University of California. To begin my journey, I took a bus from Aleppo, where my family and I were living, to Damascus to catch my flight. Two hours into the trip, the bus came upon a column of Syrian military trucks. Not wanting to lose time, the bus driver pulled into the left lane. With lights flashing and the horn blaring, he forced all opposing traffic onto the shoulder of the highway. Everyone else seemed relaxed, but I was semi-horrified—that was a stunt no driver in Canada would ever contemplate! A few minutes later we approached a curve by a small bridge, with a bus suddenly in the other lane. A serious collision was inevitable. The other bus driver panicked such that his bus flipped perpendicular onto the highway, exploding into flames upon impact. Ahead of us was a literal wall of fire, and I was totally convinced I had only a few seconds to live. Would I experience all the pain upon impact, or die first and then be with the Lord? I instinctively leaned forward and covered my face with my hands in anticipation of flying glass. I prayed to Jesus, releasing my spirit to him, and for my wife and daughter, who I was sure I would never see again until heaven. Amazingly, in those seconds I was surrounded by such a solid peace, which I knew to be the presence of Jesus. The bus driver managed to avoid a direct head-on collision, so we ended up in the ditch, and didn't even roll! All ten or so people in the other bus were killed, while those ahead of me in the bus were badly cut and bleeding. The Syrian military had the accident site sealed off within minutes, whereas the ambulance from nearby Homs came almost an hour later. I suffered only some glass in my scalp, and minor cuts. The Lord sustained me in the midst of all the blood and screaming passengers in the bus. I spent a good hour on the Damascus highway shivering in the cool, Syrian night, talking with some fellow passengers, East German engineers on their way back to East Berlin. What a place to practice my German! I finally arrived in California, had the interview, but in the end the position was re-classified. I will never forget that night as long as I live.

Some years later, while back in Canada, I began to desire more of God, especially to deal with some deep emotional and personal issues. I had all the biblical knowledge I could use, but for some reason or reasons that I could not fathom, it was not sufficient. In time, the Lord answered my prayer, surprising me in a way I could never have imagined. Now the Lord healed me on the inside, dealing with past pain and bondage. Finally the gospel was penetrating my whole being, including my heart. Now I can see how the Lord used other people and circumstances for me to experience more of his healing and transforming presence. Trained as a research scientist with an earned doctorate in quantitative genetics, and having spent many years developing computer software, this has not been an easy discovery for me. I have now come to realize that my Christian faith and experience was quite rationalistic and abstract. When one of my good IVCF friends from many years back heard that God was using me in the ministry of healing prayer, she was amazed and remarked that I was the last person she ever would have expected that God would use in such a ministry. But then, with God all things are possible! If someone would have told me years ago that I would one day be involved in the ministry of healing prayer, I would have said that they have "really lost it." But the Lord had other plans, and he has clearly called me into this ministry. The last number of years have been a remarkable journey, seeing Jesus heal and transform his loved ones in ways that I had never dreamed possible. This book recounts some of the stories of people truly touched and healed by Jesus in powerful and amazing ways.

Theological Turmoil

When the topics of "healing" and certainly "deliverance" come up, there is often much confusion in the Church. There is usually more heat than light in discussions, with strong and differing opinions over critical issues. Some Christians are quite skeptical and wary of spiritual healing, not encouraged in the least by "faith healers" and their apparent dubious practices and claims. Some Christians teach against receiving any medical attention or treatment at all, since they believe doing so signals a lack of faith. Other Christians strongly believe that modern medicine is quite sufficient and there is not much, if any, need for healing prayer or "spiritual healing." How then do we reconcile spiritual healing and modern medicine? Most Christians would agree to at least intercessory prayer for those who are ill. Are the Scriptures more or less silent on emotional healing, more focused on physical "organic" healing? Why doesn't God always heal? While all Christians would agree that churches should be safe places of nurture, healing, and edification, there is much talk about spiritual abuse. Is it for real? Is the "spirit of the Pharisees" found in the contemporary Church? If so, how do we recognize this for the safety of our souls? Do any illnesses have demonic sources? How Biblical is "deliverance ministry"? Can Christians in any way be demonized? Should we as disciples of Jesus ever engage in rebuking demons, or is faith, repentance, prayer, and "classical" spiritual warfare the true biblical answer?

A very fundamental question to all these debates is whether the ministry of healing prayer and deliverance are part of the Great Commission. How closely should the Church today follow the example of Jesus and the apostles in this type of ministry? Not a few evangelical Christians would challenge any such notions, arguing that some of the spiritual gifts ceased with the completion of the New Testament and the closing of the apostolic era. Some would even go so far as to claim that Christians with the "power" or "sign" gifts actually have mediumistic gifts and hence are influenced by evil spirits. In their view, faithful disciples of Jesus can readily omit the ministry of healing and deliverance, as modeled by Jesus and the apostles, from the Church's life and mission today. Meanwhile, others argue that such an omission is clearly wrong, and furthermore, that none of the gifts of the Spirit ever ceased. How does one navigate through this seeming mental minefield? Why do such seemingly simple issues from the Scriptures cause such strong doctrinal disagreements and ensuing theological turmoil?

These are not abstract, academic questions, since the pain that some of us deal with is certainly not abstract. These questions ultimately lurk behind the very real and personal questions often posed by real people with real pain. I will endeavor to bring answers to questions like the foregoing. In doing so, I will draw on true-life stories and testimonies of Christians who have experienced the healing and transforming power of Jesus. The names and some of the details of the individual's circumstances have been changed to guard their confidentiality.

To begin, we will turn our attention to Jesus, our model and perfect example in ministry.

Chapter One

The Ministry of Jesus

Helen's Healing

Helen was in bondage to a fear of death for as long as she could remember. In addition, it was difficult to establish relationships with others, including other women. She would always feel alone, and the feeling was intensified when in a crowd or gathering. We prayed with her for some time, waiting on the Lord for his direction. Just as I was about to give up, the Lord revealed to her that before she was born, there was an attempted abortion. That understanding, plus the healing presence of Jesus to deal with the fear that she felt from the womb onwards (Luke 1:41), brought a deep healing.

The Holy Spirit as counselor (John 14:16) then revealed the root of her feeling alone and abandoned. When she was only a few years old, her mother, out of annoyance and anger, shut her in a dark closet for several hours. As a small child, this had an understandable major impact. She could now clearly remember this long-forgotten painful event. It had so touched her emotions and inner being as a child that intense feelings of abandonment, aloneness, and rejection impacted her mind and spirit. Forgiveness to her mother had long been extended, so Jesus healed her from the power and pain of this past event in a way that was uniquely meaningful for her. To complete the healing, Jesus even revealed to her why her mother did such a thing. The Holy Spirit reminded her of things about her mother that she knew, but had not fully taken into account. This was not to rationalize the hurt and pain, but to reveal the full context of her mother's life. Helen was then able to let the incident go and receive complete healing.

Jesus knew exactly what to do. Most importantly for Helen, she encountered the same Jesus that she encountered when she came to first know him as Savior and Lord. The goal here was to be released from things of the past so that she could move ahead in the present with Jesus.

The "Magna Carta" of Jesus

The fourth chapter of Luke's Gospel records how Jesus, filled with the Spirit, was led into the wilderness to be tempted by the devil. After unsuccessfully tempting Jesus three times, the devil left him and in the power of the Spirit, Jesus returned to Galilee and went to Nazareth. Right at the beginning of his growing ministry, on a Sabbath, he went into a synagogue. On that day, the scroll of the prophet Isaiah was handed to him. He read the following:

> *The Spirit of the Lord is on me, because he has anointed me to preach good news to the poor. He has sent me to proclaim freedom for the prisoners and recovery of sight for the blind, to release the oppressed, to proclaim the year of the Lord's favor* (Luke 4:18-19).

Jesus then rolled up the scroll, gave it back to the attendant, and sat down. As everyone was looking at him, he said, "Today this scripture is fulfilled in your hearing" (Luke 4:21).

In Luke 4:18-19, based on Isaiah 61:1-2, Jesus defines the three major thrusts of his ministry: preaching (preach good news), healing (recovery of sight for the blind), and freedom (release the oppressed, year of the Lord's favor). As his ministry unfolds, it is clear that this means liberation from sin and all its consequences. By referring to Isaiah, Jesus identified himself as the Messiah, the suffering servant as portrayed in Isaiah 53 and onwards. Jesus did not read out, "and the day of vengeance of our God" (Isa. 61:2b), because that refers to the final judgment when Jesus returns a second time. The passage in Isaiah 61:2b continues:

> ...to comfort all who mourn, and provide for those who grieve in Zion—to bestow on them a crown of beauty instead of ashes, the oil of gladness instead of mourning, and a garment of praise instead of a spirit of despair (Isa. 61:2b-3a).

It also reads "He has sent me to bind up the brokenhearted...." The ministry of Jesus is a ministry of wholeness and personal transformation, from salvation to the healing of the whole person. This includes healing of heart and soul involving the emotions—mourning, grief, despair, and more. The Lord heals the brokenhearted (Ps. 147:3) and is close to them while also ministering to those crushed in spirit (Ps. 34:18). God is the Father of compassion and of all comfort (2 Cor. 1:3-4).

As Luke records how Jesus' ministry unfolds, the emphasis on healing and deliverance is quite pronounced. Jesus casts out a demon (Luke 4:35) from a man in a synagogue and heals Simon's mother-in-law by rebuking her fever (Luke 4:39). Then "...the people brought to Jesus all who had various kinds of sickness, and laying his hands on each one, he healed them. Moreover, demons came out of many people" (Luke 4:41), evidence of healing and deliverance. He healed a leper (Luke 5:13), "...and the power of the Lord was present for him to heal the sick" (Luke 5:17), and then he healed the paralytic (Luke 5:25). He healed a man's shriveled hand (Luke 6:10), the centurion's servant (Luke 7:10), and at Nain raised a widow's dead son (Luke 7:14). His ministry became so pronounced that crowds surrounded him, to touch him, and receive his healing power (Luke 7:18-19). Jesus delivered a demon-possessed man in the tombs (Luke 8:27), raised Jairus' daughter from the dead (Luke 8:42), healed a woman of her bleeding (Luke 8:44), healed a man with dropsy (Luke 14:2), healed the ten lepers (Luke 17:11), and the blind beggar on the road to Jericho (Luke 18:35). After the transfiguration, Jesus healed a boy suffering seizures and convulsions caused by an evil spirit (Luke 9:39).

His ministry gained such momentum that John the Baptist sent his disciples to ask whether Jesus was the one who was to come, or should they expect someone else (Luke 7:19). Jesus replied:

> "Go back and report to John what you have seen and heard: The blind receive sight, the lame walk, those who have leprosy are cured, the deaf hear, the dead are raised, and the good news is preached to the poor" (Luke 7:22).

Jesus pointed them back to Isaiah 29:18-21 and Isaiah 35:5-6, identifying himself as the fulfillment of the Old Testament hope as the Messiah with his healing ministry. Matthew also highlighted Jesus' healing ministry, how Jesus drove out spirits with a word and healed all the sick (Matt. 8:16). This fulfilled the prophecy that he would take upon himself our infirmities and carry our diseases (Isa. 53:4). He was not just communicating promises, words, concepts—but truth with power, healing, and life-restoring miracles witnessing to his presence and ministry. Jesus taught people about the Kingdom, and then *invited them to experience the presence and reality of the Kingdom*. The gospel of Jesus is more than just doctrine, since it has the power to make people whole. The Kingdom of God is much more than words, involving the power to *save and transform* (1 Cor. 4:20). Spiritual truth is combined with spiritual power.

Peter summarized the ministry of Jesus to Cornelius with:

> ... *how God anointed Jesus of Nazareth with the Holy Spirit and power, and how he went around doing good and healing all who were under the power of the devil, because God was with him* (Acts 10:38).

MacNutt made the following observation of Peter's summary:

> ...he sums up the entire public ministry of Jesus in terms of what he did rather than of what he said, for Jesus established the Kingdom of God through the power of healing as well as through preaching. The healing of Jesus, then, is central to the doctrine of the gospel. To deny this is, in effect, to deny the gospel—to change it from Good News into Good Advice which lacks the power to transform man into a new creation. In short, Jesus did not heal people to prove that he was God; he healed them because he was God (emphasis mine).[1]

Jesus as the Ultimate Model of Ministry

Jesus is our ultimate model of ministry, and thus we must first understand how he ministered. The ministry of the Church should be patterned after Jesus.

Anointing. An anointing from God was foundational for everything that Jesus accomplished and was required right at the beginning of his ministry.

Jesus apparently had no ministry of power until after his anointing by the Holy Spirit. He cast out no demon, he healed no sick person, he raised no dead, he calmed no storm nor fed the multitude miraculously until after his baptism in power by the Holy Spirit. Immediately following this anointing, Jesus began a ministry which was accompanied by extraordinary manifestations of power.[2]

The Spirit of the Lord anointed Jesus to preach (Luke 4:18). Jesus was anointed with the Holy Spirit and power (Acts 10:38, cf. Isa. 11:2).

Authority. Jesus taught with authority (Mark 1:21-28) and rebuked evil spirits with a command—a word of authority (Mark 1:27)—to the amazement of everyone. Jesus had authority to forgive sins when he said to the paralytic, "Get up and walk" (Mark 2:10). He even had authority over the wind and the waves that he rebuked with, "Quiet! Be still!" (Mark 4:39). In raising Jairus' daughter, Jesus had authority over death (Mark 5:21-24).

Power. Prior to the healing of the paralytic brought on a mat through the roof, "the power of the Lord was present for him to heal the sick" (Luke 5:17b). People were coming from all over Judea, Jerusalem, and from the coast of Tyre and Sidon, and "the people tried to touch him, because power was coming from him and healing them all" (Luke 6:17-19). A woman with a hemorrhage was healed by touching Jesus, whereupon Jesus acknowledged that someone had touched him because some power left him (Luke 8:43-48). Spiritual power was important in face of opposition from the kingdom of darkness and in the desire to extend the Kingdom of God. Jesus used his power to extend love. Jesus certainly had the spiritual gift of miraculous powers (1 Cor. 12:10,28) and miracles, and all the gifts of healings (1 Cor. 12:9).

Love. Jesus was so incredibly effective because he was moved by love and compassion as he encountered people. When a leper came and begged him on his knees for healing, Jesus was filled with compassion and even touched his hand (Mark 1:41), and healed him. Jesus had compassion on two blind men who asked for mercy and healing (Matt. 20:34), and they were healed. When Jesus entered the town of Nain, he met a funeral procession for the only son of a widow. Understandably, the mother was grieving and crying, without a husband and now not even a son to support her, and the family line in jeopardy. When Jesus saw the widow "his heart went out to her" and he told her to stop crying, whereupon he raised the son from the dead while in the coffin (Luke 7:11-15). Jesus didn't even ask her if he could do this, he just went ahead and brought forth life. Jesus had compassion on a crowd of people and then healed the sick (Matt. 14:14). Jesus also had compassion for people who were without caring leadership, harassed or helpless (Mark 6:34; Matt. 9:36), and who were hungry after days of listening to his teaching (Matt. 15:32). Love was at the heart of all that Jesus did (1 Cor. 13).

Discernment. Jesus could discern the truth in any situation, and fully exercised the spiritual gift of discernment. He knew when an evil spirit was present, or when there was no evil spirit involved. He could discern the true spiritual state of a person, as he did concerning Nathaniel (John 1:47), or the influence of Satan upon Peter (Matt. 16:23).

Wisdom and Knowledge. Jesus ministered healing and deliverance with wisdom, knowledge, and spiritual insight. He could always discern the true issues and the best means for the person needing healing. He knew when sin was an issue, so in healing the paralytic, he first said "Son, your sins are forgiven." Yet, sin was not always a factor in the illness or bondage—it wasn't for Peter's mother-in-law with a severe fever, or the man with a shriveled hand, or the man born blind, where Jesus expressly said neither he nor his parents had sinned (John 9:1-7). He knew when deliverance was the issue, as in the case of the demon-possessed man of the Gerasenes; the woman crippled by a spirit of infirmity (Luke 13:10-13), the boy with the epileptic seizures (Mark 9:14-29), and the man who could not talk (Matt. 9:32) because of a demon. But many times deliverance was not the issue or need at all, like for the ten lepers (Luke 17:11). He would at times ask diagnostic questions. To the father of the boy with an evil spirit, he asked, "How long has he been like this?" (Mark 9:21). Jesus often had a word of knowledge. He knew "in his spirit" what the Pharisees and the teachers of the law were thinking before anything was said (Mark 2:8; Luke 5:21; 6:8). In his encounter with the woman at the well, Jesus had a word of knowledge that the woman had five husbands and was not then living with a husband (John 4:17). Jesus had the spiritual gifts of the message of knowledge, the message of wisdom, and the ability to distinguish between spirits and the presence of spirits (1 Cor. 12:8,10). The Spirit of the Lord rested on Jesus with manifestations of wisdom, understanding, counsel, and knowledge (Isa. 11:2).

Truth. Jesus had a strong teaching and preaching ministry, and spoke the truth into the lives of people. His truth was a counter to the lies of Satan. In knowing the truth, people are set free from the bondage of lies (John 8:32). Jesus spoke the truth (John 5:19,24-25; 6:26, 32, 47, 53; 8:34, 45; 10:7; 12:24). To know Jesus personally is to know the truth (John 14:6). This is profoundly different from Greek thought, which understands truth as concepts and ideas that are apprehended primarily by logic and reason.

Obedience. Jesus had to know who, if, when, and how to heal. Jesus did not heal everyone, nor did he always heal as asked. He refused to be pressured by people or manipulated in any way. At the pool of Bethesda (John 5:1-5), where there were many disabled people, Jesus chose only one person for healing, and asked even that one if he wanted to be healed. It would appear almost unloving that he didn't offer healing to the others. Why did he not launch many healing crusades? How did he know which person to ask? When a Canaanite woman first asked to have her daughter delivered from a demon, falling at Jesus' feet and begging him to do so, at first he didn't even say a word (Matt. 15:23). He was not a "push-button machine," responding and healing by request. When Mary and Martha sent word that Lazarus was very sick, and implied that he should come soon, Jesus stayed where he was two more days (John 11:6). When some people brought a deaf-mute man to him, they requested that he lay hands on him (Mark 7:31-37), but instead he put his fingers in the man's ears, then spit and touched his tongue, thereby not doing what was asked. Sometimes he healed when he was not, strictly speaking, even asked, like raising the widow of Nain's son from the dead, and healing the man with the shriveled hand (Mark 3:1-6), and the crippled woman on the Sabbath (Luke 13:10-17). Jesus did exactly what the Father commanded him (John 14:31), and said only what the Father wanted him to say and even how to say it (John 13:49).

Faith. Jesus often healed through, or in cooperation with, the faith of the person to be healed, or of those who brought the person to him, or of those who petitioned on their behalf. For the woman with the hemorrhage (Mark 5:34), Jesus affirmed that it was her faith that healed her. With blind Bartimaeus (Mark 10:52), his faith healed him, and the two blind men were healed according to their faith (Matt. 9:27). Jairus just believed and his deceased daughter was healed (Luke 8:50). There was no mention of faith concerning Peter's mother-in-law and healing from her fever, or for the deliverance of a man with an evil spirit in the synagogue. The invalid at the pool at Bethesda (John 5:1-15) initially had no faith in Jesus, but rather faith in the curative powers of the water. Only after being healed and then grilled by the Pharisees did he know who Jesus was. Thus, his healing did not come from his faith in Jesus. Not only did Jesus have the gift of miraculous power, he also had the gift of faith (1 Cor. 12:9).

Prayer and relationship. How else could he discern—know what to say and do—if not in close communion with the Father? Jesus had a close, sinless relationship with the Father. Jesus had the same character as the Father—love, grace, truth, light, and more. Even though Jesus and the Father were one (John 10:30), Jesus prayed often and did only what the Father was doing. Jesus often went to a lonely place and prayed (Luke 5:16), or prayed early in the morning. Thus, how Jesus ministered, what he said and did, flowed out of his relationship with his Father.

Listening. Building on prayer and relationship, Jesus was the great listener, acutely observing what the Father was doing. Jesus always sought the will of his Father and did nothing of his own accord (John 5:30). Jesus did nothing by himself, but did only what he saw his Father doing because "whatever the Father does the Son does also" (John 5:19). Jesus only and always spoke just what the Father told him to (John 8:26,28), and was always under his Father's direct command in all that he said (John 12:49-50). Jesus knew exactly when to precisely do what the Father asked him to do (John 2:4; 7:6,8,30; 8:20). Jesus focused always on doing the Father's will, and not his, even when it was incredibly costly (Luke 22:42; Matt. 6:10). Jesus is seen in the Gospels as the Great Listener, always listening and waiting upon Father God.[3] This was absolutely central to everything he did, and determined the use of all his spiritual gifts, anointing, and empowering.

No consistent method. As Jesus knew the precise need, he ministered by various means for each situation. The ways he ministered allowed people to relate to him, to connect with him, and to be affirmed. The means were also sacramental as a channel of grace or a way to mediate the presence and power of God. Sometimes he touched only, sometimes he spoke only, sometimes he did both, and sometimes he did something else. For the healings by the seaside, where he healed many, all who had diseases pressed upon him to touch him (Mark 3:10). At Nazareth, he laid his hands on a few sick folk and healed them (Mark. 6:5). Sometimes he healed by word only. For the demoniac in the synagogue he said, "Be quiet, and come out of him!" (Mark 1:25). Sometimes he healed by touch and word. For Peter's mother-in-law, he rebuked the fever, took her hand and helped her get up (Mark 1:29-31). For the two blind men who asked for mercy, upon confessing their belief, he touched their eyes and said, "According to your faith will it be done to you" (Matt. 9:29). For the crippled woman healed on the Sabbath, he pronounced healing and put his hands on her (Luke 13:10-17). In a few instances he healed with saliva. In healing the deaf-mute, Jesus put his fingers into the deaf-mute's ears and spat and touched his tongue (Mark 7:33-34). There was no consistent method for all situations. *The healings revolved around his presence, not methods.*

Following Jesus as Our Model

Melanie had been gang-raped at age thirteen, date raped, and then married an alcoholic who abused her over many years. It was understandably difficult for her to share her story. As I listened, and began to empathize with her, I sensed the Lord telling me to begin by simply declaring what he thought of her. I looked straight at her and reassuringly told her that in spite of all this abuse, she was still his precious child, a daughter of Zion, a beloved member of the Body of Christ. Upon hearing this truth, she instantly wept with deep sobs. That began a deep release of much pain and shame, and was the beginning of significant healing for her. Following Jesus in this ministry is key. It is never about learning a method, but rather, following his direction.

In ministry, Jesus is our example and model. While ministry skill and knowledge are important, the issues of the heart are most foundational. The Lord cares more about our character than our charisma, analysis, or calculation. Jesus was so incredibly effective because, among other things, he was so incredibly compassionate. The next chapter is entirely devoted to love and compassion since it is so central and important.

Endnotes

[1] Francis MacNutt, *Healing* (Notre Dame: Ave Maria Press, 1974) p. 108.

[2] David Pytches, *Come Holy Spirit: Learning How To Minister In Power* (2nd ed. London: Hodder & Stoughton, 1995) p. 42.

[3] Klaus Bockmuehl, *Listening to the God Who Speaks* (Colorado Springs: Helmers & Howard, 1990) pp. 48-50.

Chapter Two

Compassion Deficit Disorder

A Startling Personal Revelation

Some years ago, as a deacon, I went with Shirley, a fellow deacon, to visit Mary who had requested ministry from our church. During the visit, Mary expressed many needs and concerns. Shirley took the lead in listening to and praying for Mary. On the way home, Shirley, who had an abundance of empathy and compassion, continued to discuss Mary's concerns and what she must be feeling at a deeper level. Upon returning home, I made myself a cup of tea, relaxed, and began to reflect on the evening. The more I reflected, the more disturbed I became. I was stunned to realize that my heart was quite cold and that I hadn't been particularly moved during that visit. Here I was, a lay leader in a church, with a noticeable *compassion deficit*. Convicted, I began to pray that the Lord would soften my heart and help me to connect with the emotions and pain of those around me. I have prayed this often, and the Lord has been merciful to increase my compassion and empathy, especially for the hurting and wounded.

A few days later I asked the Lord to show me some of the pain and woundedness of people in the city where I lived. That very day, as I was returning to my office after an errand downtown, a woman passed me on the sidewalk. Her head was down, with an anguished look on her face. She was trying not be noticed by anyone, with tears literally streaming down her face. That one glimpse was enough to remind me about the pain and emotional hurt in my city. In fact, that memory sort of haunts me. Over the years I've learned to appreciate, and learn from, believers who show great compassion. I used to think that knowledge and ministry skill were most important, but I now believe that one's capacity to truly love and show compassion is more important.

The Compassion of Jesus

Love is at the heart of the Kingdom of God, and Jesus' desire to heal was certainly motivated by his love and compassion. Jesus was moved by compassion as he ministered to people. When a leper came and begged him on his knees for healing, Jesus was filled with compassion and even touched his hand (Mark 1:41), and healed him. Jesus had compassion on two blind men who asked for mercy and healing (Matt. 20:34), and they were healed. When Jesus entered the town of Nain, he met a funeral procession for the only son of a widow. Understandably, the mother was grieving and crying, without a husband and now not even a son to support her, and the family line in jeopardy. When Jesus saw the widow "his heart went out to her," and then told her to stop crying, and raised the son from the dead while in the coffin (Luke 7:11-15). Jesus had compassion on a whole crowd of people, and then healed the sick (Matt. 14:14). Jesus also had compassion for people who were without caring leadership, harassed or helpless (Mark 6:34; Matt. 9:36), and who were hungry after days of listening to his teaching (Matt. 15:32).

The story of Lazarus in John 11 reveals much about Jesus' compassion. Lazarus of Bethany, the village of Mary and Martha, was sick (John 11:1-2). Lazarus was the brother of Mary, who poured perfume on the Lord and wiped his feet with her hair (John 12:2). They sent word to Jesus that one he loved was sick (John 11:3). The message did not include Lazarus' name—this must have been an exceptionally close relationship. There was no specific demand as to what to do and when, although it was an indirect plea for help. Jesus replied that the sickness would not end in death since it would be a means to glorify God's Son (John 11:4). We know that Lazarus will die, but that's not the final end, the conclusion. The glory will be seen in Jesus' miraculous power over death, which will stir up the Jews to plot Jesus' death, and initiate events that will lead Jesus to the cross and thus redemption for all people (John 11:45-53).

Jesus' love for Martha, her sister, and Lazarus is mentioned in John 11:5, supplementary to Jesus' acknowledged love for Lazarus (John 11:3). Why this apparent repetition? John emphasized Jesus' love so that his response of delaying his return by two days would not seem inconsiderate or unloving (John 11:6). Apparent inaction, delay—how could he do that when the one he loved was so seriously sick? Consider Martha and Mary, waiting for Jesus, and of course, Lazarus seriously ill, with Jesus now not showing up, not arriving, and nothing happening. What kind of love is this? Wouldn't one expect Jesus to immediately leave for Lazarus' home?

Upon Jesus' arrival (John 11:17), Lazarus had already been in the tomb for four days. Lazarus died soon after the messengers left Martha and Mary—a day to travel, two days of delay, and one day to arrive, equals four days. The four days is significant because in those days, there was a Jewish belief that "the soul stays near the grave for three days, hoping to be able to return to the body. But on the fourth day, it sees decomposition setting in and leaves it finally."[1] Jesus was first met by Martha and then Mary who came quickly when she heard that Jesus was asking for her (John 11:29). When Mary meets Jesus, she falls at his feet and says "Lord, if you had been here, my brother would not have died." Mary is definitely more emotional than her matter-of-fact sister. Her words show her belief that, had Jesus been there, Lazarus would have been healed, but no more is implied (John 11:33). "When Jesus saw her weeping, and the Jews who had come along with her were also weeping, he was deeply moved in spirit and troubled." Jesus went through a deep emotional experience in response to the tragedy of death, an apparent victory of the enemy, plus the apparent hopelessness and pain of those in the situation. Thinking then about Lazarus' death, he asked "Where have you laid him?" They told him to come and see (John 11:34).

The Greatest Male Spiritual Leader and Warrior Weeps

"Jesus wept" (John 11:35), is the shortest verse in the Bible. The Greek word used for "weeping," *dakruo* is found only here in the New Testament and means "to burst into tears," as a quiet weeping, in contrast to wailing with loud voices and distress, not unlike professional mourning of the times.[2] Even though Jesus knew Lazarus would be resurrected, he wept; he fully entered into their sorrow, their pain, their grief, and their sadness. He connected emotionally, without holding back, not inhibited by others.

Jesus as a male spiritual leader is our role model, our perfect example of ministry, the truly masculine man. Yet, as a mature spiritual leader, he wept openly for all to see. As they saw how Jesus wept, they acknowledged his love for Lazarus (John 11:36). The tears of Jesus become even more significant for us when we remember that Jesus is also the Lord of Lords and King of Kings, a strong warrior of the Kingdom of God standing against the kingdom of darkness. How much of a warrior is Jesus? Gordon Dalby wrote about how US Green Berets would define the ideal warrior:

> They cited loyalty, patience, intensity, calmness, compassion and will. They agreed that the true warrior knows himself, knows his limitations... Self-mastery, according to the Special Forces men, is a warrior's central motivation. He is always practicing, always seeking to hone his skills, so as to become the best possible instrument for accomplishing his mission. The warrior takes calculated risks and tests himself repeatedly. He believes in something greater than himself: a religion, a cause.[3]

Dalby goes on to show how Jesus fills the role of an ideal warrior to perfection.

> The gospel accounts reveal Jesus' courage, in returning to Jerusalem, where He knew the religious authorities wanted to eliminate Him; His righteousness, in turning from Satan's temptations; His fellowship, with his disciples; His discipline, in early morning prayer; His determination, even when rejected in his own home town; His strength, in casting out demons; His energy, in calling forth Lazarus from the tomb; His glory, in being baptized with the Father's blessing; His anger, against the temple money-changers; and His overcoming the enemy, in meeting death and rising victorious. And Jesus never killed anyone, nor destroyed anything. In fact, Jesus is the authentic warrior, in whom God has given us power to battle victoriously the struggles of this world.[4]

We need to reflect on Jesus' weeping in the context of the whole gospel where Jesus is the ideal warrior. In this account with Lazarus, Jesus is on his way to Jerusalem. He is walking right into the line of fire. Hence his clear courage, boldness and total loyalty to his Father's mission. Yet this ideal warrior Jesus, a true male spiritual leader, wept openly and was not afraid to display immense compassion and empathy.

The example of Jesus goes against our culture where "it's not cool for men to cry." One of my former pastors wept during a sermon out of deep concern for the lost. It was sad how some people interpreted that as weakness. *If we, especially men, are ashamed to cry, are we then ashamed of the example of Jesus?* After the stone was moved away, Jesus prayed to the Father, and called Lazarus forth. He came out of the tomb, grave clothes and all. By a word of authority, Jesus showed his power over death, and that he truly is the resurrection and the life.

The Story of Lazarus: A Personal Application

Apply the story of Lazarus to yourself; make it real in your heart. Prayerfully reflect on the following points.

Jesus loves you, even if it appears he's not arriving on the scene, or you think he's delaying. We know very little about Lazarus—he wasn't a disciple, an accomplished person—he just happened to be Mary and Martha's brother. He just happened to be there, and Jesus loved him. Same with you and I; we're just here, and Jesus loves us—no requirements. Maybe we've all been there, in the midst of our own pain and sorrow, and we say to ourselves "where is my Jesus?" As Jesus loved Lazarus, Martha, and Mary, so he loves you.

Jesus knows your pain and your hurt, past and present, and he can fully connect with it. Jesus confronted Saul with these words: "Saul, Saul, why do you persecute me?" (Acts 9:4). Paul said "Who are you Lord?" Jesus said, "I am Jesus, who you are persecuting." Paul did not physically hurt Jesus, but when anyone hurts a Christian who is a part of the Body of Christ, Jesus himself feels it. When you hurt, or are persecuted, never forget that Jesus also feels it. Jesus is not a remote Savior and Lord seated far away on the throne of heaven. "Jesus is one with us in our need; he feels our pain; he lives our experience from the inside; his tears at that moment truly express the emotion of his heart."[5]

Jesus has wept with you. Is this the Jesus that you know? I have often prayed with people in the healing of pain from memories. In some cases, Jesus appeared to them in the memory, weeping with them in the situation. That has always been very moving and healing.

Your tears and your sorrow especially move Jesus as you come to him. It was Mary who fell at his feet and wept; Martha did not. It was at Mary's presence that Jesus was moved and then wept. The text also emphasizes that it was Mary who anointed Jesus with oil, and with her own tears—she obviously had a deep, emotional attachment to Jesus. So we should not hold back our tears, for Jesus will certainly be ever present. Can you imagine Jesus standing in front of you, seeing you, looking down to you, and weeping with you? Is this the Jesus that you know?

You may experience pain and suffering, even as Jesus loves you. Jesus loved Lazarus, yet Lazarus fell ill and actually died. Mary and Martha did grieve, as part of Jesus' larger redemptive mission. But again, he is present and identifies completely with us.

There is no waste in your suffering and pain. Lazarus' death in the end was used to glorify God, to point to Jesus as the resurrection and life. Why did God allow cancer in my life? Among other things, I was able to witness to people in a cancer ward and the experience has made me really appreciate life and health and strengthened my desire to live for Jesus alone. Is this the Jesus you know, who would actually weep with you plus redeem your suffering?

How intense can Jesus' compassion be for each of us? On some occasions, I've been on healing prayer teams with women who can identify with the pain and sorrow of the person being prayed for. They actually felt it in their abdomen—it can be really intense. This is actually quite biblical. One key Greek word used for compassion is *splanchnizomai*, and originally meant, "the inward parts of sacrificial animals" (*splanchna*), then, also human inward parts (bowels, liver, kidney), which are the place of natural passions.[6] In the New Testament, *splanchnizomai* very much relates to the idea of mercy. It describes the attitude of Jesus and the actions of key persons at turning points in three parables.[7] *Splanchnizomai* describes the merciful master who canceled his servant's debt, upon seeing his servant on his knees before him, pleading (Matt. 18:27). The word describes the father's heart attitude—"filled with compassion"—upon seeing, in the distance, his returning prodigal son (Luke 15:10). To note the intensity of feelings from *splanchnizomai*, it is also used to describe the anger of the master who delivered the unmerciful servant over to jailers for torture (Matt. 18:34), and concerning the prodigal son over his older brother's anger (Luke 15:28). The word conveys strong intensity of feeling, of intense compassion, or in a few cases actually anger. The feelings and emotions of Jesus were very intense and deep as he encountered human need and sickness.

Compassion, Wombs, and Father God

What about the compassion of Father God? When you think of him, are you tempted to focus on smoke, fire, wrath, judgment, and a consuming fire? Remember that Jesus is a perfect representation of Father God. In John 14:6-7, Jesus declares himself as the way to the Father, telling Philip that as he knows Jesus, he knows the Father. Philip said, "Lord, show us the Father and that will be enough for us" (John 14:8). Jesus answered, "Don't you know me, Philip, even after I have been among you such a long time? Anyone who has seen me, has seen the Father" (John 14:9). The Son is the "radiance of God's glory and the exact representation of his being... " (Heb. 1:3). So the compassion, the gentleness, the tenderness of Jesus is totally true of Father God.

The Old Testament uses four different words for compassion, three of which come from the same root word as for womb (*rehem*), not unlike other cognate languages in the Ancient Near East that show a connection between the womb and compassion.[8] The word for compassion (*raham*) is used by itself and in the plural (*rahamim*) and in another form. Deuteronomy 30:3 uses *raham* where, if you obey God, he will bless you and "will have compassion upon you" as a translation for "a womb upon you." So, the way a woman feels about her child in the womb, is the way God feels about us—tender, protective, nurturing, gentle, loving, and more.[9] This means that Father God also has maternal, motherly, and deeply gentle feelings towards those he loves. Can you grasp the significance of this? *Rachum*, "full of compassion," is used in all the verses in the Psalms. God the Father redeems lives from the pit and then crowns them with love and compassion (Ps. 103:4). To those who fear him, he will have compassion just as a father has compassion on his children (Ps. 103:13). The Lord God is full of great compassion (Ps. 116:5; 119:156), and extends it to all of his creatures (Ps. 145:9). The Lord desires to extend grace and compassion to his people (Isaiah 30:18), whether in provision (Isaiah 49:10), affliction (Isaiah 49:13; 51:3), or with deep compassion calling his people back after judgment (Isaiah 54:7). Truly, God the Father shows compassion and love alongside all his other attributes and actions.

Modeling Jesus' Compassion In the Church

As Jesus modeled compassion and love that resulted in healing, we should do likewise. Healing, driven by love and compassion, must be on the Church's agenda as it was on Jesus' agenda. We must enter into the compassion of Jesus. How much compassion do we show in Church life? How often are our decisions affected by the hurt and pain of those around us? How often are our hearts moved and troubled by the deep healing need of others? What are we moved and troubled by, if not the needs for healing and deliverance? Are we moved more by the TSE, Dow Jones, NASDAQ, and S&P 500 than the needs of people around us? What is the true index of our hearts? The Scriptures command us to authentically, with sincere love (Rom. 12:9), identify with the full range of emotions of those around us—to rejoice with those who rejoice and to mourn with those who mourn (Rom. 12:15). Paul served the Lord with great humility and tears (Acts 20:19), and wrote to the Corinthians out of great distress and anguished heart, and with many tears (2 Cor. 2:4). As God shows compassion and comfort (2 Cor. 1:3), the Church should show tenderness and compassion (Phil. 2:1) and indeed clothe herself in compassion, kindness, humility, gentleness, and patience (Col. 3:12). We must be tenderhearted (*eusplanchnos*) with one another (Eph. 4:32; 1 Pet. 3:8), among other Christian virtues. Joel expected the priests, as leaders, to weep as part of their contrition before the Lord (Joel 2:15). Nehemiah, hearing about the disgraceful and desperate situation of Jerusalem and the ruins, sat down and wept (Neh. 1:4). How often do we weep or have a deep emotional response for the ruined lives we encounter? If love and compassion operate in our hearts and thus in our churches, then we will be moved to seek the healing of our brothers and sisters in Christ as Jesus consistently modeled.

We must guard our hearts (Ps. 4:23) that determine our passion and compassion. Our hearts must be pure (Ps. 24:2; Matt. 5:8) and undivided (Ps. 86:11). The heart is the heart of the matter. *If there is no or little passion for the lost, there is not much evangelism. If there is no or little compassion for the hurting, there is not much healing.* Do the same things that move God's heart move our hearts? What moves our hearts, or your heart? Do we notice the pain and hurt of those around us, or is that lost in the machinery of Church life? Jesus himself wept—how often do you see church leaders weep over the pain and sorrow of those in their church, let alone weep for those who are lost and perishing? What would happen if they did?

When I lived in Morocco, North Africa, I remember a missionary to the Muslims telling me of his flight into Casablanca as he was beginning his assignment in Morocco. As his plane started to descend to the Mohammed V airport, he suddenly and inexplicably began to experience pain in his kidneys. The pain became progressively intense, almost excruciating, before landing. Exactly when the plane landed, the pain totally disappeared and the Lord spoke to him saying, "This is the intensity by which I love the Moroccans." He never, ever forgot those words, especially when he was confronted with difficult and uncomfortable situations and people in Morocco.

I was at a church conference where the speaker was instructed by the Lord to pray for the release of true passion and true tears for the lost. As he prayed, immediately some one hundred or so people started to wail very loudly, with many tears. The presence of God was unmistakable. I have often enough heard people cry very deeply, but this was something else—so intense, so real. This gave me another picture of the heart of God for the lost and hurting. Do we have more than enough information, knowledge, resources, and skill in the Church, but remain deficient in what's most important—compassion and love? Jesus appeared to be more concerned about hardness of heart than skill and knowledge, as important as they are. Compassion and Godly passion, coming from soft hearts, must be molded in God's desires and in obedience to him. Regarding evangelism, Edwards wrote that since passion is insufficient, churches use programs to compensate or substitute for it:

> Today we run our training courses in evangelism, telling people just what to say and how to present the gospel. These are all very necessary simply because we have no passion for evangelism.[10]

Dispositions of the heart cannot be manufactured.

There is no shame in experiencing or exhibiting the emotions of God the Father and his Son. A revealing exercise for any church might be for its leaders to spend time together in listening prayer to hear from the Father how much pain and sorrow is in their congregation, and also of those who are outside the Church. How much does it bother us that it seems so easy for people to perish without Jesus?

Jesus wept—are we ashamed to follow his example? The Church is often too preoccupied with skills, information, knowledge, and programs. Jesus was preoccupied with love and compassion. Mother Theresa once said, "It is better to do small things with great love, than great things with small love." The world values IQ—Intelligence Quotient—the higher the score, the better. I wonder if Jesus values another IQ—the *Indifference* Quotient—the smaller the score, the less the indifference to people and their pain and thus the greater the love. Will the world be more challenged by our knowledge or our love?

If God was a psychiatrist, I expect that He would label the systematic lack of true compassion as *Compassion Deficit Disorder.* There would be Type I to Type IV Compassion Deficit Disorder.

Type I is typical of those who have some level of compassion, but are moved to do very little about it. Type IV would be fore those who have hardened hearts that are almost totally insensitive to the hurts and wounds of others, and are moved only to superficial action. Might there be whole churches or church leaders with Type I to Type IV Compassion Deficit Disorder?

We can have great charismatic and spiritual experiences, both individually and corporately, but if we do not have love, we have nothing (1 Cor. 13:2-3). Nothing is nothing. I once read the true story of a Christian woman dying of cancer. Many in the church interceded, with no apparent change. Then the Lord convicted the pastor, instructing him and others in the church to visit the family, bless them, and show tangible love. They did so with cooked meals and caring visits, and she was totally healed in a few days. We must not overlook the power of love.

Jesus was profoundly effective because, among other things, in his compassion he knew the power of love. Modern medicine and psychotherapy are now finally beginning to appreciate what Jesus simply and clearly taught and modeled over two thousand years ago. Hart, citing the renowned psychotherapist Karl Menninger, wrote:

> Karl Menninger, after decades of work in psychotherapy, lays aside all learned talk of psychic maladies and of therapeutic techniques, and utters one simple overarching truth: It is unlove that makes people unwell, and it is love and love alone that can make them well again. His contention is buttressed by more general studies and surveys, in which it has been shown that those therapists are most successful in bringing health back to their clients who are best able to convey love... This explains in part why some psychotherapists seem to do so little for people even after

years of appointments, and some complete amateurs are able to make a significant difference in a short time.[11]

As we grow in true compassion and love, we become more effective for the Kingdom of God. While knowledge and skill in ministry must not be devalued, it is important to have the same priority that Jesus did. *He accomplished much because he loved much and obeyed always.* Since love and compassion are so important as repeatedly emphasized by Jesus and taught often throughout the New Testament, the potential for healing in the Church is greater than often realized. I believe that the teachings of Jesus, appearing simple at times, have a depth and profundity that often escapes us.

Concerning the vital connection between compassion and healing prayer, Jack Deere wrote:

> I frequently meet people who are enthusiastic about praying for the sick. They devote a significant amount of their time each week to praying for hurting people. But some of them see very little healing taking place. After talking with them for a little while, it is not difficult to see why they have so little success. Often their primary motivation in praying for the sick is to see something exciting, something supernatural, or to prove to their theological opponents that God does heal after all. These are not New Testament motivations for healing. God is not in the business of gratifying our desires for excitement nor in helping some of his children in winning arguments over others. He is in the compassion business. To the degree that you can enter into his compassion for the sick and the hurting, you can be a vessel through which the healing power of Jesus can flow. If you really want to be used in a healing ministry, ask your heavenly Father to let you feel his compassion for the hurting.[12]

I know of one pastor who prays with people and can often indicate the exact emotion, and its degree, that the person receiving ministry will soon feel. There is much to learn in deeply identifying with the wounds and pain of our brothers and sisters in Christ.

When Jesus revealed the new heaven and the new earth to the Apostle John, he announced,

> *Now the dwelling of God is with men, and he will live with them. They will be his people, and God himself will be with them and be their God. He will wipe every tear from their eyes. There will be no more death or mourning or crying or pain, for the old order of things has passed away* (Rev. 21:3-4).

It is significant that as God describes the new order of things and the future dwelling of his people with himself, that he focuses on the pain, hurt, woundedness, bondages, and all consequences of sin (tears, death, mourning, crying, pain). God is very much aware of the hurt and woundedness in this world, the very things that are addressed by Jesus' ministry of healing and deliverance. If such concerns mirror the heart of God from the beginning of creation (Gen. 6:6), through salvation history, and to the end of all things, then those concerns should be our concerns.

The cry of people's hearts, the pain in their inner being, are not unnoticed or neglected by God the Father and God the Son. No tears are wasted in the presence of God, no sorrow lost in the economy of God, no life wasted in the face of God.

Endnotes

[1] Leon Morris, *The Gospel According to John*. Revised edition. The New International Commentary on the New Testament. (Grand Rapids: Eerdmans, 1995) p. 485.

[2] Morris, p. 495.

3 Gordon Dalby, *Healing The Masculine Soul* (Milton Keynes: Word Publishing, 1988) p. 122.

4 Dalby, p. 125.

5 Bruce Milne, *The Message of John. Here is your King!* (Downer's Grove: InterVarsity Press, 1993) p. 164.

6 H.H. Esser, "Mercy—Splanchna" in *The New International Dictionary of New Testament Theology, Vol. 2* (Grand Rapids: Zondervan, 1976) pp. 599-600.

7 Esser, p. 599.

8 M. Butterworth, in Willem A. VanGemeren (ed.), *The New International Dictionary of Old Testament Theology & Exegesis Volume 3* (Grand Rapids: Zondervan, 1995) pp. 1093-1095.

9 Jack Deere, *Surprised By The Power Of The Spirit* (Grand Rapids: Zondervan Publishing House, 1993) p. 119.

10 Brian H. Edwards, *Revival! A People Saturated With God* (Darlington: Evangelical Press, 1990) p. 152.

11 Thomas N. Hart, *The Art of Christian Listening* (New York: Paulist Press, 1980) p. 18.

12 Deere, pp. 120-121.

Chapter Three

Re-Thinking the Great Commission

More Than Crusades and Missionaries

There are times when something may be so familiar that one never investigates further. Many Christians have frequently heard about the Great Commission. It's assumed everyone knows what it's all about. We readily think of missionaries going off to Africa, and all manner of evangelistic crusades, witnessing, maybe even apologetics. This is what I thought for decades. Certainly this is important, since the gospel must be preached and the world introduced to Christ. But what if there is more to the Great Commission? What if bringing people to Christ is not even the main emphasis? Let's take another look at this all too familiar passage—Matthew 28:18-20:

> *Then Jesus came to them and said, "All authority in heaven and on earth has been given to me. Therefore go and make disciples of all nations, baptizing them in the name of the Father and of the Son and of the Holy Spirit, and teaching them to obey everything I have commanded you. And surely I am with you always, to the very end of the age."*

Jesus had authority over all people (John 17:2), sin (Matt. 9:6), death (Mark 5:21-24), sickness (Matt. 8:2-4), evil spirits (Mark 1:27; 5:1-20), the Sabbath (Mark 3:1-6), even creation (Mark 4:37-41), and more. No one taught like Jesus did, with authority (Mark 1:22). Jesus modeled the authority and power to extend the Kingdom of his Father. Therefore, having all authority in heaven and on earth (Daniel 7:14), he could command his disciples and delegate that authority.

The Great Commission is a disciple-making commission, since the disciples were clearly commanded to make more disciples, and from all nations or ethnic groupings. How is this done? First of all, to preach the gospel so that people will come to faith in Jesus, repent of their sins (Acts 2:38), and become connected to the Body of Christ by baptism (Acts 11:16), confessing Jesus as Lord and Savior. This is clearly Trinitarian, involving the Holy Spirit, the Father, and the Son. But this is only the beginning, since the Great Commission goes beyond evangelism and witnessing. Jesus himself defines the next more involved stage of discipleship as *"teaching them to obey everything I have commanded you."* Jesus made it clear, we are to obey everything he *commanded* his disciples. The question then becomes, what all did Jesus command his disciples to do? In following acknowledged principles of biblical interpretation, considering the immediate context we should ask: what did this mean to the eleven disciples as Jesus spoke to them on the mountain in Galilee?

From Matthew's Gospel, this must surely include Jesus' teaching and commands from the Sermon on the Mount. After the Beatitudes (Matt. 5:2-11), Jesus commanded his disciples to be true witnesses (Acts 1:8) such that their light shines before men and they praise God the Father in heaven (Matt. 5:14-16). Life in and for the Kingdom of God would demand serious discipleship, including upholding the law and the prophets (Matt. 5:17-20) with a righteousness that exceeds that of the Pharisees and the teachers of the law. Disciples must control negative emotions like anger in their hearts (Matt. 5:21-22), maintain right relationships (Matt. 5:23-26), avoid adultery in their hearts or marriages (Matt. 5:27-32), speak with complete honesty and integrity (Matt. 5:33-37), not always press their rights (Matt. 5:38-42), love their enemies (Matt. 5:43-48), avoid outward religious performance and hypocrisy (Matt. 6:1-16), avoid idolatry (Matt. 6:19-24), not worry for life's provisions (Matt. 6:25-34), judge righteously (Matt. 7:1-5), be careful when sharing deep spiritual truths (Matt. 7:6), ask in dependence all things from the Father who gives generously (Matt. 7:7-12), avoid religious systems in favour of Jesus' life in the Kingdom (Matt. 7:13-14), and discern and watch out for false prophets (Matt. 7:15-20).

From John's Gospel, we note a very key and central command of Jesus to his disciples: "love one another as I have loved you. By this all men will know that you are my disciples, if you have love one for another" (John 13:34). This too is part of the Great Commission, and is so important that Paul (1 Cor. 13; Col. 3:5-17) and James (James 3:13-4:17) gave it serious attention. When Christians cannot love one another, the gospel is hindered and the world will not believe that they are truly disciples of Jesus. Fulfilling the Great Commission has *two* sides—the positive proclamation of the gospel by the Church and the lives of its members plus the minimization of any negative counter-witness from the Church. To the extent that any church has disunity, strife, and lack of love, it is counter-productive for the Great Commission. Discipleship involves not hindering the gospel (1 Cor. 9:12), ensuring no one can malign the Word of God (Titus 2:5), and making the teaching of God attractive by how we live

(Titus 2:10). Christians study the biblical text while the world studies the life text of Christians. Jesus also commanded the disciples to remain or abide in him (John 15:1-7) and bear much fruit—fruit that will last. Jesus knew that actions speak louder than words. As disciples, all of our effort for Jesus comes directly from our union and communion with him.

But there is still more that the disciples would clearly have understood as being part of what Jesus had commanded them. Matthew records how Jesus, early in his ministry, preached the good news of the Kingdom, and healed every sickness and disease, including those with seizures, and demonic oppression (Matt. 4:23-24). In the chapter *"The Ministry of Jesus,"* we saw how much attention and importance Luke gave to the ministry of healing and deliverance of Jesus. Matthew then made it very clear that this was a major part of the ministry of Jesus in writing how "Jesus went through all the towns and villages, teaching in their synagogues, preaching the good news of the Kingdom and healing every disease and sickness" (Matt. 9:35). In the gospel of Mark, a full forty-seven per cent of the text covers healing and deliverance accounts, when you exclude the crucifixion and resurrection narratives.[1]

Jesus said that the harvest is plentiful, but the workers are few, and so the disciples should pray that the Lord would send out workers into the harvest field (Matt. 9:37-38). What did he then do? He commanded the twelve disciples to do what he had been modeling all along. He gave them authority to drive out evil spirits and to heal every disease and sickness (Matt. 10:1). He commanded them to go only to the lost sheep of Israel, to preach that the Kingdom of heaven is near, to heal the sick, raise the dead, cleanse those with leprosy, and drive out demons (Matt. 10:6-8) among other instructions (Matt. 10:9-42) for the mission's conduct. This was essentially a carbon copy of his ministry. Working in the harvest field, then, includes the ministry of healing and deliverance. When John the Baptist sent his disciples to Jesus to inquire whether Jesus was the Messiah, he replied in terms of his healing and preaching ministry (Matt. 11:2-5). Not only did Jesus command his disciples to heal and deliver, it was quite clear that this was the expectation of the disciples from the people in that day. In Mark's Gospel, after the transfiguration, a father expected and asked the disciples to drive a demon from his son (Mark 10:17-18). Jesus then commanded a deaf and mute spirit to leave the boy (Matt. 10:26-29). It was clearly understood in those days that a disciple should do just as the master.

Luke's Gospel shows the same pattern. Jesus healed and delivered many people, and then he commanded the disciples to do what he did. He gave them power and authority to "drive out all demons and to cure diseases" (Luke 9:2). He later appointed seventy-two others, who obviously were not the disciples, to heal the sick and preach the good news of the Kingdom (Luke 10:1,9). This clearly involved rebuking demons (Luke 10:17), for which Jesus had given them authority and the promise of protection (Luke 10:19).

It becomes very clear, then, that the disciples would have understood that the ministry of healing and deliverance, which Jesus had modeled and already commanded them to do, would be an integral part of the Great Commission. They would certainly have understood this as part of "everything I have commanded you," since it was obviously such a major part of Jesus' ministry. A clear and straightforward reading of the Gospels with the basic rules of biblical interpretation makes this an inescapable realization. The Great Commission applies to making disciples in all nations, and thus extends borders beyond the nation of Israel (Matt. 10:6). The Great Commission is as much a healing and deliverance commission as an evangelization commission. Thus every church should have a ministry of healing and deliverance as well as gospel preaching and evangelism among any other ministries.

To be clear about terms, what is evangelism? Although this may sound like heresy, evangelism is not winning converts or bringing people to Christ, even though that *is* a desired objective. Evangelism is the proclamation of the good news of Christ, whether received and believed or not, and irrespective of any method. "If we want to be biblically accurate, we must insist that the essence of evangelism lies in the faithful proclamation of the gospel."[2] The actual conversion is part of the Holy Spirit's ministry of convicting the world of sin and righteousness (John 16:8). Christians are called to faithful witness, proclamation of the good news, and discipleship.

Getting Beyond Snake Handling

Mark's version of the Great Commission has some different emphases when compared to Matthew's version. But is it a part of the Word of God? Scholars do not agree whether these verses, part of the "longer ending" (Mark 16:9-20), really belong to the Gospel of Mark. The otherwise shorter and abrupt ending, "...they were afraid" (Mark 16:8) seems unnatural for a gospel of good news. Furthermore, it is entirely possible that the original fragile papyrus roll was damaged so that the last few inches, and hence the last verses, were torn off and lost, accounting for the omission in the earlier manuscripts.[3] Some scholars contest these verses, since the vocabulary, style, and theological content are unlike the rest of Mark's writing. While this is an important consideration from the viewpoint of textual and linguistic criticism, this is not as much a concern as many would believe. The Great Commission, as recorded by Mark, reads:

"*Go into all the world and preach the good news to all creation. Whoever believes and is baptized will be saved, but whoever does not believe will be condemned. And these signs will accompany those who believe: in my name they will drive out demons; they will speak in new tongues; they will pick up snakes with their hands; and when they drink deadly poison, it will not hurt them at all; they will place their hands on sick people, and they will get well*" (Mark 16:15-18).

Some writers and scholars find the reference to snakes and poison problematic. Does this literally mean that as a sign of a true follower of Jesus, one can or must handle snakes directly or drink deadly poison, and yet not die? Would a Christian ever be expected to do this to "prove" his belief in Jesus? It has been argued that these signs were true of only the apostles, except for drinking poison, since they have not been true of all believers over the centuries. Therefore, this applied only to the apostles to confirm the message of the gospel and themselves as the earliest messengers.[4] The apparent requirement that an allegorical interpretation must be true of all the signs in Mark 16:15-18, and not one or some, has been used to justify a literal interpretation of all the signs.[5]

I disagree with that interpretation, and would also argue for a metaphorical, as opposed to allegorical, interpretation of the snakes and poison part of this version of the Great Commission. First, there is no logical reason why the whole passage must be either all allegorical or all literal. These are the words of Jesus, and I see no reason why Jesus could not communicate one of the signs as metaphorical and the rest as literal. Why impose such logic on Jesus? Actually, Jesus starts with a figure of speech in that the gospel must be preached to all *creation*—who would then argue that we should also preach to cats and dogs? Hence, Jesus himself mixed metaphor with literal meaning in this very passage. Second, as discussed below, a metaphorical interpretation is simply more superior and hermeneutically sound than a literal one. Third, the literal application has problems in that it seemingly forces Christians into handling snakes and drinking deadly poison. This reality is not even demonstrated for the apostles. There is no biblical reference anywhere to any of the apostles drinking deadly poison and surviving. The one and only reference to snake handling is by Paul, who accidentally picked up a viper along with some brushwood for a fire (Acts 28:3-6). Vipers may well appear like sticks of wood. Paul shook the viper off into the fire, not wanting to "handle" the viper at all, yet did not die. Did this event help to authenticate Paul as a messenger of the gospel? Actually, this "sign" caused those present to make the idolatrous declaration that Paul was a god (Acts 28:6). Further, the Scriptures are very clear that the healing and deliverance signs were performed by the seventy-two (Luke 10:1,9,17,19) and non-apostles, as recorded in Acts. Thus, not all these signs were the special provenance of the apostles and one cannot then argue that all these signs accompanied only the apostles. How can these signs apply to all believers without imposing guilt trips for requiring great faith or some special level of spirituality?[6]

Using a metaphorical interpretation, Jesus is really talking about protection. Jesus himself frequently used metaphors—he referred to the yeast of the Pharisees as the teaching of the Pharisees (Matt. 16:6-12), and to the Pharisees as a brood of vipers (Matt. 12:34) or snakes (Matt. 23:33). They were not, literally, snakes or vipers. So it should be no surprise that he could use metaphor in Mark 16:15-18.

One would expect that the disciples knew the Old Testament well enough concerning all the metaphors and Hebraisms regarding protection. In using Scripture to interpret Scripture, one is reminded of passages like Psalm 91. This Psalm talks of God's protection over those who love him and trust in him. God will save his people from the fowler's snare (Ps. 91:3), deadly pestilence and plague (Ps. 91:3,6-7), enemy arrows (Ps. 91:5). Indeed, if you take refuge in the Lord and dwell in him, "no harm will befall you, no disaster will come near your tent" (Ps. 91:10). Further, "You will tread upon the lion and the cobra; you will trample the great lion and the serpent" (Ps. 91:13). Do we take that literally as well? It's then not only a question of whether all Christians are expected to handle snakes and drink deadly poison (Mark 16:18), but whether any Christian has ever died from pestilence or plague or violence. Must we then also require that no Christian has died in a famine in the last two thousand years (Ps. 33:18-19; 37:19)? Psalm 91 gives metaphors and figures of speech that talk of God's protection and care of his people as a general rule, yet there might be exceptions. Jesus walked in God's ways and was sinless, yet he did experience harm (flogging and crucifixion) in spite of Psalm 91:10, and surely not because he lacked faith or was not spiritual enough. Since we are covered by God's feathers and are under his wings—do we then believe God is a giant bird (Ps. 91:4)? This is clearly metaphorical language, figures of speech.

If Mark 16:18 must be literal, then why not insist on lion trampling (Ps. 91:13) as well as snake handling? Just as the different figures of speech in Psalm 91 are signs of God's protection of his people, the figure of speech in Mark 16:18 is a sign of God's protection over his eleven disciples and all future believers. This interpretation could still allow for literal protection from a snake or poison. Hence, the metaphorical interpretation serves to expand protection to believers well beyond just snakes and poison—like plague, violent acts, bus accidents, lions' dens (Dan. 6:19-23), etc.

When I worked in the Syrian Arab Republic, I was required to represent my institute at a meeting for the governor of Kamishly province, near the Iraq border. The dignitaries arrived an hour late and in several Mercedes Benz, with many bouquets of flowers and some typically "mushy" Arabic greetings. Always on the alert against hepatitis and diarrhea, I ate only food that I could peel or that was thoroughly cooked, which in this case included chicken. Late that evening at home back in Aleppo, I suddenly developed intense chills followed by intense body heat. Competent medical help was not available, so I prayed fervently during this strange and painful condition that I had never experienced before. It went on for some hours. I had barely any rest but felt well enough to go to work the next day. Midmorning in my office I was suddenly and instantly hit with the most excruciating abdominal pain I had ever experienced. I more or less had to be carried into the nurse's station, where I was given a powerful drug that alleviated the pain. I learned a week later from a professor of microbiology that the cause was *clostridium botulinum*, food poisoning from the chicken. I was told that this is one of the most dangerous poisons known and that I should be dead. The Lord protected me and no harm came to me. In this case I was literally, not metaphorically, protected from deadly poison. Well, back to Psalm 91.

Interestingly enough, Satan used Psalm 91:11-12, the protection of God's angels, to tempt Jesus to jump off the temple roof (Luke 4:9-11). Quoting Deuteronomy 6:16, Jesus replied that one should never put God to the test (Luke 4:12). Thus, Christians should never, ever put God to the test (cf. 1 Cor. 10:9) or presume on his protection by intentionally handling dangerous snakes or drinking deadly poison or trampling over lions, for example. The Apostle Paul certainly didn't. My closest encounter was while watching snake charmers in Al Jafna square, Marrakech,

Morocco—and I was never interested in getting too close. To request Christians to handle snakes to "prove" that the passage applies to Christians today, as well as the apostles originally, amounts to requesting them to succumb to the temptation of Satan (Luke 4:9-12). That is not wise.

The protection promise is clear in Jesus' reply to the seventy-two, who had returned from powerful ministry: "I have given you authority to trample on snakes and scorpions and to overcome all the power of the enemy; nothing will harm you" (Luke 10:19). These are figures of speech which point to protection as empowered servants of Jesus, given authority from Jesus to overcome evil spiritual forces.[7] The figures of speech—snakes and scorpions—are especially relevant here because they often signify evil and Satan himself. A sign of the Messiah's ultimate triumph over evil will be when "the infant will play near the hole of the cobra, and the young child put his hand into the viper's nest" (Isaiah 11:8). This is hardly a relaxing verse for mothers! Evil speech is like the poison of vipers (Rom. 3:13) or poison (Jas. 3:8), while evil rulers have the venom of a cobra (Ps. 58:4). The disciples would have clearly understood the words of Jesus in Mark 16:18 as protection, most certainly protection from evil power and Satanic forces. No surprise, since such evil resistance would be expected for those who seek to bludgeon the kingdom of darkness with God's great assault weapon, the gospel of Jesus.

Jesus was indeed very concerned about protection for his followers. In his high priestly prayer, Jesus acknowledged how he had protected his disciples (John 17:12), and then asked the Father to protect all future believers by the power of his name (John 17:11) and from the evil one (John 17:15). It would seem logical and consistent then, to again promise in Mark 16:18 his protection upon his eleven disciples and all who would follow. This would give the eleven apostles and all future disciples full confidence, encouragement, and boldness to proclaim the greatest message on earth to all creation, not a small task without danger and hardship.

Some writers argue that this passage applies only to the eleven disciples and not to future Christians since this was a private meeting between Jesus and the eleven. In addition, the overall context of the passage is Jesus' specific rebuke to his disciples for their "lack of faith and stubborn refusal to believe those who had seen him after he had risen" (Mark 16:14).[8] Masters wrote:

> Mark 16:17-18 is really a very embarrassing text for charismatic healers, for while they claim that Christ has promised these signs for all time, they cannot survive snakebites and poisons. Until they can, they should realize that they are wrestling this text out of its proper context, namely that of a private exhortation to the future apostles. The version of the great commission that applies to all disciples—of every day and age—gives us no instruction to perform healing signs.[9]

There are strong reasons for rejecting any such view. First, it is not the disciples' disbelief as a whole that is in question, but only their disbelief in the resurrection of Jesus. Second, if the passage really was for the disciples only, Jesus was saying that any one of them might well end up being condemned (Mark 16:16), hardly an edifying or reassuring thought. A better interpretation is that Jesus was just restating the truth of John 3:16, that those who do not believe will perish. We also know from John 2:11 that the disciples had already put their faith in Jesus, and did eventually believe the Scriptures about his resurrection (John 2:22). The disciples already had gone out and rebuked demons and healed the sick when first commissioned. In Luke's account, Jesus did rebuke two of them for being slow to believe, but then was gracious to them in patiently expounding the Scriptures (Luke 24:25-27), and later appeared to all and helped them to believe by eating some fish (Luke 24:36-43). Thus the rebuke in Mark 16:14 is better seen as a section in itself, with Mark 16:15-19 as subsequent affirmation, assurance, and commissioning of the disciples. Would we not rather see Jesus as the Good Shepherd here, building up his followers, than handing out condemnation? If anything, Jesus' rebuke to the disciples for their stubbornness to believe and hardness of heart should be a warning to us today for any unbelief in the power of the Kingdom of Jesus to heal and deliver directly in his name.

The idea that this was a private meeting between Jesus and his disciples while they are eating and thus does not apply to us is problematic.[10] Since Jesus talked in private to the disciples about the signs of the end of the age (Matt. 24:3-25:46), should we then conclude that it only applied to them and thus we are exempt from keeping watch (Matt. 24:42), for example? Would we ever consider exempting ourselves from the Great Commission (cf. also Acts 1:8) since it was also addressed privately and directly to the disciples? Should we then wonder whether Paul's personal and private letter to Philemon has any application to us? *Such a hermeneutic undermines the authority of the Scriptures by nullifying its effective authority to us today.*

Mark's version of the Great Commission serves to emphasize what Matthew had clearly intended in recording Christ's overall call to make disciples. Jesus then commands the eleven to preach the good news to all creation, not unlike "all nations" as in Matthew, and then those who believe the message and repent will be baptized. This is the essence of Luke's version, wherein "repentance and forgiveness of sins will be preached in his name to all nations, beginning at Jerusalem" (Luke 24:47).

The first sign that will accompany true believers is the ability to cast out demons, showing that they are among those who have received spiritual authority from Jesus. This is nothing new or different from what we understand from Matthew 28:18-20.

The second sign is the ability to speak in "new tongues." This is a sign of the filling and empowerment of the Holy Spirit (Acts 2:3-4; 10:46; 19:6) in general. It is also a very obvious and public sign, which was yet to happen at Pentecost, and would be new for the disciples. But since not all Christians have the gift of tongues (1 Cor.12:10,28,30), this signifies the filling and empowerment of the Holy Spirit with the manifestation of spiritual gifts as a whole. By definition, every Christian is indwelt by the Holy Spirit.

The third sign is the protection of the Lord, especially from evil spiritual forces, as explained above in reference to the snakes and poison. Whenever disciples of Jesus rebuke evil spirits and move in the power of the Holy Spirit, they may well incur the attacks of Satan. This promise and reminder of Jesus is crucial in that his followers will be able to sustain the attacks of the enemy (1 John 4:4). This assurance will give his followers boldness and encouragement to do what Jesus has commissioned. In Matthew's account, Jesus reassures his followers of his continual presence to the end of the age (Matt. 28:20; cf. Josh. 1:5). With his presence comes protection and empowering.

The fourth sign, completely in line with the example of Jesus and the Great Commission of Matthew involves healing the sick. Specifically, the laying on of hands and then people will "get well." Note that this passage points to gradual healing and not always instant healing.

In retrospect, these signs become a shorthand list for discipleship, not so different from Matthew 28:18-20. Everything considered, Mark 16:15-18 is not an "embarrassing text" at all, but complements the other Gospels and clearly underlines the vital ministry of healing and deliverance.

One cannot escape the centrality of the healing and deliverance ministry as part of the Great Commission. The mastery of orthodox theological doctrine is not among the signs (John 5:39). Belief itself is just not enough (James 2:14-26). Matthew 28:20 reads "teaching them to obey," not "teaching them to believe." In order to obey, one must first believe. Thus, the command to obey presupposes belief. The Great Commission is realized, and its power released, when disciples of Jesus believe and then obey. Although John's Gospel does not have an obvious Great Commission statement, it is still there. John Stott wrote:

> The crucial form in which the Great Commission has been handed down to us (although it is the most neglected because it is the most costly) is in the Johannine. Jesus had anticipated it in his prayer in the upper room when he said to his Father: "As thou didst send me into the world, so I have sent them into the world" (John 17:18). Now, probably in the same upper room, but after his death and resurrection, he turned his prayer-statement into a commission and said: "As the Father has sent me, even so I send you" (John 20:21).[11]

While we are not sent into the world as Savior or Lord, which uniquely belongs to Jesus, we certainly are sent as servants as he was (Luke 22:27). Jesus served in deed as well as words—preaching, teaching, healing the sick, showing compassion, feeding the hungry, blessing children, delivering people from all sorts of oppression, even raising people from the dead. Thus, from all four Gospels, we see that healing and deliverance is intended as part of the ministry of the Body of Christ.

John's Gospel links love, obedience, and discipleship. Jesus gave a new commandment—to love one another as he loved us (John

13:34; 15:12,17), which would be a sign of our discipleship (John 13:35). We demonstrate our love for Jesus by obeying his commands (John 14:21) and teachings (John 14:23). Since Jesus modeled and commanded healing and deliverance (as well as showing mercy, forgiving others, fasting, praying, loving one's enemies, etc.), which flowed out of his love and compassion, his followers are commanded to likewise enter into his healing and deliverance ministry. Nowhere did Jesus indicate that the ministry of healing would be excluded from his commands or teachings to his disciples.

Must all of these signs accompany every Christian and must every Christian be involved in these ministries? While every true Christian has the authority to rebuke a demon (see the chapter *"Deliverance Ministry: Myth or Mandate?"*), can lay hands on people for healing, has the protection of Jesus, has spiritual gifts and the filling of the Spirit, these signs will be more pronounced for those who have a stronger gifting and/or calling in these ministries. The important thing is practicing the ministry of healing and deliverance in the local church.

James 5:14-18 gives instructions for healing prayer in the Church, where those who are so weak and ill (Greek *astheneo* and *kamno*) and need to be "raised up" that they are essentially confined to their home, should ask the elders to come and pray for them.[12] In general, James 5:16 allows for healing prayer in the Church in addition to the elders. Healing might again be relational, since there might be sin that can be forgiven (James 5:15). The passage emphasizes the importance of prayer offered in faith and the name of the Lord.

Realizing the Great Commission With Great Resources

In the chapter "The Ministry of Jesus," we saw how Jesus ministered with an anointing of the Holy Spirit, authority, power, love, wisdom and knowledge, truth, obedience, faith, prayer, and various means, as opposed to a consistent method of ministry in healing. The ministry of the Church as seen in the Great Commission then becomes an extension of the ministry of Jesus. As we follow the example of Jesus, corporately as the Church, this can be accomplished only with the spiritual resources that God provides. *Those whom Jesus commissions, he empowers and anoints.* The spiritual gifts then become the necessary means to accomplish the commissioning of Jesus. How can we ever begin to realize 1 John 2:6, "Whoever claims to live in him must walk as Jesus did" apart from all the spiritual resources that God could give us? Apart from all the empowering of the Holy Spirit, with all the spiritual gifts, how can we ever realize John 14:12-14—

> *"I tell you the truth, anyone who has faith in me will do what I have been doing. He will do even greater things than these, because I am going to the Father. And I will do whatever you ask in my name, so that the Son may bring glory to the Father. You may ask me for anything in my name, and I will do it."*

Jesus talked about the coming of the Holy Spirit (John 14:16-21) as key to this promise.

So what was Jesus doing? Among other things, he must have had in mind his own clear and often repeated example of healing and deliverance. Wilkinson notes three important Greek words that express different aspects of the healing miracles of Jesus. *Dunamis* (power or potential to enact a change) describes the supernatural power as the source and cause of the healing; *semeion* (sign) points to the significance of the miracles in their divine origin, and *erga* (work) expresses the activity of God in the world.[13] John used *semeion* in connection with the healing and deliverance ministry of Jesus which was also among his *erga*, or works as included in John 14:12. Hence the need for belief and empowering on our part. Like the apostles, we must be clothed with the power of the Holy Spirit (Luke 24:50), as befits our character and calling for his purposes.

Seeking the spiritual gifts is never about proving spiritual superiority or desiring the dramatic. If we seek obedience first and always, we can hardly go wrong. If we seek spiritual experiences or manifestations in themselves first, we will most likely go wrong. Receiving the Spirit and his gifts is linked to obedience (Acts 5:32). Should there not be as much discussion about emptying of self as being filled with the Spirit? Spiritual lust is always a very real temptation, as is using spiritual power like magic as we stray from our relationship with Jesus. Christian discipleship has more to do with long-term character development and perseverance than "carpet time." There is a temptation to view the presence of the Spirit in cultural terms, like function or performance. So we readily acknowledge the use of the power gifts, but often fail to appreciate the Spirit's power in helping us endure trials with humility or hardships with contentment.[14] As Houston wrote:

> As we enjoy the presence of God the Holy Spirit, we learn to see him more for the relationship we have with him than for any particular phenomena he brings.[15]

In contemporary terms, *do we readily acknowledge Christians who persevere and endure in trying situations and who remain faithful to Jesus to the end as "charismatic"?* Do we see this empowering of the Spirit as much as the more dramatic or public manifestations? I don't think so. Finally, there can be a new legalism wherein Christians must have *prescribed spiritual experiences* to be considered truly anointed, for example. It almost becomes another form of conservatism.

There is a danger of operating with counterfeit spiritual gifts. This can come by mediumistic gifts operating in one's life before coming to Christ and not renouncing them upon conversion.[16] I have experienced this a few times, in praying with Christians who really had psychic or clairvoyant gifts, thought to be gifts of the Spirit. Often they were reluctant to renounce these "gifts," since their identity was wrapped up in their performance in the church. One must also be aware of the laying on of hands by those not fully known or trusted, since some Christians operate with a *mixture* of gifts of the Spirit and mediumistic or counterfeit gifts.

Since Jesus moved fully in the power and anointing of the Holy Spirit, and expects his Church to fulfill the Great Commission through the Holy Spirit and discipleship, one might simply conclude that all the gifts of the Spirit should operate in the Church today. However, this point is strongly contested, as we shall see in a later chapter, *"Vanishing Spiritual Gifts?"*

We must pattern ourselves after the model of Jesus and conform to his ministry. Just as Jesus was in close communion with his Father, we must abide in Jesus in order to bear any lasting fruit, for apart from him we accomplish nothing (John 15:5). The challenge to the Church is to walk in love and unity—simple enough, but not often accomplished. As important as the Great Commission is, more important still is the Great Commandment (Matt. 22:36-38). As we first love the Lord with all our hearts, minds, and wills do we then realize God's calling and commissions.

Obedience must remain foremost. Discipleship is so fundamental to the Great Commission, requiring growth in holiness and practical obedience. While healing and deliverance are so important in the Great Commission, more important still is the call of God on our lives to obey him, follow him, and live for him. Our righteousness, purchased by the costly blood of Jesus, brings responsibility. In stressing the gifts of the Spirit and the role of the Holy Spirit, there is the danger of forgetting God the Father. Reflecting on the renewal movement and the work of the Spirit in bringing us into Christ's likeness, Smail wrote:

> ...What matters most is our obedience. Our renewal experiences and our spiritual gifts have significance only in so far as they are the sources or expressions of a new obedience to the Father which proves that we really are sons.[17]

Jack told me of a church known for years for its commitment to solid biblical teaching and continued practical love, but not known for the more "observable" manifestations of the Spirit. Jack and his family enjoyed the genuine fellowship, warmth, and unity. He told me that at first he wondered why the Lord had sent him there, since he was used to a more overt presence of the spiritual gifts in past churches. Then one Sunday the Lord directed him to pray for a person's healing, and give a prophetic word. He asked the pastor and leaders, who were a bit hesitant, but agreed. The Lord honored their openness, and since then the church has grown and blessed many, with joyful members of that church growing in their new-found spiritual gifts. The key here, Jack emphasized to me, was a solid prior foundation in teaching and ministry of the Word, love, and unity—in short, demonstrated obedience over time. Jack told me of another church a few years back that had much less obedience in practical love and unity, but a greater focus on the manifestations of the Spirit. That church experience caused him a lot of stress, especially the disunity and eventually a church split. One cannot generalize, for that is one person's experience.

The basic principle remains; we must link obedience with discipleship and the gifts of the Spirit. *Jesus defined the authentic love of his followers to him in terms of their obedience to his commands and teaching* (John 14:15,23). There are no shortcuts to obedience.

Endnotes

[1] Ronald A.N. Kydd, *Healing through the Centuries. Models for Understanding* (Peabody: Hendrickson Publishers, 1998) p. 2.

[2] John R. W. Stott, *Christian Mission in the Modern World* (Downer's Grove: InterVarsity Press, 1975) pp. 38-40.

[3] George E. Ladd, *The New Testament and Criticism* (Grand Rapids: Eerdmans, 1967) p. 58.

[4] John F. MacArthur, Jr., *Charismatic Chaos* (Grand Rapids: Zondervan, 1992) pp. 123-124.

[5] MacArthur, p. 122.

[6] MacArthur, p. 124.

[7] Norval Geldenhuys, *The Gospel of Luke. The New International Commentary on the New Testament* (Grand Rapids: Eerdmans, 1951) p. 302.

[8] David Powlison, *Power Encounters. Reclaiming Spiritual Warfare* (Grand Rapids: Baker Books, 1995) p. 96.

[9] Peter Masters, *The Healing Epidemic* (London: The Wakeman Trust, 1988) p. 65.

[10] Masters, p. 63.

[11] Stott, p. 23.

[12] John Wilkinson, *The Bible and Healing. A Medical and Theological Commentary* (Grand Rapids: Eerdmans, 1998) pp. 242-244.

[13] Wilkinson, pp. 86-88.

[14] James Houston, *The Transforming Friendship. A Guide to Prayer* (Batavia: Lion Publishing, 1989) p. 120.

[15] Houston, p. 122.

[16] Kurt E. Koch, *Christian Counseling and Occultism. A Complete*

Guidebook to Occult Oppression and Deliverance. 21st edition (Grand Rapids: Kregel Resources, 1994) p. 17.

[17] Thomas A. Smail, *The Forgotten Father* (Vancouver: Regent College Bookstore, 1995, reprint and first printing. First published by Hodder and Stoughton, 1980) p. 152.

Chapter Four

The Ministry of Wholeness in the Church

Jeremy's Story

I met Jeremy through some mutual friends because, as a survivor of cancer, they thought I could identify with his struggles. Jeremy had low-grade lymphoma cancer, and his chances of being cured were close to nil. In fact, seven months earlier his chemotherapy was stopped since his tumors quit responding to the treatments. I asked if he had received healing prayer that involved the presence of Jesus to deal with anything in his life that may be related to the cancer. He replied that he had not, and later agreed to a prayer ministry session. A few days later, a ministry colleague and I prayed with Jeremy. The Lord revealed significant losses and deep painful memories, and most significantly, brought a deep healing to the most wounded parts of his soul. The presence of the Lord was such that Jeremy wept and wept, experiencing the healing and restoring power of Jesus. The Lord clearly revealed his love and affirmation to Jeremy in a way that was unique and powerful for him. I concluded that all the loss and pain that Jeremy had experienced had affected his immune system, and then I laid my hands on Jeremy and prayed directly for his healing from cancer.

Two months later Jeremy had a series of medical tests. The tests were expected to confirm the spread of the cancer, finalize the schedule for a bone marrow transplant, and stage him for that procedure. Jeremy had a CT scan and a Gallium scan, both of which came back negative. The doctor couldn't understand why the results were negative and ordered a bone marrow test. The first test also came back negative and so they ran a second test to be sure. Everything was clear. The doctor said he couldn't explain why after ten months without treatment he could have a clean slate of health. The doctor from another hospital phoned to set up the time for the transplant. When told it wasn't necessary because the cancer was gone, the doctor seemed almost angry that his schedule was upset.

Was this just a spontaneous remission? Everything points to the significance of the prayer time where Jeremy received prayer ministry as a *whole person*. Under the guidance of the Holy Spirit, and using the gifts of the Spirit, Jeremy had an encounter with Jesus that changed his whole being. To really comprehend this, we need to understand health and healing in biblical terms.

But what exactly is "health"? This may appear as an unnecessary question, since health and healing are much discussed, debated, and studied. We might want to readily assume that what is so common, and concerns everyone, is clearly understood. But it is probably a surprise for many of us that the biblical view of health can be quite different from our understanding. For years I was under the impression that the Bible does not teach much about health, but that was because I had a very limited, culture-bound, view of health. The biblical view is more profound and integrative than often realized. Many of us first think of physical health, focusing on the biological dimension of life. As important as that is, it is only part of the picture. Let us take a brief look at the Old Testament.

Health As a Relational Concept

The Old Testament describes and defines the characteristics of healthy people, instead of details on characteristics or attributes of health *per se*.[1] The Bible sees health in the context of one's whole being, personhood, and most importantly, relationships. While we might think that health is fundamentally a biological concept, the Scriptures teach that health is fundamentally *a relational concept.*

There are six main characteristics of healthy people, as understood in the Old Testament. The first, and most important, is "well-being," or being at peace, based on the important Hebrew word *shalom*. A key attribute of those who are truly healthy, *shalom* denotes peace, safety, and harmony for the totality of one's being. This covers the physical, emotional, spiritual, and relational dimensions of life. As Wilkinson observes:

> The usage of the word shalom in the Old Testament denotes the presence of wholeness, completeness, and well-being in all spheres of life whether physical, mental, and spiritual...[2]

You cannot really have *shalom* if your soul is in inner turmoil, or you are in pain, or in bondage to a compulsion or addiction, or have painful recurring memories, or if you are in conflict with others. If you can truly say that "all is well with my soul," then you may be experiencing true *shalom*. Since we live by grace, we must also realize that ultimately true *shalom* is a gift of God, and comes from a relationship with him:

> True shalom or well-being comes from God for only in God do we find our true wholeness and complete fulfill-

ment. In God alone can we know the wholeness of our being and the rightness of our relationships which make up what the Old Testament means by health.[3]

In our relationship with God we are at peace knowing that our sins are forgiven, that he cares for us and has compassion upon us, that he provides for our needs, and knows the deepest yearnings and issues of our hearts. Indeed, God delights in the well-being of his servants (Ps. 35:27).

The next most important characteristic is righteousness, from the Hebrew *sedeq*. Healthy people are those who have a right relationship centred on the nature and character of God.[4] Righteousness in one's life will determine one's attitudes, behaviour, decisions, actions, and quality of relationships with others. The standard of all this should be God's will and commands as we relate to God, others, ourselves, and creation. A right relationship with God brings shalom as we trust in him (Isaiah 26:3) and walk uprightly (Isaiah 57:2). The fruit of righteousness will be peace (Isaiah 32:17).

Third, flowing from righteousness is obedience to God's laws.[5] This meant freedom from disease as Israel was admonished: "If you listen carefully to the voice of the Lord your God and do what is right in his eyes...I will not bring on you any of the diseases I have brought on the Egyptians, for I am the Lord who heals you" (Exod. 15:26). If Israel was faithful and obedient, worshiping only God and renouncing all false gods, God would take away sickness, miscarriages, and barrenness (guarantee fertility), and bless them with many years (Exod. 23:25-26). Disobedience will bring all sorts of diseases, fevers, and afflictions (Lev. 26:14-16; 23-26), while obedience brings a prosperous and blessed life (Deut. 5:32), free from disease (Deut. 7:12-15). The best form of preventative medicine is obedience to God's ways and law.⁶ As just one example, it is well known that sexual promiscuity often results in sexually transmitted diseases (STD), which can result in cervical cancer for women. Abortion increases the incidence of miscarriage, cancer, and infertility. In addition to obedience to God's moral laws, there are also his physical laws, such as relating to hygiene concerning infected food, dead animals, contact with dead bodies, and disposal of human waste (Lev. 11:4-7; Num. 19:11-13; Deut. 23:12-14).

Fourth, there is strength which is often related to health, or *shalom*, and should be understood as a gift of God— "The Lord gives strength to his people; the Lord blesses his people with peace" (Ps. 29:11).⁷ Then, fertility, as noted in Exodus 13:26 and Deuteronomy 7:12-14. Finally, longevity as promised to all those who obey God's laws (Exod. 20:12; Deut. 5:16).

Health is thus more than just a biological concept, which comes from a reductionistic or materialistic view of life. As Wilkinson summarizes:

> First of all and most important of all, health consists in a right relationship to God expressed in our obedience to his will and our worship of his name. These result in holiness for righteousness is the content and expression of holiness, which is spiritual wholeness.⁸

Worry can cause ulcers, distrust in God can cause anxiety, unbelief in God's protection can cause fear or phobias, inability to receive God's forgiveness can cause vain regrets or depression, anger or hostility in our hearts can cause cardiovascular problems, and so forth. How we relate to God and others will affect how much *shalom* we have in our life. Our relationship to God, and living by His grace and mercy, has more to do with our health than anything else. Our walk of humility, obedience, and gratitude to God has more to do with our health than medical or biological technique. *Health must be understood in terms of the whole person.*

In the larger view, health as relationship can be seen in terms of reconciliation or entering in a covenantal relationship.[9] Thus, reconciliation with God brings forgiveness, meaning, grace, peace, love, and more. Reconciliation with other people brings fellowship, mutuality, trust, acceptance. Reconciliation with God's created order means health from good nutrition, hygiene, clean unpolluted environment, and health promoting behaviour and lifestyle. Poor stewardship of the earth and violation of God's laws in creation causes malnutrition, pollution, and bodily disruptions and disorders. Health is a function of one's relationship with God, others, and creation.

I would add that health also involves reconciliation with oneself. I can remember praying with a woman who could not stop smoking. Why? Because deep down, she hated herself, and was thus trying to self-destruct by smoking. Her healing involved encountering the presence of Jesus to identify and overcome the roots and causes of the self-hatred. She began to understand that loving her neighbour required learning to love and accept herself.

PsychoNeuroImmunology of the Old Testament

We realize that people are integrated, with their body, heart, mind, and soul very much inter-connected at a deep level (Hebrew, *nephesh*—the whole person). Not only do we have a soul, we *are* a soul. Medical science is beginning to realize this more and more, and especially from a new field of research, PsychoNeuroImmunology (PNI), which describes the effects of stress on the functioning of the immune system. This is a study of the interaction of the mind and emotions (psycho), and the brain and central nervous system (neuro), and the body's cellular defense against disease (immunology). Researchers are finding a strong interaction between mind and body at the root of both health and disease:

> There is considerable evidence that emotions, attitudes, and negative stress can all adversely affect the functioning of the immune system.... Anxiety, depression, and repressed emotions have been demonstrated to play a particularly important role in suppressing immune system functioning. Specific diseases that have been shown to be strongly correlated with such psychosocial factors are rheumatoid arthritis (which is associated with anger, suppressed emotions, nervousness, reserve, perfectionism, and restlessness), cardiovascular disease (which is highly associated with repressed hostility), and cancer (which is associated with nonassertiveness, the inability to express emotions, and hopelessness or depression).[10]

While association does not always mean causation, this research tells us that we must consider relational and emotional issues in physical healing. In contrast to the above, it is laughter, relaxation, feelings of peace and contentment, connectedness to God and others, and a positive attitude to oneself which all contribute toward good health.

This research confirms clear teaching in Proverbs: "Do not be wise in your own eyes; fear the Lord and shun evil. This will bring health to your body and nourishment to your bones" (Prov. 3:7). "...These words of wisdom are life to those who find them and health to a man's whole body" (Prov. 4:22). "The fear of the Lord adds length to life, but the years of the wicked are cut short" (Prov. 10:27). "Hope deferred makes the heart sick, but a longing fulfilled is a tree of life" (Prov. 13:12). "A heart at peace gives life to the body, but envy rots the bones" (Prov. 14:30). "A happy heart makes the face cheerful, but heartache crushes the spirit" (Prov. 15:13). "A cheerful look brings joy to the heart, and good news gives health to the bones" (Prov. 15:30). "Pleasant words are a honeycomb, sweet to the soul and healing to the bones" (Prov. 16:24). "A cheerful heart is good medicine, but a crushed spirit dries up the bones" (Prov. 17:22). "A man's spirit sustains him in sickness, but a crushed spirit who can bear?" (Prov. 18:14). No wonder that Christians who more frequently attend church have better immune systems and tend to live longer.[11] Ulcerated colitis is frequently caused by psychological stress.[12]

> A great deal of evidence exists to show that diabetes, a disease that produces many physical complications, can be triggered by emotional crisis.[13]

Our attitude to life, God, and others, and how we live, will affect our bodies more than we often care to think. We must learn to shun evil like bitterness, unforgiveness, anger, resentment, and hostility before it does damage to our physical bodies. We must look to God and ask to reveal if there is an "offensive way" in our hearts as well as any anxious thoughts (Ps. 139:23-24). *The quality of our health is often reflected in the quality of our relationships.* Thus we see the strategic importance and necessity of healing prayer to address the relational and spiritual issues, which may be involved with the physical ones. While not all illness is caused by sin or relational problems, they must be discerned when they do impact one's health.

Wanda came for prayer for chronic back pain. As we prayed, the Holy Spirit brought to mind her uncle Jack. Unrelated? A "rabbit trail"? It turned out that he had sexually defiled her on one occasion at a very young age. The incident was buried deep in her past, plus the unforgiveness with the associated resentment and anger. When she spoke out forgiveness, thus freeing herself from the incident and allowing healing to begin, her back pain began to disappear. Simply praying for physical healing would not have helped Wanda.

Anger: Relating Emotions and Health

Medical research has shown that prolonged, unresolved anger can lead to a variety of unfortunate physical symptoms and diseases. Ferder wrote:

> Many studies have shown, and continue to show, that poorly handled anger can lead to a variety of debilitating physical symptoms and diseases. Ulcers, migraines, tension headaches, some forms of arthritis, skin disorders (eczema, hives, rashes), asthma, low back pain, neck and shoulder pain, colitis, spastic colon, chronic constipation or diarrhea, and vascular diseases all have strong links to prolonged anger mobilization. The problem is that the body systems were not meant to store anger. The stomach, for example, was meant to hold food, not anger. When we use it as a storehouse for anger energy, it will eventually rebel. [14]

With anger, muscles tighten throughout the body. You may become used to this condition to the extent it seems normal, but it stresses the body over time. The prolonged body stress and tension, which involves adrenaline, can result in neck and shoulder soreness and lower back pain. If a person has any of the above symptoms or illnesses, it does not automatically mean there is anger, but then, one should not be surprised if there *is* anger. We deceive ourselves if we think we can deny the anger such that there is no more effect.

If we try to hide, deny, or bury it, our body will nevertheless remember, and the effects live on. These are the sorts of illnesses that we invite upon ourselves if we disobey God.

> While a feeling might be put out of a person's mind, it cannot be put out of the body. The energy from the hidden feeling remains trapped in the stomach, the chest, and the neck. We can try to dull it with aspirin or Maalox, but the energy and the chemical correlates of trapped emotional reactions stay alive and scream for release. Sooner or later uncomfortable feelings are exchanged for uncomfortable symptoms as the victims of repressed feelings become plagued with a variety of emotionally related physical problems and diseases.[15]

If this is not enough, medical research is increasingly showing that angry or hostile persons have two other biological characteristics that could be damaging to health: a weak parasympathetic nervous system (PNS) and a weak immune system.[16] The PNS helps to calm a person down, and the immune system helps to fight off diseases, especially afflictions like cancer. Anger is a toxin to the body.[17]

This all points to the incredible relevance and importance of healing prayer that has as much to do with our emotions as the rest of our being. Since over sixty per cent of illnesses are chronic and can cause serious health problems, healing prayer is especially important in facing issues of forgiveness, repentance, bitterness, and more, which are often the underlying causes.

Leanne Payne tells the story of a woman suffering from arthritis. She had come repeatedly for healing prayer over several years, yet with no result as the arthritis worsened. Then one day at a healing prayer service the Lord strongly and clearly reminded her of her unforgiving and petty attitude to her invalid landlady for whom she prepared a noon meal daily. Leanne wrote:

> On the day of her healing, she painfully bent her arthritic knees before the altar, and as we prayed with her, she realized her need to forgive the upstairs invalid and to ask God's forgiveness for her reactions. This she did, and she was instantly healed of her very painful arthritic condition.[18]

This highlights the significance of healing prayer, where one prays for a *whole person in the context of their entire life and relationships*. For that lady, medical treatment was of little help. This example also demonstrates the power of forgiveness. Spiritual power, rooted in love and guided by the Spirit in the presence of Jesus, comes not only through the "power gifts" but also through avenues like forgiveness and the cross.

Is Your View of Salvation Too Small?

When we then see the example and teachings of Jesus, it should be no great surprise that the ministry of healing and deliverance is part of the Great Commission. We need not split theological hairs over issues like whether there is healing in the atonement or whether the miracles of today must be like those of the apostles. It is a continuation of God's long-standing desire to heal (Ps. 103:1-3; Ps. 107:20; Exod. 15:26), take away sickness (Exod. 23:25), and restore health (Jer. 30:17).

This is part of the Great Commission first and foremost due to the love and compassion of Jesus as we have seen in the chapter, "Compassion Deficit Disorder." It is the character and nature of Jesus and God the Father to show love by not only saving people, but healing them and freeing them from evil oppressive forces. God is no less compassionate, generous, or loving today as he was then. Death is a reality for all people, and for many people sickness and illness are realities as well. Regimes, ideologies, philosophies, theological systems, fads, and more, will come and go over the centuries. But sickness will always be a universal concern in this fallen world, and when people are especially vulnerable. Jesus healed "all who were oppressed by the devil" (Acts 10:38). The Scriptures do not tell us that Satan has gone on a holiday or is any less active today, thus the type of ministry that Jesus modeled is no less relevant today.

When people are in great need, Satan often comes with counterfeit or distracting promises or schemes that can deceive people and cause many to perish. Hence, the Church must practice the true healing presence of Jesus. As the Kingdom of God advances in the lives of people, demonic opposition will appear in many ways. Disciples of Jesus must have the confidence and knowledge that comes in dealing with evil spiritual forces. There is no neutral ground anywhere, for the whole universe is all part of the Kingdom of light or the kingdom of darkness. Until Jesus returns, there will be conflicts between the Kingdom of Jesus and the defeated, but not yet banished, kingdom of darkness.

The connection between preaching and salvation with healing and deliverance in the Great Commission is also no surprise when one considers the dynamic connection with salvation. Christians are saved from sin's guilt and penalty (Ps. 103:12), condemnation (Rom. 8:1), and the power of sin (Titus 2:11-3:6). We will be saved from the coming wrath of God (Rom. 5:9; 1 Thess. 1:10), eternal death (Rom. 6:21,23), and from the certainty of the final judgment (Rev. 20:11-15). We are forgiven, reconciled, justified, accepted, adopted into God's family, and joint heirs with Jesus because of the finished and complete work of Christ on the cross. But we have not experienced all of salvation. As J.I. Packer wrote, "We are fully into salvation, but salvation is not fully into us. The foretaste is ours now; the fullness remains future."[19]

The New Testament uses the Greek verb, *sozo*, "to save," 106 times, and sixteen times in the context of healing.[20] The verb has a wider sense than just salvation from sin and the judgment of God, but covers the concepts of salvation, healing, wholeness, rescue, and preservation. There is an organic, integral connection with healing and deliverance. Salvation is also seen in Jesus' miracles of healing where *sozo* is used. Deliverance from hemorrhage (Mark 5:34), blindness (Mark 10:52), demon possession (Luke 8:36), and death (Mark 5:23) were evidence of salvation (Matt. 11:4-5). Many translations use the word "heal" instead of "save" when *sozo* is being used. In Matthew 9:21-22 (cf. Mark 5:25-34; Luke 8:43-49), the woman who had been bleeding for twelve years, wanting to be healed (*iatrous*) upon touching Jesus' cloak, heard Jesus say, "Your faith has healed *(sozo)* you." Matthew wrote, "And the woman was healed *(sozo)* from that moment." When the blind Bartimaeus came to Jesus, Jesus said, "your faith has healed *(sozo)* you." Jairus pleaded Jesus to place his hands on his daughter so that she would be healed *(sozo)* and live (Mark 5:23; Luke 8:50). Mark records how, in Gennesaret, people continually brought the sick to Jesus, and "all who touched him (Jesus) were healed *(sozo)*" (Mark 6:56; Matt. 14:36). When the demon-possessed man was delivered from demons that went into pigs, Luke refers to the man as cured (*sozo*, Luke 8:36). Peter prays for the healing of a crippled beggar, who is healed, (Acts 3:2-10) and in defending himself before the Sanhedrin, refers to the man as healed (*sozo*, Acts 4:9-10). From Acts 4:12, "Salvation is found in no one else, for there is no other name under heaven given to men by which we must be saved," we see in the context of Peter's situation that healing is dynamically linked to salvation. Paul saw that a man crippled from birth had faith to be healed (*sozo*, Acts

14:9), and he was healed. The prayer offered in faith will make the sick person get well (*sozo*, Jas. 5:15). To the leper who returned to give thanks, Jesus said that his faith made him well (*sozo*, Luke 17:19). In the examples given above in each case where *sozo* was used, the person healed wanted healing and had faith.

Therapeuo is the commonest and most comprehensive Greek verb used for healing in the Gospels, occurring thirty-six times.[21] It is used to describe healing of physical disease by doctors (Luke 4:23; 8:43) as medical healing, healing by Jesus whether physical or from the demonic (Matt. 4:24; 12:22; 17:16; Luke 6:18), or by the disciples of Jesus of physical disease (Matt. 10:8; Mark 6:13; Luke 10:8). *Iaomai* occurs twenty times, and appears to be synonymous with *therapeuo*.[22] When the person who was healed did not make an extended effort, a lesser Greek word (*iatros, therapeuo, hygiaou*) than *sozo* was used.

The truest healing, for the whole person, comes when one's spirit realizes the presence and power of Jesus, and need of him, and thus fellowship with him. Considering all the biblical data, "healings and demon exorcisms were the negative side of salvation; the positive side was the incoming of the power and life of God."[23] In other words, anything from the kingdom of darkness is "pushed out," and the abundant life of the Kingdom of Jesus "received in." Salvation involves every part of man's being—healing for physical and inner needs, as well as deliverance from demonic forces. *Sozo* thus points to the restoration of a person to a state of wholeness—in communion and relationship with God (reconciliation, justification, sanctification), and his whole being (body, mind, soul, spirit) healed, and made whole. Salvation involves being saved from sin and all its consequences in this fallen world—judgment, demonic powers, emotional wounds, physical illness, and so forth. Jesus wants to save the whole person, to restore the whole person, to heal the whole person.

As Foster wrote:

> Healing Prayer is part of the normal Christian life... it is simply a normal aspect of what it means to live under the reign of God. This should not surprise us, for it is clear recognition of the incarnational nature of our faith. God cares as much about the body as he does about the soul, as much about the emotions as he does the spirit. The redemption that is in Jesus is total, involving every aspect of the person—body, soul, will, mind, emotions, spirit.[24]

Isaiah 53:4-5 also shows the organic connection between healing and salvation:

> *Surely he took up our infirmities and carried our sorrows, yet we considered him stricken by God, smitten by him, and afflicted. But he was pierced for our transgression, he was crushed for our iniquities; the punishment that brought us peace was upon him, and by his wounds we are healed.*

Infirmities and wounds are part of Jesus' work on the cross, along with taking upon himself the penalty of sin as transgressions and iniquities. The work of Jesus on the cross was comprehensive, covering sin and all its consequences. Matthew emphasized this in Matthew 8:17 by referring therein to Isaiah 53:4.

The common view of salvation as merely the forgiveness of sins makes it hard to fully grasp the significance of wholeness, healing, and deliverance. "Salvation is not just forgiveness, but a new order of life." [25] A more complete and biblically comprehensive view sees salvation as eternal life (1 John 5:11-12; John 10:10). We are saved by the life of Jesus, and not only by his death (Rom. 5:10). With the death and the resurrection of Jesus, the new life of the Kingdom of God is incarnated into each believer. "The idea of redemption as the impartation of life provides a total framework of understanding."[26] Whatever hinders the fuller impartation of the life of Christ—lies, bondages, wounds, pain, sorrow, traumatic memories—needs healing, deliverance, and sanctification. Jesus intended wholeness in all of its dimensions when he said, "I have come that they may have life, and have it to the full" (John 10:10). *Experiencing the abundant life of Jesus is the most inclusive statement of wholeness and salvation.*

Divine Healing And Medicine: Avoiding Spiritual Schizophrenia

Divine or spiritual healing, as part of the Great Commission, should not in any fundamental way conflict with modern medicine. Unfortunately, in some Christian circles, there is the belief that seeing a doctor and benefiting from modern medical practices shows a lack of faith. For Christians seeking healing from modern medicine, such attitudes only worsen their situation by adding guilt and condemnation. In an extreme example, there is at least one church which teaches "faith healing" which holds that modern medicine is actually an extension of witchcraft or black magic and, therefore, following a doctor's treatment plan makes one vulnerable to demonic influence.[27] As a result, over ninety people in that church have died from easily treatable illnesses. This is tragic. A law was recently passed in Colorado that makes faith healing a crime when medical treatment is withheld.[28] The law was precipitated by the death of a thirteen-year-old girl from treatable diabetes. Her parents were members of a Christian church whose belief would not allow for medical treatment for their daughter. The opposite error is to seek modern medical help but not healing through prayer at all. How can we reconcile these concerns to spiritual healing in the life of the Church?

Fundamentally, God is the source of all true healing, whatever the means. Doctors do not, strictly speaking, cause any healing at all. Their job is to set the body's healing processes in motion to make healing possible. No doctor actually monitors and moves a patient's cells around, or causes the patient's organs to function, etc. Doctors use medical procedures and various drugs, resulting from scientific and medical research, which come ultimately from studying and experimenting within God's created order. Hence, God's truth from "natural revelation" is the ultimate source of the medical knowledge. Many of the first scientists and doctors were Christians, who had a very real sense of God's presence and direction in their research and really saw themselves as *priests of creation*. Science assumes a knowable world, with repeatable results for research and testing hypotheses, which is ultimately a reflection of God's consistency, order and faithfulness in his creation. All truth is God's truth, so when Einstein came across the equation $e=mc^2$, he discovered what God had already built into his universe. It's only called Einstein's equation because he discovered it. One of my most worshipful moments in my scientific career was when I discovered a set of trinomial-extended probability equations which proved to be fundamental to my computer simulation in quantitative genetics. The Lord revealed it to me after two weeks of prayer and scientific reflection. This became the key to my doctoral dissertation. I, for one, know the presence of the Lord in scientific research. As we consider the wider scope of the Great Commission, we see that it includes scientific research for those so-called of God.[29] Before the Great Commission, there was the Culture Commission (Genesis 1:28; 2:15), and science as well as all fields of work come from obedience to that commission. Even the farmer's knowledge of cultivating and sowing is linked to the Spirit of God (Isaiah 28:24-29). Technical skill can also come from the Holy

Spirit (Exod. 31:3; 35:1; 1 Kings 7:14). The wisdom that God gave King Solomon included knowledge of the plant and animal kingdom (1 Kings 4:29,33-34). In fact, Solomon's extensive knowledge and example in natural history so influenced Sir Francis Bacon that it became "a widely accepted model for science at the beginning of the Enlightenment."[30] This was behind London's prestigious College of Physicians' original identity as "Solomon's House."[31] The significance is that such knowledge of creation, both pre-scientific and scientific, is not unspiritual.

Historically, medicine and spiritual healing were in harmony when many of the early physicians were monks and the first hospitals were founded in monasteries.[32] The rift later developed from the Scientific Revolution by the philosophy of men like Descartes, Hume, and Locke who only accepted knowledge via empirical measurements and the scientific method. Without recognition of God's immediate revelation and the dynamics of experiencing God, the rift widened such that it has become an issue today.

If we believe that God has little or nothing to do with science and medicine, and that we must live by faith in "direct divine healing," we unwittingly believe and uphold a secular humanistic view of the world. The secular mind would banish God to personal piety and devotion at most, and claim man's prominence in science, medicine, engineering, etc. So when Christians seek healing apart from medicine, because "God is not in it," they give silent agreement to the secular agenda. Such a view from Christians actually undermines the place of Jesus as Lord of all truth and every scientific discipline and area of research. As part of the Great Commission, the Body of Christ should have disciples who seek to establish the Lordship of Jesus and the ethics of the Kingdom of God into those areas. That is all part of being salt and light to the world. The question is then not whether Christians should seek medical help or not. Rather, it is about hearing God's voice and knowing his will, and the ethics, correct diagnosis, care, and sensitivity from physicians and others, and appropriate treatment for any given situation. Following the principles of nutrition, diet, exercise, rest, sanitation, and hygiene, but suddenly not medical help in healing, is an example of "spiritual schizophrenia." *It is not either faith or medicine, but faith and medicine in the presence of God* as we live in his creation.

We must be willing to accept that our pathway to healing can be supernatural and instantaneous, but it may also, and often does, involve the supernatural combined with the natural.[33?]

Healing through medicine acknowledges Christ as co-Creator of the universe. Since all things hang together through him, and all things were created in him and for him and by him (Col. 1:16), Christ is involved in all forms and levels of healing. Christ is Lord of all medical and scientific research, and all such results point to him, whether scientists and researchers so engaged acknowledge him or not. True medical knowledge, as well as all other scientific knowledge, ultimately submits to Jesus as Creator. Luke was himself a physician (*iatros*, Col. 4:14). Paul advised Timothy medically, to stop drinking only water and drink a little wine for his stomach and to alleviate his frequent illnesses (1 Tim. 5:23). King Hezekiah was deathly ill and Isaiah prophesied that he would die (Isaiah 38:1). Hezekiah prayed earnestly to the Lord, who then granted him another fifteen years as well as deliverance from Assyria (Isaiah 38:2-4). The Lord also graciously provided a sign, a shadow going backwards, to confirm his word (Isaiah 38:7). But significantly, the Lord commanded through Isaiah that a poultice of figs should be prepared and applied to the king's boil, and then he would recover (Isaiah 38:21; 2 Kings 20:7-8). This was a healing remedy well known in the ancient world.[34]

The Lord brought Isaiah to Hezekiah at the right time to prescribe the remedy. All things considered, it was still a divine healing of the Lord. As Oswalt remarks:

> ...though it is not explicitly stated, we are led to believe that the miracle of healing was achieved through the application of a poultice of figs. This is an important point in any theology of healing. All healing is of God. Sometimes he intervenes directly to produce health. At other times he works through intervening means, as here. But it is misleading to limit divine healing to those instances where no intervening means appears.[35]

Whatever the situation or need for healing, as Christians we should always first seek God and his direction. We are always dependent upon him, and should come to our Father with expectant, believing hearts. Hezekiah came to the Lord with prayer and tears (2 Kings 20:4-5), such that the original prophecy of the Lord regarding his health and time of death was actually changed.

To not consult modern medicine would dishonor those Christians who have responded to the call of God to be medical missionaries, doctors, nurses, or surgeons, etc. It can actually lead to dishonoring Jesus as Creator. Further, "The refusal to use medical means to promote healing may be a gesture of faith—more often it is a gesture of spiritual pride."[36] It would be pride in the sense that others might have to go through the usual medical treatment and perhaps loss of modesty, but not oneself due to "superior faith" or "special status" among God's people. The story of Naaman the leper, commander of the army of the King of Aram, who went to visit Elisha for healing is quite instructive (2 Kings 5:1-14). Elisha didn't even see him, and through a messenger commanded him to wash himself seven times in the river Jordan. Naaman became angry since he expected to see Elisha personally, pronounce a healing through an invocation to God, and be healed immediately on the spot. After all, he was a man of stature and importance and had arrived with much wealth and prestige. Instead, he was humbled by not even seeing Elisha and having to wash himself in a small unpretentious river compared to those of his great nation. Clearly, pride stood in the way of his healing. But when he humbled himself and obeyed God's means for his healing, he was cured of leprosy. If Naaman had not buried his pride, his pride would have soon buried him.

The prophets were not above applying the medical and scientific knowledge of the times. When Elisha realized that a poisonous apple had been mistakenly included in a stew, he knew enough that adding flour (2 Kings 4:38-41) would neutralize its effect.[37] Elisha purified a spring at Jericho by adding salt (2 Kings 2:19-22). Physicians are mentioned in the Old Testament, as in Isaiah 1:6 where wounds and sores are cleansed, bandaged, and treated with oil. The healing balm of Gilead was renown (Gen. 37:25); balm in general was used for healing (2 Chron. 28:15) and used by physicians (Jer. 8:22). The Bible itself gives no grounds for divorce between medical and spiritual means of healing.

Even in this very modern age, our final faith and hope is in the Lord; hence, the continual need for healing prayer. It is a simple fact that modern medicine cannot always cure, especially terminal illnesses or inoperable conditions. Sometimes modern medicine will itself cause illness (*iatrogenic*), or a wrong diagnosis or treatment is used. Alarmingly, depending upon how statistics are compiled, the fourth or sixth leading cause of death after heart disease, cancer, and stroke is "death due to drug reactions, including psychiatric drugs."[38] Spiritual healing is for the whole person and can bring healing in places and ways that modern medicine simply cannot. There is also the possibility of demonic sources of illness, as seen clearly in the Gospels, and therein the spiritual power of Jesus is the only sure recourse. Whatever the means of healing, we are always to pray and seek God. Our faith is in God, not faith in faith. We must guard against trying to use "faith" where wisdom is called for. One should seek the best medical attention and the best healing prayer while listening to God in expectant faith.

An edifying practice for any church would be to anoint and bless in the congregation all who have been called to the medical field—doctors, nurses, physiotherapists, surgeons, and so forth. Service in the medical professions brings its own dilemmas, stresses, and pressures, and the body of Christ would do well to encourage those in its midst who are called to the ministry of healing.

Overcoming Theological Roadblocks to Healing

Illness as God's will. A view held by some is that illness is always God's sovereign will, and hence it is wrong to seek healing or ask for healing prayer. Or at least, one might feel guilty in expecting healing. But just as the Apostle John wrote to Gaius with the desire that he would enjoy good health (3 John 1:2), we can pray with confidence for good health as well. Just as Jesus prayed for the sick and healed them, we can and must do so likewise. If it really is God the Father's sovereign will that people remain ill, then Jesus himself violated his Father's will. If one then argues that it was different for Jesus' time, then what is the basis for the difference today? Jesus healed out of his compassion and love, reflecting the Kingdom of his Father. Would we ever believe that his love has been minimized for centuries? When we are ill, the Scriptures command us to seek healing prayer (Jas. 5:13-18). Why would God give the gifts of healings if they were not to be used? Any belief that illness is God's sovereign will violates the healing and deliverance part of the Great Commission. How can one insist on God's sovereignty in illness when one has a responsibility to preach the gospel (Rom. 10:14-15), make choices in sanctification (Col. 3:5; 1 Cor. 9:27), maintain unity and love (Eph. 4:2-3), and work (Eph. 4:28; 1 Thess. 4:11), for example? So much of the Christian life involves responsible decisions, so why exclude healing?

Sometimes the idea of God's sovereign will is used to rationalize a spiritualized form of fatalism and justify inactivity. This "divine determinism" results in despair, passivity, needless suffering, and undermines the ministry of healing prayer.[39] There might be exceptions in the sense that God has allowed an illness for his purposes, like Paul's illness that God used to establish the Galatian Church (Gal. 4:13), but the general expectation is that God desires to heal. Some illnesses will lead to death, and illness and death will not be conquered until the coming of the new heaven and earth (Rom. 8:18-21; Rev. 21:1-4).

Sanctification through sickness. Another view holds that there is sanctification through sickness. Therefore, one is hesitant to ask for healing since this interferes with God's work of sanctification. Purifying one's soul then becomes a goal. As a general principle of belief, this also falls apart, given the same initial reasons above (3 John 1:2; Jas. 5:13-18). One may well learn of God's faithfulness, strength, presence, and more from an illness, but this is not the typical reason that illness comes into our life. Illness has much more to do with sin, the fallen state of this world, and the devil himself with evil spirits of various forms of infirmities. Trials and testing (Jas. 1:2-4) build our faith and mould our character, and is not what James had in mind, although sickness cannot be ruled out totally. Persecution (Matt. 5:11,44; Luke 11:49; 21:12; John 15:20; Acts 12:1) is not sickness, and comes with belonging to

Jesus. Suffering for the Kingdom (2 Thess. 1:5) or the gospel (2 Tim. 1:8; 2 Tim. 2:9) or because we belong to Jesus (1 Pet. 4:12-14) has to do with persecution and sickness at all. Jesus himself was perfected by suffering (Heb. 2:10) and not sickness, and though such suffering builds character and perseverance (Rom. 5:3), it is again not sickness.

Our bodies don't matter. Another view says that God is not really interested in our bodies, so why be so concerned about healing? But God cares about the whole person. Jesus healed many physical illnesses, and again, we must follow his example. This view devalues the incarnation and the physical healing ministry of Jesus as recorded in the Gospels and is more like gnosticism. Since God created matter, and dwells in it (John 1:14), matter does matter.

Punishment. I have met a few people who believed that God was punishing them, and that there would be no relief ever from the illness. Such a belief comes from a harsh, unloving view of God's character. Even when illness is the direct result of sin (Ps. 38:3), there is still forgiveness and God's grace and presence.

All such beliefs can be major roadblocks to healing and receiving God's love. The bottom line still remains—we must pray for healing and deliverance because it is an integral part of the Great Commission. But why doesn't God always heal?

Why God Does Not Always Heal

At a conference, Sherry was somewhat skeptical of the healing ministry, and asked me whether I believed that God always healed. I replied that while we should assume God wants to heal due to his love and compassion, there are times when healing does not occur. Apparently some "faith healers," who believed that God will and must always heal, had bothered her. If he doesn't, they indicated, it's because the person receiving prayer "lacks faith."

I have known of some Christians who received prophecy that they would be healed, yet they died of cancer. This is simply fact and should not be hidden or overlooked or denied. Was the prophecy given not of God? Did someone not pray hard enough? We can ask all kinds of questions in our quest to know why. First, let's firmly remember that no matter the outcome, Jesus loves us (remember the story of Lazarus in the chapter, *"Compassion Deficit Disorder"*), will never forsake or leave us (Deut. 31:6; Ps. 27:19; 37:28), and nothing can separate us from his love, not even illness or death (Rom. 8:38). Indeed, precious in the sight of the Lord is the death of his saints (Ps. 116:15). This is much more important than knowing "why."

Imagine Jesus coming to you just when you have learned that you have a serious illness. What if he offered you one of two things— to be reassured of his presence through all that will come, or to know why this is happening? Which would you choose? I'm almost certain you would choose the former. While there is nothing wrong with asking the Lord why there is an illness, this is far less important than the assurance of his presence and love, no matter the outcome. We do well to realize that the larger problem of suffering for Christian belief appeared as of the seventeenth century, when Christian thinkers attempted to make Christianity intellectually respectable apart from the significance of the life and presence of Christ.[40] I still do not really know why I had cancer plus months of chemotherapy and time in a cancer ward. But more important, I am thankful for the healing and his real presence during those months. If Jesus did not know why his own Father had forsaken him (Matt. 27:46; Ps. 22:1), we might not always know why we suffer.

Nevertheless, I have seen much healing, both physical and, especially, emotional and spiritual. From Christian healing ministries over the centuries and even now, there are even well-attested accounts of people being raised from the dead. The good news is that while God does not always heal, he nevertheless heals frequently. It is beyond the scope of this book to consider the whole issue of suffering, evil, and sickness. But I would like to offer some reasons why healing does not always occur.

Lack of faith. At times this may be a factor, but given the additional reasons below it is not always the case. One should not judge the person with an illness as lacking faith if there is no healing. I expect the Lord will reveal this to the person involved. The lame man at Bethesda did not even know who Jesus was and therefore certainly had no faith in his healing power at all (John 5:2-14). Of the ten lepers, only one came back and thanked Jesus (Luke 17:12-17). At other times, faith and belief were necessary to bring about a healing, like the disciples and the demonized boy (Mark 17:14-20). Jesus healed when he saw the faith of those who brought the paralytic (Matt. 9:2) or the faith of the woman with the bleeding (Matt. 9:22). When there was unbelief, he could not do any healing miracles (Matt. 13:58). The challenge to us is to grow in faith, to exercise it more and more and ask the Lord to help us in any unbelief (Mark 9:24). The most instantaneous healings that I have seen are those where someone, usually the person with the need, has a strong faith that God is about to bring a healing. Faith must be in Jesus and his love for us, not faith in faith itself, or faith in our ability to "claim" a healing, or faith in our power to think positive thoughts. The latter are actually examples of the works of the flesh and have more to do with the human potential movement, mind control, and transcendentalism. The Gospels clearly show that there was not always an absolute and direct connection between faith and healing. In "faith formula" thinking, "when faith becomes a technique to manipulate the power of God, it becomes destructive."[41] The result is guilt and blame when a healing does not occur, or possibly gratitude in one's power to believe when healing does occur.

Redemptive suffering. "Physical healing is not in itself the highest value in the world. At times God uses sickness for a higher purpose."[42] Seemingly countless interpretations have been proposed for Paul's "thorn in the flesh." An exhaustive medical and theological analysis reveals that Paul's thorn in the flesh was most likely benign tertian or vivax- type malaria.[43] That interpretation agrees with all the biblical and medical data—sudden onset, migraine headaches, aches, pain like a thorn, recurrent, and chronic. Malaria was endemic in the regions where he traveled. I am familiar with those regions as well, having traveled in them myself, even visiting Paul's hometown of Tarsus (I would not advise a special trip there. It wasn't terribly exciting; I just happened to be in the neighborhood). The Apostle Paul, himself, was subject to illness like we all are, and not from lack of faith or sin. The redemptive value was that it kept Paul from the temptation of pride, made him rely on God's strength, deepened his prayer life, and displayed the power and grace of God to others (2 Cor.12:7-10). The Lord's reply, after three requests for healing by Paul, was that he would have to live with the condition but no less in God's continued strength and grace. What Satan meant for evil, God allowed and redeemed for His purposes. Nothing happens to the believer outside of God's will, and all works for good in the end (Rom. 8:28). God did not allow the malaria to worsen such that it curtailed his ministry, as it very well could have. It seems that because of the illness allowed in God's sovereignty, Paul first preached to the Galatians (Gal. 4:13) and, therefore, a new church was born. This example from Paul's life directly defies any "faith formula" type of thinking. As was true of Paul, there are situations where illness must be considered in the wider context of spiritual direction and pilgrimage. Yet the majority of illnesses do not have an overwhelming redemptive value that pre-empts healing.

Janet suffered an illness for some years, and by her own admission is so thankful there was not a quick and as yet complete healing. Why? Because her life was so busy and on the fast lane that she really never had much time for God. This wakeup call from God changed all her priorities and has caused her to go deeper with God. She firmly believes that, otherwise, she would have been lost in the world and its rat race. Perhaps God could have used another means, but I hesitate to question her assessment of her life.

Sin. When sin is the issue, it must be addressed. Unforgiveness, bitterness, resentment, and more, can be major roadblocks to healing (Ps. 38:3). When we hold unconfessed sin in our lives, we cover ourselves with a cloud so that our prayers cannot reach God (Lam. 3:44). When we cherish sin in our hearts, the Lord will not listen to us (Ps. 66:18). Fortunately, the Lord desires to forgive, cleanse, heal, and restore us from the effects of sin in our lives. But of course there are times when sin is not the issue at all (Job 1:8; John 9:2-3).

Too general prayers. Often, specific healing will need specific prayer. In praying for the whole person, the Holy Spirit must reveal the exact root or cause, when there is one. Prayer more like a "shotgun approach" is much less effective. This is part of what Paul meant by always praying in the Spirit (Eph. 6:18). Healing prayer should be directed by the Spirit and reflect the mind of Christ. Jeremy's healing, as recounted in the beginning of this chapter, is an example of this. If someone is stated as not having enough faith or not "claiming their healing hard enough," perhaps the person administering healing did not take time to listen to the Spirit. That could be an example of shifting the blame to the person in need. One must guard against trivializing the issues of the soul.

Misdiagnosis. One needs true discernment to uncover the real issues and causes. If deliverance is the real need, any other prayer or diagnosis will not help. Or maybe sin is the issue and not deliverance at all, or both. Or for physical healing, it may be a relational issue from the past. Again, this requires the spiritual discipline of listening to the Spirit and praying just as Jesus would in the given situation.

Refusal to seek medical help. Sometimes God will bring healing through creational means, and one must be open to his will. It's not then about lacking faith, but of obedience and listening to the Father. This could be why there may be no apparent response from healing prayer. But as discussed above, whatever the means, all healing comes from God and we must not prescribe which pathway or combinations thereof he will employ. Apparent spirituality in seeking "healing by faith only" could be a cover for disobedience.

Rejecting God's means of preserving health. God designed our bodies for the principles of nutrition, diet, hygiene, exercise, rest, and more. If we allow too much stress in our lives due to a complex lifestyle too conformed to the world—such that it affects our blood pressure or immune system—we need more wisdom and the practice of the spiritual discipline of simplicity before any healing prayer. If we neglect proper nutrition, for example, we are actually disobeying God's truth in creation and dishonor the way he has built our bodies. While God may be merciful enough to heal us of any effects from improper diet, one cannot overlook the practical and medical daily issues of living.

Timing. Some people are healed only after a longer time waiting in prayer. In some cases, God healed later because they were then ready to understand more in their spiritual journey. Sometimes healing is instantaneous; sometimes there is a delay. The ten lepers were healed gradually as they went to the priest, and one of them soon noticed the healing (Luke 7:12-15). Not all of Jesus' healings were instant. Some healings are gradual over time, and may require repeated times of prayer. In our age of instant results, fast therapeutic accomplishments, instant communication, push-button technology, and more, we must fit into God's agenda and timing and not the reverse.

The wrong person. Since healing prayer requires the gifts of the Holy Spirit, there will be different giftings. I know of a few people who have an especially strong anointing of the Spirit for praying for infertility, for example. Others pray more for physical illnesses, others more for emotional and relational needs. In a few cases a person has come to me for prayer out of conviction that the Lord clearly spoke to them that I was to pray for them. I'm uncomfortable with this, since I fear it will draw too much attention to me and less to Jesus, but if I am to so pray, then I must obey the Lord. Among those cases, a lady at a conference came to me for a very specific physical need that would require some painful surgery. She was convinced that Jesus would heal her, and that I should pray for her. I did, anointing her with oil and praying for healing. She said she knew that the healing took place by the Lord's revelation to her as I prayed. Tests later proved that the healing had occurred and no surgery was required.

Insufficient anointing or empowering. Those administering healing prayer must spend time in Jesus' presence and grow in the spiritual gifts. Presumption in the healing ministry can undermine its effectiveness. I can remember one healing prayer service where the Lord used me to bring deep and often very quick emotional and physical healing to a number of people. Elated, I had presumed the same would happen the next week. It didn't, and as I reflected on that evening, I saw how presumptuous I had become. All ministry comes out of continual dependence upon Jesus. True anointing or empowering does not require dramatic manifestations. The goal is lasting fruit from truly changed lives. The goal is to experience the deep love of Jesus. Beyond that, we seek to bring glory to Jesus and his Father.

Healing not really wanted. Jesus asked the lame man at the pool of Bethesda if he wanted to get well (John 5:6). That may seem like a strange question, given he was in need of healing. But part of the healing process is a desire to get well. In some cases, people are not healed because they like the attention, role, or identity that comes with their illness. A colleague of mine told me of a man who was blind, and when challenged, he somewhat angrily agreed that he did not relish the idea of regaining his sight because he would then have to get a job, would lose a lot of attention and empathy, be required to make other changes in his life, and so forth.

Other avenues of healing required. We must not overlook fellowship, relationships, hospitality, and related avenues of healing. The larger social environment is part of the healing as well, since, as we have seen in the beginning of this chapter, health is a relational concept. I know of a few people who have changed incredibly, overcoming past fears and insecurities, and are now more peaceful and healthier. That occurred through lots of hugs and fellowship with Christians of integrity, patience, and much love. The environment of a church as a whole should be such that it is a healing fellowship. This is another reason why cell or home groups are so important in a church.

The fact that not all people are healed is not any grounds for criticism or reservations about the ministry of healing prayer. The bottom line is still that we should pray for healing and deliverance in obedience to the Great Commission. In a word, obedience.

Waging War with Wounded Warriors

Much has been written about equipping the saints (Eph. 4:21) in terms of skills, knowledge, mentoring, and such. A key assumption in the life of the Church is that the saints who are engaged in its ministries and callings have a "basic" level of wholeness. When we think of the Church as an army of God, engaged in spiritual combat, serious thought must be given to the ability of Christian soldiers to effectively wage war. No true general would ever think of going to battle without being certain that the soldiers are fit for battle—healthy, strong, and well trained. It seems that the Church does so whenever insufficient attention is given to healing, restoring, and nurturing its members.

In the New Testament, equipping has a wider scope than often appreciated. The making of disciples, a goal of the Great Commission, will of necessity involve healing, sanctification, personal transformation, and greater degrees of spiritual wholeness. Equipping thus involves mending/restoring, establishing/laying foundations, and preparing/training.[44] As Ogden wrote:

> Any equipping ministry begins with the assumption that we are all broken people because of our own self-destructive sin or having been victimized by the sin of others …Therefore an equipping ministry makes provision for restoring all who bear the damage of physical, spiritual, and emotional brokenness. Our ministry will be only as effective as we are whole in Christ.[45]

Church Growth or Church Faithfulness?

Jesus expects his Church to grow both in number and depth, but Jesus himself will build his Church (Matt. 16:18). Our age, obsessed with success and quantifying results, tempts church leaders to stress numbers, or church size, above all else. A successful pastor or priest is deemed by many to be the head of a large congregation or parish. While Jesus said to *feed* the sheep, there seems all too often to be a preoccupation with *counting* the sheep. Not surprisingly, many church leaders flock to a "successful" church to study the model or example, and then attempt to emulate it in their church in order to produce the same results. Effectively, this is *church cloning* or *spiritual franchising*, whereby church leaders attempt to manufacture what God is doing in other churches—not much unlike McDonald's or Burger King across North America.[46] Posterski and Nelson recount how this has not worked in Canada:

> In Canadian evangelical churches, many visions and plans are drowning in efforts to emulate Bill Hybel's Willow Creek congregation. Many other Canadian congregations are attempting to ride the wave of Rick Warren's California Saddleback purpose-driven church.[47]

Poterski and Nelson note some flawed church approaches, like Disneyland Churches where entertainment is the core of church life and seeks to attract people on that basis; Restaurant Churches where the focus is on menus—meeting the needs of as many people as possible; Teaching Center Churches where doctrine, preaching, and truth are the core; Hothouse Churches where deep commitment is the life of the community; or, Community League Churches where church life revolves around social action and outreach into the community.[48]

How does all this relate to the ministry of spiritual healing and deliverance in the Church? Simply, whatever God is calling a church to do as its unique calling or identity, spiritual healing and deliverance—both integral parts of the Great Commission and commanded and expected by Jesus—must be a part of church life. Given the power of personal testimony from people both saved and healed, and the potential for God to build his Church in the power of his Spirit, a church open and obedient to the healing and freeing ministry of Jesus may experience significant growth and blessing. Yet healing and deliverance must come from genuine compassion and obedience, not as a *means to engineer church growth*. Does it not seem prudent to do what Jesus clearly modeled and commanded, before anything else?

Carsten is the pastor of First Baptist Church, Dauphin, Manitoba, a small but slowly and steadily growing church. Over many years the Lord has led and equipped him in a ministry focused heavily on the healing and transforming presence of Jesus. While the church does have the usual programs like Sunday School, Prayer Meetings, House Groups, Music Ministry, and several committees, etc., plus the occasional outreach activity, this is all secondary to the church experiencing more of Jesus. Often, he can spend at least half of his time each week in healing prayer with people that are drawn by the Holy Spirit to this church. As more and more people experience the direct love and healing presence of Jesus in his congregation, marriages are strengthened and thus there is little need for marriage counseling. There are also fewer conflict issues in the church, since issues of sin and woundedness are steadily being dealt with one by one as people come, a welcome relief after congregational upheaval in earlier days. Rather than spending time and energy on programs and activities and special appeals to get people into the church, the Holy Spirit draws them to the church and often for healing prayer. Carsten considers this a very rewarding use of his time, since most of his time is spent trying to keep up with those whom the Spirit brings to him instead of using cold call visitation or other means to draw people in. This church is offering what cannot be found elsewhere, except in other churches that have the same kind of ministry. This responds to the real spiritual hunger of people who seek true spiritual reality. Outreach for this church has been strengthened because few people can deny the testimony of deeply changed and transformed lives. As family members and co-workers hear what Jesus has done, they sometimes come themselves for healing prayer. Even non-Christians come, and some, upon experiencing the presence of Jesus, accept him as their Lord and Savior. Carsten is also an equipping pastor and is steadily training others in this ministry. The church family and leadership agree with him that the center of their church must be the saving, healing, and transforming presence of Jesus. This unanimous agreement is a key element of this church's effectiveness in the healing prayer ministry. This church has a strong ministry focus on true worship, a desire to know Christ and the power of his resurrection (Phil. 3:10), and to be a people of the genuine presence of the Lord.

Ken Blue wrote about his attempt to start a new church mission in Vancouver.[49] For five years, he and the church leadership tried virtually every conceivable evangelistic strategy, with some church growth and significant rewards but no significant impact on the community. The needs were so great that counseling and community support did not really help the people in their community who needed spiritual, emotional, and physical healing as well as deliverance from powerful spiritual bondages. In that community of competing religious faiths, it was only the healing and delivering power of Jesus that began to make a difference and became a main emphasis of the new church's ministry.

Not every pastor must be so heavily involved in healing prayer. Rather, those with the gifting and anointing for this ministry must be equipped and given the full opportunity to operate in the church. Some pastors have primarily the spiritual gifts of preaching and teaching, so their role is to teach and encourage those in the ministry of healing prayer.

Many have criticized the organizational and technical approach to "church growth." The danger is rational and technical bondage. But church growth that focuses on experience, manifestations, and signs and wonders can unwittingly end up trading the danger of rational and technical bondage with the danger of experiential bondage. The focus must always be on the authentic presence of Jesus and experiencing more of his saving and transforming love. Satan is quite pleased when the Church does everything and anything except exactly what God the Father expects.

The core of church life must be the person and presence of Jesus, and his saving and healing work. The primary calling of the Church is to be faithful to the commands and commission of Jesus, our first love (Rev. 2:4), before all other programs or activities. In some respects, church growth has become needlessly complex. Is there not a greater need for church faithfulness experts than church growth experts?

Endnotes

[1] John Wilkinson, *The Bible and Healing. A Medical and Theological Commentary* (Grand Rapids: Eerdmans, 1998) p. 11.

[2] Wilkinson, p. 12.

[3] Ibid.

[4] Wilkinson, p. 13.

[5] Wilkinson, p. 14.

[6] Wilkinson, p. 15.

[7] Ibid.

[8] Wilkinson, p. 19.

[9] James F. Jekel, "Biblical Foundations for Health and Healing," *Journal of the American Scientific Affiliation*, Vol. 47(3), 1995, pp. 150-158.

[10] David G. Benner, *Care of Souls. Revisioning Christian Nurture and Counsel* (Grand Rapids: Baker Books, 1998) p. 59.

[11] Reginald Cherry, *Healing Prayer. God's Divine Intervention In Medicine, Faith, and Prayer* (Nashville: Thomas Nelson, 1999) p. 15.

[12] Morton Kelsey, *Healing and Christianity: A Classic Study* (Minneapolis: Augsburg Press, 1993) p. 205.

[13] Kelsey, p. 221.

[14] Fran Ferder, *Words Made Flesh. Scripture, Psychology and Human Communication* (Notre Dame: Ave Maria Press, 1986) p. 82.

[15] Ferder, p. 54.

[16] Redmond and Virginia Williams, *Anger Kills* (New York: Harper Paperbacks, 1993) p. 75.

[17] Williams, p. Xvi.

[18] Leanne Payne, *Restoring The Christian Soul Through Healing Prayer. Overcoming the Three Great barriers to Personal and Spiritual Completion in Christ* (Wheaton: Crossway Books, 1991) p. 82.

[19] James I. Packer, *Rediscovering Holiness* (Ann Arbor: Vine Books, 1992) p. 46.

[20] Colin Brown, *The New International Dictionary of New Testament Theology, Vol. 3.* (Grand Rapids: Zondervan, 1978) pp. 211-213.

[21] Wilkinson, p. 78.

[22] Wilkinson, p. 79.

[23] George E. Ladd, *A Theology Of The New Testament* (Grand Rapids: Eerdmans, 1974) p. 77.

[24] Richard J. Foster, *Prayer: Finding The Heart's True Home* (San Francisco: Harper, 1992) p. 203.

[25] Dallas Willard, *The Spirit of the Disciplines. Understanding How God Changes Lives* (New York: New York, 1991) p. 32.

[26] Willard, p. 38.

[27] John F. MacArthur, Jr., *Charismatic Chaos* (Grand Rapids: Zondervan, 1992) p. 237.

[28] Julia C. Martinez, "Owens signs faith-healing bill," *Denver Post Capital Bureau*, www.denverpost.com, 17 April 2001.

[29] David O. Moberg, "The Great Commission and Research," *The Journal of the American Scientific Affiliation.* Vol. 51(1), 1999, pp. 8-16.

[30] Lytton John Musselman, "Solomon's Plant Life: Plant Lore and Image in the Solomonic Writings," *Journal of the American Scientific Affiliation*, Vol. 51, 1999. p. 26.

[31] Musselman, p. 27.

32 Dale A. Matthews with Connie Clark, *The Faith Factor. Proof of the Healing Power of Prayer* (New York: Viking, 1998) p. 17.

33 Cherry, p. 23.

34 John N. Oswalt, *The Book of Isaiah Chapters 1-39. The New International Commentary on the Old Testament* (Grand Rapids: Eerdmans, 1986) p. 691.

35 Oswalt, p. 691.

36 Foster, p. 204.

37 Wilkinson, p. 60.

38 Peter R. Breggin and D. Cohen, *Your Drug May Be Your Problem. How And Why To Stop Taking Psychiatric Medications* (Cambridge: Perseus Publishing, 1999) p. 60.

39 Ken Blue, *Authority to Heal* (Downer's Grove: InterVarsity Press, 1987) pp. 33-40.

40 Alister McGrath, *Suffering & God* (Grand Rapids: Zondervan, 1992) p. 42.

41 Ken Blue, p. 42.

42 Francis MacNutt, *Healing* (Notre Dame: Ave Maria Press, 1974) p. 250.

43 Wilkinson, pp. 204-226.

44 G. Ogden, *The New Reformation. Returning The Ministry To The People Of God* (Grand Rapids: Zondervan, 1990) p. 101.

45 Ogden, pp. 104-105.

46 Don Posterski and G. Nelson, *Future Faith Churches: Reconnecting With The Power Of The Gospel For The 21st Century* (Winfield: Wood Lake Books, 1995) p. 168.

47 Posterski, pp. 170-171.

48. Ibid., p.p. 170-171.

49 Blue, pp. 13-17.

Chapter Five

Vanishing Spiritual Gifts?

The Contemporary Spiritual Gifts and Healing

I vividly remember one of the first people to whom I administered healing prayer. Janice, herself a health professional, had been suffering for over ten years from an obsessive-compulsive disorder. She had sought help from different sources, including several counselors, pastors, and a telephone crisis line, but all to no avail. This disorder consumed several hours of each day, causing considerable emotional and mental turmoil and draining her energy. When she came to see me, she said that she was desperate and felt as if her life was "falling apart." After listening to her story, I suggested that we ask Jesus by His Spirit to reveal the source(s) of this apparent disorder. After a few minutes in prayer, a long-forgotten memory came back, and the Lord enabled me to see the connection between the current disorder and this past event. I asked Jesus to come and bring his healing and freedom from the emotional and mental bondage, which he did. By the time she left, there was a new joy in her face, for she was no longer under the power of this disorder. Ten years of bondage terminated in less than an hour!

Dunkerley[1] recounts the true story of Rev. Peterson Sozi who pastored an illegal church that met in a garage in Kabowa, off the Kampala-Entebbe Road in Uganda during the reign of Idi Amin. One Sunday, after preaching on Acts 3, Peterson greeted a twelve-year-old boy on crutches, over whom he spoke just as Peter did in Acts 3—"In the name of Jesus Christ of Nazareth, walk." The boy began to walk immediately, then ran and jumped, holding his crutches in the air, in the presence of many witnesses. The boy's father, as it turns out, was a member of the State Research Bureau, Amin's secret police. He began to tell his friends that Jesus was performing miracles in a garage in Kabowa. As a result, this well-known and undeniable miracle actually led to the salvation of military and security men who joined the growing congregation.

I have prayed a number of times with people who clearly felt heat over various parts of their body. I was just as surprised as they were! For whatever reason, the Spirit gave this as a sign for their healing. The situations that I recall involved healing for an eye, a back, and for cancer. I never seek such manifestations at all, or ever ask if it is happening. The goal is experiencing the healing presence of Jesus and, in the long term, holiness, as those purchased by the blood of Christ. But I see these instances as examples of gifts of healings.

The ministry of healing prayer involves the healing presence of Jesus and the operation of the gifts of his Spirit. I, for one, make no apologies for an intentional reliance on the gifts of the Holy Spirit, including the gifts of healings. More and more Christians worldwide are becoming involved in healing prayer ministry, and are growing in their knowledge and experience of the gifts of the Holy Spirit as they seek to bring healing and wholeness to people. For a growing number of churches, this is understood as the normal, obedient part of church life, based on the model and clear commands of no other than Jesus himself.

The spiritual gifts that I refer to are listed in 1 Cor. 12:7-10. Many books have been written on the subject of the spiritual gifts, and on this passage in particular. Different groupings have been proposed for these gifts. A popular grouping has gifts of instruction (wisdom and knowledge), then gifts of supernatural power (faith, healings, miracles), and then gifts of inspired utterance (prophecy, discerning prophecies, tongues, and interpretation of tongues). Another grouping has been illumination, action, and communication.[2]

The *spiritual gift of wisdom* brings God's wisdom and understanding into a situation, and the word of knowledge is a revelation about something or someone that could only have come from God. The latter is especially useful in healing prayer to give direction and understanding. The *gift of faith* is not saving faith per se, but the ...

> mysterious surge of confidence that rises within a person in a particular situation of need or challenge and that gives an extraordinary certainty or assurance that God is about to act through a word or action.[3]

Fee describes it as a "supernatural conviction that God will reveal his power or mercy in a special way in a special instance."[4] The spiritual *gifts of healings* refer to healing for different types of illnesses and also healing for a particular time and place. In either case, it points to a manifestation of the Holy Spirit as healing through God's people. The *spiritual gift of miraculous powers* (*dunamis*) is God's more extraordinary empowering for the purposes of his Kingdom, including miraculous healing.[5] It is especially important here to note that "*dunamis* is used in the synoptic Gospels to describe the works of healing which Jesus performed."[6] It is not the power or ability to cast out demons since that comes with authority and our position in

Christ who has defeated the enemy. The *spiritual gift of prophecy* relates not to additional revelation as part of the completed written Word of God (Jude 3), or anything that ever stands above the Scriptures. Rather, it concerns God speaking encouragement, warning, direction, exhortation, or knowledge of future events to communities of believers or more personally to any of his believers. The spiritual *gift of distinguishing between spirits*, controversial among some scholars, is crucial to discern the presence and role of evil spirits or test and discern teaching or prophecy.[7] The *gift of tongues and interpretation of tongues* has to do with Spirit-inspired utterance.[8] Romans 12:6-8 has another list of spiritual gifts, which includes serving, teaching, encouraging, giving, leadership, and mercy. I exclude Ephesians 4:11 because that's God's gift of people, not spiritual gifts per se.

Some Christians hold that some of the spiritual gifts, particularly those of communication (wisdom, knowledge, prophecy, tongues, interpretation of tongues) and supernatural power (faith, healing, and miracles) have ceased to operate since the apostolic era. There are some Christian circles where healing prayer using the spiritual gifts of healing and related gifts is not only discouraged and discredited, but actually proclaimed as unscriptural for the Church today. Some would even go so far as to say that the desire for such gifts actually opens one up to evil spiritual influences. Either the gifts of healing and related gifts operate today, or those claiming to have those gifts are deceived, or misrepresenting the Spirit, or using evil spiritual power. Such a view directly calls into question the ministry of spiritual healing, and must be challenged. Most importantly and tragically, this view becomes responsible for the needless suffering of Christians who would otherwise be healed. In effect, a means of grace becomes blocked within parts of the Church. This is not simply an academic question, for it involves the very real pain of Christians today within the Body of Christ.

If Janice had not received healing prayer using the gifts of the Spirit, she might have ended up in a psychiatric ward, or worse. If the young Ugandan boy had not received prayer in the name of Jesus, he might still be unable to walk. I can remember one healing prayer conference in particular when I and others on the ministry teams were praying with people well past midnight three evenings in a row. There was such a desire to be touched and healed by the direct, deep love of Jesus, especially by people from churches where healing prayer was not offered. The Lord was truly present with his healing power, and brought deep emotional, spiritual, and physical healing. At many conferences I see a hunger among God's people to experience more of Him. One can only guess how much illness and suffering among Christians would be alleviated if the gifts of the Holy Spirit were fully utilized in the Church.

The denial of the contemporary operation of some of the gifts of the Holy Spirit, including gifts of healings, comes from a purportedly biblical teaching known as cessationism. In short, some gifts of the Spirit ceased after the apostolic era. Cessationists argue for this view, whereas continuationists hold that all the gifts of the Spirit have continued until today. Both cessationists and continuationists would agree that the writing of Scripture has ceased and therefore any addition to the written Scriptures has ceased.

A Brief History of Cessationism

For centuries it has been believed and taught in some seminaries and churches that some of the gifts of the Holy Spirit, including healing, ceased upon the death of the apostles or certainly upon the completion of the New Testament. Most scholars agree that the New Testament was completely written by about 100 A.D., with most having been written twenty to forty years before.[9] Where and when did this belief originate? For the reader with a passion for history or historical theology, here are just a very few comments on a complex subject. For readers with little interest in these matters, I won't be offended if you just skip this section.

Some writers trace the basic idea of cessationism back to Judaism from the Maccabean era onward, characterized with a growing ambivalence to prophecy and miracles. This was due partly to the apparent absence of such operation of the Holy Spirit since the time of the Old Testament prophets, and in reaction to Jewish "charismatics" who used their spiritual experiences to confirm their doctrinal credibility.[10] The early church fathers used the Jewish admission of the cessation of prophecy and miracles in their midst as proof that God had transferred his favor from them to the Christian Church. But in the process, they endorsed the belief that the primary, if not exclusive, function of miracles is to substantiate the theology of its bearers.[11] Augustine (354–430 A.D.) initially supported cessationism but later repudiated it. Gregory the Great (540-604 A.D.) recorded many miracles, but taught that the miracles were meant to initiate the growth of the Church. In the now growing Church, miracles would be replaced by piety and the study of Scripture[12], and miracles were understood to "prove the gospel, not to express it." Thomas Aquinas rewrote Christian theology using the world view of Aristotle, with this result:

> If God is known primarily through intellectual activity rather than experience, there is little place for any gifts of the Spirit. As described by Paul, they fit more easily into a Platonic world view than an Aristotelian one. The medieval church developed a final and certain total outlook based on past revelation elaborated by human reason; it needed nothing more. There was no need for God to continue to communicate with human beings. One might

expect further revelations or healings, but only under extraordinary supernatural conditions.[13]

Aquinas taught mainly, but not always consistently, that the main purpose of miracles was to prove or affirm Christian truth, especially the deity of Christ.[14] The Reformers were challenged by the medieval Catholic Church which demanded miracles to authenticate teaching. The medieval Roman Catholics pointed to miracles from their tradition and history which they claimed authenticated their doctrine, like God's "seal of approval." The Reformers were not impressed with Catholic abuses of healing and related spiritual practices, like relics and veneration of saints.[15] Using the teaching of Aquinas to their advantage, the Reformers argued that the more miraculous gifts of the Spirit ceased with the apostles, and thus felt justified in challenging the authority of Catholic doctrine and maintaining their teaching. Truth was to be based on Scripture alone, not on extra-biblical teachings, or spiritual experiences, or other claims to authority. Calvin himself did not hold to a rigid cessationism. He believed that the gifts were withdrawn due to disbelief, but not totally, and might possibly be restored one day.[16] But concerning the gift of healing, Calvin wrote in his *Institutes*:

> But that gift of healing, like the rest of the miracles, which the Lord willed to be brought forth for a time, has vanished in order to make the new preaching of the gospel marvelous forever.[17]

Calvin also believed that the laying on of hands for especial empowering was a specific grace of the apostles, and, as such, ceased with the passing of the apostles. Those miraculous powers were for the new, inaugural preaching of the Kingdom of God and could not be passed on once the apostles died.[18]

John Knox, disciple of Calvin, who founded Scottish Presbyterianism, was among the leaders of the Reformation who exercised the gift of non-revelational prophecy. [19] [20] Thus, while the Reformers used some cessationist arguments, it is not true that they themselves did not exercise any of the miraculous gifts of the Spirit.

From the early 1900's, cessationism was articulated and popularized by B.B. Warfield in his book *Counterfeit Miracles*. Many believed that once the Church was planted, established, spread through the known world, and then came under the protection of civil power, the more miraculous gifts of the Spirit were no longer required.[21] In effect, the miraculous gifts of the Spirit were intended only to "jump start" the Church. Warfield rejected that view as without New Testament support,[22] and helpless due to the inherent logical inconsistencies.[23] Warfield wouldn't allow for any evidence of miracles in the early centuries of the Church, and instead linked the miraculous gifts of the Spirit closely to the apostles:

> The Apostolic Church was characteristically a miracle-working church. How long did this state of things continue? It was the characterizing peculiarity of specifically the Apostolic Church, and it belonged therefore exclusively to the Apostolic age—although no doubt this designation may be taken with some latitude. These gifts were not the possession of the primitive Christian as such; nor for that matter of the Apostolic Church or the Apostolic age for themselves; they were distinctively the authentication of the Apostles. They were part of the credentials of the Apostles as the authoritative agents of God in founding the church. Their function thus confined them to distinctively the Apostolic Church, and they necessarily passed away with it.... The possession of the charismata was confined to the Apostolic Age.[24]

Warfield's theology was influenced by the thinking of his day. A key concept of the Enlightenment was that man, by his own reason and empirical observation, could discover truth and knowledge. Instead of submitting to the authority of the Word of God, man would stand over the Scriptures and become the source of revelation. Man need not live under superstition and religion—he would be enlightened by his own intellectual powers.[25]

Inevitably, the issue of miracles soon arose. If miracles were to attest to divine truth, like an apologetic or reason for believing, what if they did not occur now? Why then believe that they ever occurred in the first place? The Protestant theologians responded to Hume and the Enlightenment skeptics, who claimed that miracles did not occur now, or in the past, *by agreeing that in the present miracles do not occur.*[26] In essence, cessationism was just one step from the full Enlightenment position, which was centered on man's ability to think and rely only on data from the five observable senses. American evangelicals embraced Enlightenment thinking in their theology through Scottish common sense philosophy—which was embraced at Princeton where Warfield taught—whereby all people possessed a common, innate understanding to grasp the basic realities of truth and God.[27] This resulted in an evangelical Enlightenment with an intellectual climate quite conducive to cessationism. The desire was to appear intellectually credible in an increasingly rationalistic academic world, but at the cost of denying any miracles in the present.

The rise of dispensationalism, in response to liberal theology, was supportive, but not totally formative, of cessationism. Cessationism holds basically that since the completion of the New Testament (now a new era), God is now working differently (no miracles, signs, and wonders as before). Dispensationalism, which has many versions and nuances, holds that God dispenses his grace and purposes in different ways in different eras. Kelsey summarizes this as follows:

> The natural reaction to this critical and liberal theology was to hang to the very letter of the Bible and maintain the literal truth of the text against all comers. To do this, fundamentalism or literal theology needed to explain how there could be such radical difference between the experiences described in the Bible and those of men today. The theory of dispensationalism provided the answer. The Biblical experiences, it held, particularly the encounters of God with men, were not natural happenings... In New Testament times, and to an extent in the Old Testament period, God allowed these things to happen by a special dispensation. He set aside the ordinary structure of the universe long enough to break through man's resistance and establish the people of Israel and, through them, the church of Christ. Then he withdrew this dispensation and the normal order was restored.[28]

Dispensationalism or cessationism, in attempting to explain the apparent contemporary lack of spiritual experiences in comparison to those as recorded in the Bible, claim the cause is no less than God himself. Rather than allowing the Scriptures to interpret or even challenge our spiritual experiences or lack thereof today, these arguments claim that, in part, the Scriptures describe what we do not experience today and must not ever expect.

Contemporary Cessationism

An increasing number of Christians began to believe that the operation of the "more miraculous" gifts of the Spirit, such as tongues and prophecy, and necessarily also healing, ceased once the early Church was established. One professor of systematic theology wrote:

> *Among the early Christians there were some who had the gift of healing and could perform miracles, 1 Cor. 12:9, 10, 28,*

> 30; Mark 16:17-18. This extraordinary condition, however, soon made way for the usual one, in which the Church carries on its work by the ordinary means. **There is no Scriptural ground for the idea that the charism of healing was intended to be continued in the Church of all ages.** Evidently, the miracles and miraculous signs recorded in the Scriptures were intended as a mark or credential of divine revelation, themselves formed a part of this revelation, and served to attest and confirm the message of the early preachers of the gospel. As such they naturally ceased when the period of special revelation came to an end (emphasis mine).[29]

A.W. Pink, like Warfield, differentiated between the ordinary and extraordinary gifts, with the extraordinary gifts for confirming the preached word of the apostles, and the apostles themselves as communicators of divine truth. Apparently this was necessary since the New Testament had not yet been written, compiled, and acknowledged as the Scriptures in entirety. Concerning 1 Cor. 12:8-10, Pink wrote, "Now that all of these special impulses and extraordinary gifts of the Spirit were not intended to be perpetuated throughout this Christian dispensation, and that they have long since ceased, is clear...."[30] Pink even claimed that seeking extraordinary gifts today opens Christians to Satanic deception:

> What the Spirit does now is to bestow ordinary ministerial gifts, which the possessor must improve and develop by study and use. To "seek power from on High," or a special "filling of the Spirit," is to run serious risk of being controlled by evil spirits posing as angels of light.[31]

A more recent writer has similarly concluded that while healings occur today, the biblical gift of healing is not present.[32] Here cessationism distinguishes between permanent edifying gifts (knowledge, wisdom, prophecy as authoritative preaching, teaching, exhortation, faith or prayer, discernment, showing mercy, giving, administration, and helps) and the temporary sign gifts.[33] Concerning the temporary sign gifts which includes the gift of healing, MacArthur wrote:

> These were specific enablements given to certain believers for the purpose of authenticating or confirming God's Word when it was proclaimed in the early church before the Scriptures were written. The temporary sign gifts included prophecy (revelatory prophecy), miracles, healings, tongues, and interpretation of tongues. The sign gifts had a unique purpose: to give the apostles credentials, that is, to let the people know that these men all spoke the truth of God. Once the Word of God was inscripturated, the sign gifts were no longer needed and they ceased.[33]

> ...those who claim the gift of healing do not really have it. Why? The gift of healing was a temporary sign gift for the authenticating of the Scriptures as the Word of God. Once that authenticity was established, the gift of healing ceased.[34]

Thomas R. Edgar, in his book on the miraculous gifts, concluded similarly to MacArthur:

> There is no evidence from any source to demonstrate that sign gifts from the Holy Spirit, such as working miracles and gifts of healing, are present today. The Biblical evidence indicates that the sign gifts were given to confirm the gospel message of eyewitnesses of the Lord to a world where the gospel was unknown.[35]

Gumprecht, in critiquing Agnes Sanford's theology of healing and discussing the application of John 14:12 and miracles which includes miracles of healing, wrote:

The ability to do miracles was given by God to establish the authenticity of their apostleship and the authority of God while the canon of Scripture was being completed. Thereafter miracles gradually ceased in the Church because Christians had the Word of God as their rule and guide and the Holy Spirit indwelling them to comfort and teach (John 14:16,17,26; 16:13-15; Matt. 12:38; 1 Cor. 1:22; 13:9,10).[36]

Masters maintained that cessationism is a mainstream orthodox belief when he wrote:

> ...let us be clear on this point—cessationism is not merely the opinion of a minority of obscurantists and pedants; it is the view which has been held by the overwhelming majority of evangelicals until this present age of unprecedented doctrinal decline. To avoid any confusion it is necessary to point out that the historic "cessationist" position does not say that miracles have ceased, but that the revelatory and sign gifts have ceased, that is, the power to speak inspired words, and the power to work miracles and perform healings. God no longer delegates the dispensing of miracles to human agents.[37]

Dickason supports a cessationist view also:

Gifts of the apostolic office and miraculous types have been removed by God. The apostles were the foundation of the church; they are not found in the superstructure (Eph. 2:20). Paul's healing gift seems later nonoperative for Epaphroditus and Trophimus (Phil. 2:27; 2 Tim. 4:20). The special gifts of prophetic revelation and a message of knowledge were rendered inoperative, and tongues were to cease at the completion of revelation and knowledge as found in the New Testament (1 Cor. 13:8-10).[38]

Dickason wrote that while we have authority in Jesus to cast out demons, we do not necessarily have miraculous powers to introduce a new message.[39] The role and purpose of miraculous powers is linked to the gospel as a new message, and once the introduction was complete, the miraculous powers were no longer needed. In agreement with other writers, Dickason holds that there are no genuine spiritual gifts of tongues today, and those that appear to operate are either artificial, psychological, or demonic.[40] This is a logical consequence of cessationism. If a spiritual gift really did cease at the completion of the New Testament, only its counterfeit operates today.

In summary, cessationists claim that some of the gifts of the Holy Spirit were temporary "sign" gifts that pointed to Jesus and the apostolic authority of the apostles, who performed signs, wonders, and miracles which often involved miraculous healing. With such credentials, the apostles were confirmed by the Church to write divine revelation which eventually formed the New Testament. When the New Testament was completed, the temporary sign gifts were no longer required. When the apostles died, the more miraculous spiritual gifts also ceased. The other spiritual gifts are the permanent gifts. Not all cessationists rule out miracles per se, since some will allow for God to answer prayer in miraculous ways. It's not whether, but which, gifts continue today.[41] In particular, cessationists tend to question the operation today of the gifts of healing and miracles and all the revelatory or word gifts. There is some disagreement among cessationists as to which spiritual gifts are among the temporary sign gifts. For example, MacArthur includes the gifts of wisdom and knowledge among the permanent gifts,[42] whereas Gaffin argues for the cessation of those gifts along with all revelatory or word gifts.[43]

How biblical is cessationism? Do the Scriptures really teach this doctrine? Can cessationists really uphold their position so strongly and clearly as God's teaching from the Scriptures? Did Jesus himself believe in cessationism? Are there any unstated assumptions behind cessationism? What are the consequences of cessationism? That is the substance of the next chapter.

Endnotes

[1] Don Dunkerley, *Healing Evangelism: Strengthen Your Witnessing with Effective Prayer for the Sick* (Grand Rapids: Chosen Books, 1995) pp. 17-19.

[2] Gordon D. Fee, *God's Empowering Presence. The Holy Spirit In The Letters Of Paul* (Peabody: Hendrickson Publishers, 1994) pp. 165.

[3] C. Samuel Storms, "A Third Wave View," Wayne A. Grudem (Gen. Ed.), *Are The Miraculous Gifts For Today?* (Grand Rapids: Zondervan, 1996) p. 213.

[4] Fee, p. 168.

[5] John Wilkinson, *The Bible and Healing. A Medical and Theological Commentary* (Grand Rapids: Eerdmans, 1998) p. 162.

[6] Wilkinson, p. 154.

[7] Fee, p. 171.

[8] Fee, p. 172.

[9] F.F. Bruce, *The New Testament Documents: Are They Reliable?* (Downers Grove: InterVarsity Press, 1960) p. 12.

[10] Jon Ruthven, *On the Cessation of the Charismata: The Protestant Polemic on Postbiblical Miracles* (Sheffield: Sheffield Academic Press, 1993) pp. 24-25.

[11] Ruthven, p. 27.

[12] Ruthven, pp. 30-31.

[13] Morton Kelsey, *Healing and Christianity: A Classic Study* (Minneapolis: Augsburg Press, 1993) p. 161.

14 Ruthven, p. 33.

15 William De Arteaga, *Quenching The Spirit: Discover the REAL Spirit Behind the Charismatic Controversy* (Orlando: Creation House, 1996) p. 84.

16 Dunkerley, p. 242.

17 J.T. McNeil, (ed.) *Calvin: Institutes of the Christian Religion.* The Library of Christian Classics, Volume XXI, Book IV:xix.18 (Philadelphia: Westminster Press, 1975) p. 1476.

18 McNeil, p. 1454.

19 Dunkerley, p. 243.

20 Douglas A. Oss, "A Pentecostal/Charismatic Response To Robert L. Saucy," Wayne A. Grudem (Gen. Ed.), *Are The Miraculous Gifts For Today?* (Grand Rapids: Zondervan, 1996) p. 168.

21 Benjamin B. Warfield, *Counterfeit Miracles* (Scribner's, 1918) Republished as *Miracles: Yesterday and Today, True and False* (Grand Rapids: Eerdmans, 1965) p. 7.

22 Warfield, p. 21.

23 Warfield, p. 35.

24 Warfield, pp. 5-6.

25 Charles H. Kraft, *Christianity with Power. Your World view and Your Experience of the Supernatural* (Ann Arbor: Servant Books, 1989) p. 25.

26 De Arteaga, pp. 90-91.

27 Mark A. Noll, T*he Scandal of the Evangelical Mind* (Grand Rapids: Eerdmans, 1994) pp. 83-107.

28 Morton Kelsey, *Encounter With God. A Theology of Christian Experience* (Minnesota: Bethany Fellowship, 1972) p. 30.

29 Louis Berkhof, *Systematic Theology* (Grand Rapids: Eerdmans, 1939, Fifteenth printing, 1977) p. 601.

30 Arthur W. Pink, *The Holy Spirit* (Grand Rapids: Baker Book House, 1970) p. 177.

31 Pink, p. 180.

[32] John F. MacArthur, Jr., *Charismatic Chaos* (Grand Rapids: Zondervan, 1992) p. 265.

[33] MacArthur, p. 243.

[34] MacArthur, p. 248.

[35] Thomas R. Edgar, *The Miraculous Gifts: Are They For Today?* (New Jersey: Neptune, Loizeaux Brothers, 1983) p. 106.

[36] Jane Gumprecht, *Abusing Memory: The Healing Theology of Agnes Sanford* (Moscow: Canon Press, 1997) p. 20.

[37] Peter Masters, *The Healing Epidemic* (London: Wakeman Trust, Elephant and Castle, 1988) p. 37.

[38] C. Fred Dickason, *Demon Possession & the Christian. A New Perspective* (Wheaton: Crossway Books, 1987) p. 263.

[39] Dickason, p. 262.

[40] Dickason, 266.

[41] Richard B. Gaffin, Jr., "A Cessationist View," in Wayne A. Grudem, (Gen. Ed.), *Are The Miraculous Gifts For Today?* (Grand Rapids: Zondervan, 1996) p. 213.

[42] MacArthur, p. 243.

[43] Gaffin, p. 42.

 Chapter Six

Unmasking Cessationism

A "Different" Seminar For Deacons

When I was chairperson of deacons in a church some years ago, we invited a senior pastor from another church in our denomination to give us a weekend seminar on spiritual warfare. After excellent biblical teaching and fellowship, he encouraged us to practice "listening prayer" as we walked through assigned places in our church building. This was a bit of a stretch for some of us, to expect that God would speak to us in a more direct manner. After a little reluctance on the part of some of us, we agreed. The pastor walked through his assigned area, which included each Sunday School room in the church's basement. We met to compare notes and debrief. To our amazement, he gave a detailed description of the dynamics of the class that met in each room, including the overall spiritual atmosphere and even the struggles that the teacher of each class faced. He had absolutely no prior knowledge about our Sunday School at all, yet what he said was completely accurate. Some of the rooms were quite bare, so there was no way of even deducing many ideas and impressions about the classes. I know this for a solid fact, because he also described the class that my wife taught at the time as one of the Sunday School teachers. Incredibly, as I was listening, it might as well have been my wife standing right there sharing her concerns over the class. She had shared most of her concerns only with me and no one in the church to date.

This was an example of a "word of knowledge" where God reveals information directly to his servants. The information was not in addition to the Word of God, for it served to edify our church by giving us more direction and also how to pray for the various classes. Of course, none of us overlooked any biblical truths or principles that could apply to our Sunday School and we all still endeavored to use our minds. Personally, I was challenged to realize that God has such spiritual gifts that could be developed to such a degree. We all realized that we needed to grow in the spiritual disciplines and gifts.

But some cessationists would give another interpretation for the above. They would insist that since such a spiritual gift had ceased from the apostolic era and is no longer required because the Scriptures were completed, therefore a psychic counterfeit gift or some psychological manipulation was operating. These are two totally different and irreconcilable views. How does one resolve this? To begin, we must critique cessationism and its assumptions.

A Strong Connection Between Signs, Wonders, and Apostolic Credentials?

From the previous chapter, we recall that cessationism necessarily requires a strong connection between signs and wonders, or the use of the more miraculous gifts of the Spirit, and their role in confirming apostolic credentials and authorship of Scripture. Is this connection really strong enough to support cessationism? At least six reasons challenge this.

First of all, Jesus taught (Matt. 24:24; cf. 2 Thess. 2:9; Rev. 13:13-14; 19:20) that the ability to perform signs, wonders, or miracles could also be a mark of false prophets and false Christs—even to deceive the elect, if that were possible. There will be those who prophesy and drive out demons in Jesus' name as well as perform miracles, but will not enter the Kingdom because they did not know Jesus nor did the will of the Father (Matt. 7:21-22). Sorcerers, wise men, and magicians in the service of Pharaoh confronted Moses with incredible miracles and powers (Exod. 7:11,22; cf. Rev. 16:14), often duplicating what God achieved through Moses. How then can signs and wonders in themselves ever be sufficient to confirm sources of revelation when they can also be signs of deception? Signs and wonders were not unique to the apostles or confirming their role in proclaiming truth.

Second, Matthew 24:24 deserves further attention, "...false Christs and false prophets will appear and perform great signs and miracles to deceive even the elect—if that were possible." Could Jesus himself have believed in cessationism in making this statement? If cessationism is really true, then anyone at all performing signs and miracles would, by definition, be a false Christ or prophet, since such true abilities ceased long ago. There would be no possibility of deception at all, since by definition its supposed manifestation is false and counterfeit. How then could it be that such powers would be exhibited to the point that even believers might be deceived? Only if miraculous powers and all of the gifts of the Holy Spirit, including the gift of miraculous powers, were still operating so that one must discern between true and counterfeit spiritual powers. This already casts serious doubt on cessationism.

Third, the apostles' ability to perform miracles was only a part of their recognition as apostles and thus authors of Scripture. The apostles received their divine authority from the calling and appointment of Jesus and His Spirit (Mark 3:13-15; 6:30), having spent time with the Lord personally (Acts 4:13) and publicly, which was key in replacing Judas (Acts 1:21-26) with Matthias. For Paul, it was a dramatic encounter and calling (Acts 9:15; 26:17-18; Rom. 1:5; Gal. 1:11-2:10) and eventual confirmation by the other apostles.

Some cessationists argue from 2 Cor. 12:12, which in the NIV reads, "The things that mark an apostle—signs, wonders and miracles—were done among you with great perseverance," that these signs then were unique to the apostles. Deere, citing other Biblical scholars, gives a more literal translation of, "The signs of an apostle were performed among you in all endurance with signs, and wonders, and miracles."[1] The word for "mark" and "signs" is the same word (*semeion*) in the Greek. Thus, the effective outworking of true apostles resulted in, and was accompanied by, God's gracious display of his power. This is a better rendering of the Greek because in the epistle as a whole, he also referred to other signs or criteria—his knowledge of Jesus (2 Cor. 11:4-6), his character in not being a financial burden (2 Cor. 11:7-9), his sufferings for Christ (2 Cor. 6:3-10; 11:23-28; Gal. 6:17), his visions and revelations (2 Cor. 12:1-10), all in comparison to the "super-apostles." Paul pointed also to his character, obedience, and commitment to Jesus as signs of true apostleship. Philip and Stephen were non-apostles who also performed signs and wonders, and thus the signs were obviously and clearly *not unique* to the apostles as their distinct "mark." The apostles performed signs and wonders *because* they were called, anointed, and empowered by Jesus as his true servants, and *not to prove* that they were so called, anointed, and empowered.

Next, when the apostles actually did perform signs and wonders, their function was other than to affirm their apostleship. In Acts 3, where Peter heals the cripple, the response is such that people began to think that Peter had divine power in himself (Acts 3:11-12). Peter then proclaims that the healing occurred in the name of Jesus and the faith that came through him (Acts 3:16) and was foremost an act of kindness (Acts 4:9). The healing thus authenticated and glorified the person of Jesus who showed compassion. The healing of Aeneas, the paralytic, by Jesus through Peter, resulted in all those of Lydda and Sharon turning to the Lord (Acts 9:35). Peter then prays in Joppa for the raising from the dead of Dorcas with the result that many people in Joppa believed in the Lord (Acts 9:39-42). At Iconium, Paul and Barnabas spoke boldly, "for the Lord who confirmed the message of his grace by enabling them to do miraculous signs and wonders" (Acts 14:3). In Lystra, Paul healed a crippled man that had faith to be healed (Acts 14:8-9). Paul prayed for the healing of Publius' father on Malta, certainly out of compassion for his host.

When Paul wrote about his ministry to the Gentiles, he gloried in how Christ, through him, led the Gentiles to "obey God by what I have said and done—by the power of signs and miracles, through the power of the Spirit" (Rom. 15:18b-19a). Thus for Paul, a key function of signs and miracles was to bring people to faith, to facilitate evangelism, by pointing back to Jesus and his message of salvation. Paul communicated the gospel in word and deed like Jesus did. God testified to the salvation message—not the apostles—by signs, wonders, and various miracles, and gifts of the Holy Spirit (Heb. 2:3-4). Many of Jesus' miracles pointed to himself and his message, such that people believed in him (John 2:23; 7:31; 10:38; 14:11), or would be moved to repent (Matt. 11:20-23; Luke 10:13). Miracles were also signs pointing to Jesus' claim to be God (John 2:11; 5:36; 20:30-31; Acts 5:20). Miracles, signs, and wonders accredited Jesus, not the apostles (Acts 2:22). Therefore, signs, wonders, and miracles were not apostle-centric, they were Christocentric, and witnessed to Christ's message, person, and his Kingdom.

From the Acts of the Apostles, we see that compassion, the desire to see people healed, and often the resulting evangelization, were the results or function of their signs and wonders. Ultimately, the healings validated the ministry of Jesus, not the apostles. Jesus healed to demonstrate the presence of the Kingdom of God, to fulfill the expected role of the Messiah (Isaiah 61:1-3), to show love and compassion. Jesus spoke about the Kingdom of God and then healed those who needed healing (Luke 9:11). Truth about the Kingdom led to experiencing the presence of the Kingdom. The gifts of healing, being among the gifts of the Spirit, testified to messianic salvation. Some cessationists agree with this conclusion, perhaps not fully aware that this undermines their position. If miracles, including healing, did point to Jesus and his message in the first century, then why should the miracles cease in any following century?

After that, *the apostles' use of the miraculous gifts was essentially inconsequential in the Church's acknowledgment of written, inspired Scripture.* The final writing and compilation of the Scriptures as we know today was not even in the minds of the apostles and the early Church. The Apostle Paul never intended all his letters to be circulated to all the Church. Some of his letters were personal correspondence to individuals only (1 Tim. 1:2; 2 Tim. 1:2; Titus 1:4), or only to certain churches or regions (Col. 4:16; Gal. 1:2; Eph. 1:1; Phil. 1:1; etc.). Luke wrote his Gospel and Acts expressly for Theophilus (Luke 1:4; Acts 1:1). It can be argued that not all the New Testament authors were aware that they were writing Scripture as we know it today. No doubt the Apostle Paul will be surprised to find out that believers for centuries have been reading his personal correspondence. Scholars agree that the apostles were unaware that they were writing "canonical" Scriptures, and so also were the first readers of the epistles.[2] By A.D. 200, twenty-one of the current twenty-seven books of the New Testament were in the canon, and in the third century James,

Jude, 2 and 3 John, 2 Peter, and Hebrews were disputed as inspired Scripture, with Revelation disputed for a time.[3] It was not until the councils of Hippo in 393, and Carthage in 397, that the current twenty-seven books of the New Testament were acknowledged by the Church as the inspired Word of God in addition to the Old Testament.[4] This was, however, a formal declaration of what had been accepted in most Christian communities by that time.[5] Scholars agree that canonicity was most likely based on the content, authorship, and use within the Church.[6,7] Reputed authorship by an apostle was not sufficient—a growing consensus from the greater Church in its use of the Scriptures was the real deciding factor.[8] Those who had seen the apostles and their signs and wonders had died. It was, then, the inner witness of the Holy Spirit that helped the Church decide what actually was Scripture. These facts pose *major problems for cessationism.*

Finally, some of the New Testament was not even written by apostles, so the cessationist argument becomes weaker still. The obvious facts that some authors of the New Testament were not even apostles (Jude, Luke, Mark), and were not known to have performed miracles, *clearly and directly undermine cessationism.* The author of Hebrews is unknown, and Peter, who really did perform signs and wonders beyond any doubt, had his second epistle rejected for some centuries. The supposed unique role, or function, of the extraordinary "sign" gifts of the Spirit as marking apostolic credentials or apostolic authorship of Scripture thus vanishes. The connection is very weak, to say the least, and simply does not support cessationism. *The facts above present major problems for cessationism.*

The Gifts of the Spirit Are For the Whole Church

If any of the gifts were unique to the apostles, one might possibly consider arguing for a unique function of the gifts specifically for the apostles. If the gifts were uniquely tied to a person or persons, then the gifts would cease when they died. Were any of the gifts of the Spirit unique to the apostles, or were they intended for the Church as a whole?

Jesus appointed seventy-two others, in addition to the twelve disciples, to heal the sick and proclaim the Kingdom of God (Luke 10:1,9,17). Upon Jesus' ascension, the Spirit was poured out on all people (Acts 2:17-18), such that sons and daughters, servants, men and women would prophesy, in fulfillment of Joel 2:28-29, in these last (end) times (Heb. 1:2; 1 Cor. 10:11; 1 Pet. 1:20). Acts 2:38-39 clearly states that the promise of the Spirit is for those listening, their children, and "all whom the Lord our God will call," which will continue for centuries as the gospel is preached. This was a new manifestation of the Spirit, from the time of Christ onwards until his return.[9] Peter said "...this is what was spoken by the prophet Joel...," making clear a partial present-tense fulfillment. A partial fulfillment does not invalidate what was fulfilled. Joel's prophecy has two parts—the outpouring of the Spirit as a "new development" (Joel 2:28-29), and the subsequent day of judgment yet to occur (Joel 2:30-31); but all in the last days between the ascension and return of Christ, who will then judge all peoples and all nations on a great day of judgment (Matt. 24:30-31). In terms of eschatology, such an outpouring of the Spirit on all believers is now a characteristic of the new age (cf. Ezek. 36:26-27; 39:29).[10] Some interpreters err by making Joel 2:28-31 one prophecy that must be entirely fulfilled simultaneously, and since it hasn't been, claim that a universal outpouring of the Spirit has not yet occurred. Judas and Silas, who were not apostles but prophets, encouraged and strengthened the Church (Acts 15:32). Philip, appointed as one of the seven by the apostles and known to be full of the Spirit and wisdom (Acts 6:3), healed many paralytics and cripples (Acts 8:7), and even had four unmarried daughters who prophesied (Acts 21:9). There were prophets in Jerusalem, one of whom was Agabus who predicted a famine (Acts 13:1) and Paul's imprisonment (Acts 21:10-11). There were also prophets at Antioch (Acts 13:1), and in Ephesus through Paul, the Holy Spirit came upon about twelve men who spoke in tongues and prophesied (Acts 19:8). Hence, the partial fulfillment of Joel 2:28-31.

The Corinthian Church did not lack any spiritual gift (1 Cor. 1:7). Christians have different spiritual gifts according to the grace given to each one (Rom. 12:6; 1 Pet. 4:10), according to God's will (Heb. 2:4), and as determined by God (1 Cor. 12:7,11). In the Church, God has appointed workers of miracles, those with gifts of healing, those who help others, and those with gifts of administration (1 Cor. 12:27-28), in addition to the appointment of apostles, prophets, and teachers. The giving of apostles, prophets, evangelists, pastors, and teachers to the Church was part of the apportioning of grace by Jesus (Eph. 4:7,11).

Considering all the biblical evidence, the gifts of healing, among other spiritual gifts, were not unique to the apostles. Warfield's concession that all the gifts were operative in all the apostolic churches[11] weakens cessationism. God's sovereign will and grace determines who receives which gift. To suggest some spiritual gifts were given to an exclusive, privileged group of believers, like the apostles, goes against the intrinsic nature of gifts. Gifts by definition are received by grace, not for special merit or status.

The Gifts of the Spirit Are For Edification

If none of the spiritual gifts were unique to the apostles, and the function of the gifts was not solely related to the need for apostolic credentials or confirmation as authors of Scripture, then what was their function? Paul teaches that the spiritual gifts were given for the common good (1 Cor. 12:7), to edify and build up the Church (1 Cor. 14:12). Paul exhorts all the Corinthians, who were eager to have spiritual gifts, to try to excel in gifts that build up the Church (1 Cor. 13:31; 14:12). Paul commands believers to eagerly desire spiritual gifts, especially prophecy, in the context and motive of love for the Body of Christ (1 Cor. 14:1). Prophecy, for example, is to strengthen, encourage, and comfort others (1 Cor. 14:3-4; Acts 15:32). Since the gifts were given for the common good, they were to be used intelligibly (1 Cor. 14:9), to edify the Church (Rom. 1:11), and in the overall context of love (1 Cor. 13:1-14:1). Is not healing of believers a common good (1 Cor. 12:7), which is why Paul said the gifts of the Spirit were manifested? Surely seeking healing of one's brothers and sisters in Christ is trying to excel in spiritual gifts that build up the Church (1 Cor. 14:20).

Jesus healed because he loved; then surely with love as a motivation, we should desire the gift(s) of healing. We are commanded to seek, develop, and exercise the spiritual gifts, including gift(s) of healing (1 Cor. 12-14). "Each one should use whatever gift he has received to serve others, faithfully administering God's grace in its various forms" (1 Peter 4:10). Healing is a form of God's grace and is among the spiritual gifts. Paul's concern was that the gifts not be used for personal prominence, competition, or any number of selfish, immature motives, but rather for the edification of others in all humility, gratitude, and obedience. The clearly taught biblical function of the gifts of the Spirit have everything to do with building up the Church.

The Gifts of the Spirit Express the Kingdom of God

The spiritual gifts help to bring the presence of the Kingdom of God in its power and strengthen the Church in its mission. Jesus did not only teach and preach about the Kingdom, he brought the reality of the Kingdom of God into the lives of people (Matt. 4:23; 9:35; 10:35; Luke 10:9) through salvation, healing, and deliverance. Driving out demons by the Spirit of God is evidence of the Kingdom of God (Matt. 12:28; Luke 11:20). Jesus taught repeatedly in the Gospels about the Kingdom of God, using many parables. The Kingdom was so important that it was Jesus' topic to the apostles for forty days before his ascension (Acts 1:3). The apostles preached the good news or gospel of the Kingdom (Acts 8:12; 19:8; 20:25; 28:23; 28:31). Like Jesus and the apostles after him, the mission of the Church is to advance the Kingdom. Jesus expects the gospel of the Kingdom to be preached to the whole world as a testimony to all nations before the end will come (Matt. 24:14). Many church leaders are focused on church growth, but that is not necessarily the same as doing the works of the Kingdom in the power of the Spirit. The Church proclaims and witnesses to the Kingdom, and must extend the Kingdom of God following the example of Jesus. Ladd wrote:

> The Kingdom takes its point of departure from God, the Church from men. The Kingdom is God's reign and the realm in which the blessings of his reign are experienced; the Church is the fellowship of those who have experienced God's reign and entered into the enjoyment of its blessings. The Kingdom creates the Church, works through the Church, and is proclaimed in the world by the Church.[12]

The more extraordinary "miraculous" gifts of the Spirit (Gk. *dunamis*, for "miracles, mighty deeds, power") were, and still are, necessary because the power of Satan still stands in opposition to the Kingdom of God (Acts 10:38). Jesus called Paul to turn people from darkness to light, and from the power of Satan to God (Acts 26:17-18)—in other words, truth and power encounters. The apostles operated by the power of the Spirit (Acts 1:8; 4:7; 6:8; 8:13; 19:11), just as Jesus did (Luke 4:14; 24:19; Mark 6:2). Miracles or works of power (*dunamis*) operated in the Galatian church because they believed the gospel message (Gal. 3:5). The Christian life involves experiencing the "powers of this coming age" (Heb. 6:5). That is not ordinary or of this world. Following Jesus and the apostles' example, the Church should do the works of the Kingdom using all the power of all the spiritual gifts. As Ruthven wrote:

> Jesus' central mission in the New Testament is to inaugurate the Kingdom by word and deed...miracles manifest the essential core activity of his (Jesus') mission: to displace the physical and spiritual ruin of the demonic kingdom by the wholeness of the Kingdom of God.[13]

Curiously but not surprisingly, the theology of the Kingdom of God is often either overlooked by cessationists, or not seriously considered in their reasoning.

The Spiritual Gifts Continue Until Christ Returns

Cessationists maintain that there are fundamentally two groupings of spiritual gifts—the temporary or "sign" and the permanent or continuing gifts. MacArthur, for example, refers to the "temporary sign gifts" and the "permanent edifying gifts."[14] An immediate problem with this grouping is that the Apostle Paul nowhere specifies such a grouping. In 1 Corinthians 12, he lists all the spiritual gifts, with no hint at all of such a grouping based on duration, stating that they are all gifts of the Spirit given to the Church as a whole for the functioning of the Church as a whole. The notion of temporary versus permanent must be seen as an addition to Paul's writings—it is simply not there. This is an example of *eisegesis*, or reading something into Scripture. Paul specifies no grouping, not even the continuationist groupings; but those groupings are for convenience only.

One could reason, like the cessationists do, that the duration of the spiritual gifts should be determined by their reason, function or need for their operation. Given that the function of the spiritual gifts is edification and strengthening, then the gifts would necessarily operate as long as the Church needed edification and strengthening. The Corinthians did not lack any spiritual gift as they eagerly waited until Christ would return (1 Cor. 1:7) or be revealed. When we are in the Lord's full presence and his Kingdom has come in all its fullness and power, with all its complete knowledge, peace, wholeness, perfection, and more, then the gifts will no longer be needed (1 Cor. 13) because of the new reality totally centered on the presence of Jesus. Everything that could possibly cause opposition, weakness, and discouragement will be banished from the all-encompassing presence of the Kingdom of God (Rev. 21:4). Just as Christ loves us now, he most assuredly will love us into eternity, and thus love will never cease. But the need for the spiritual gifts will cease (1 Cor. 14:1) only upon his return. Fee argues that, in 1 Corinthians 13, Paul puts the spiritual gifts into eschatological perspective while discussing the necessity of love (1 Cor. 13:1-3), the character of love (1 Cor. 13:4-6), then the permanence of love (1 Cor. 13:8-13). Fee then writes:

> ...agape characterizes our existence both now and forever. Accordingly, love is superior, not because what exists only for now (charismata) is lesser, but because what is both for now and forever (agape) must dictate the charismata is to function in the life of the church... we are still in the present, where gifts are one of the ways the Spirit builds up

the community; but love must prevail as the reason for all such manifestations. Therefore, Paul will go on in Chapter 14 not only to correct an imbalance with regard to the gifts, but to urge their proper use.[15]

Paul's reference to love never failing but prophecies ceasing, tongues being stilled, knowledge passing away, until "perfection" comes (1 Cor. 13:8-10), refers to Christ's second coming (1 Cor. 15:20-28; 1:7). Only then will we know fully and be fully known, and all in God's Kingdom and presence will be perfect or complete.

Some have suggested that by "perfection" (*teleion*), Paul meant the closing of the New Testament canon. This is impossible, since this idea would not have even occurred to Paul or his readers. The concept of "canon of Scripture" for the New Testament was not in the minds of the apostles and early readers of what is now acknowledged as Scripture. To suggest this was taught or intended by the New Testament writers thus violates a basic rule of biblical interpretation, wherein we ask, "What did it mean to the first readers?" Such an interpretation is an example of eisegesis wherein a future event is read into the Scriptures—an anachronism which is hermeneutically impossible.

Healing is an expression of the love and compassion of God the Father and Jesus, as well as bringing glory to Jesus. Is it even remotely possible that the love and compassion of Jesus is now diminished by removing the gift of healing after the apostolic era? If not, then healing as an expression of Jesus' love and compassion has continued through his Church, and must continue with all spiritual giftedness. Have the works of Satan and his fallen angels to bring illness, sickness, bondage, and much suffering upon this world, including Christians, ceased or lessened from the time of the apostles? Do we not agree with 1 John 5:19 "...the whole world is under the control of the evil one"—or has that ceased for today?

Then healing and deliverance to counter the works of Satan, which was why Jesus came (1 John 3:8), must continue through his servants both then and now. This should be exercised with boldness. As Pinnock wrote:

> While it is true that the ministry of the apostles was foundational and unrepeatable, their signs and wonders were directed to human needs that persist to this day. Why would the relevance of the Kingdom to these needs vary? Why would the sick not always need prayer and the possessed deliverance? (The Holy) Spirit has not gone into retirement, or the power of the Kingdom into recession.[16]

To emphasize the dynamic and ongoing connection between the gospel and God's power in the miraculous, Ruthven concluded:

> An examination of Scripture reveals that miracles do not prove the gospel, but are an essential element of it. Miracles represent, in actuality, the displacement of the rule of Satan by the rule of the Kingdom of God, whether in the realm of the physical, emotional, moral, or spiritual; the gospel articulates those events. Hence, to remove the presence of God's charismatic power from the Christian gospel is to destroy its very essence as biblically described.[17]

Jesus proclaimed the gospel of the Kingdom in the anointing and empowering of the Spirit. When he left the earth to be seated on the throne of God, he expected his disciples, then his apostles, and then the Church at large to continue his mission following his example with the same Spirit. The Kingdom of God will then be most fully and powerfully advanced when all the gifts of the Spirit are used in obedience to Jesus in love for him and his people. None of the spiritual gifts are then not tied to the first century only, but all subsequent centuries because they are part of the expression of the Kingdom of God when exercised in obedience, believing faith, boldness, and in intimate personal relationship with Jesus. As long as Satan has power on earth, and the gospel of the Kingdom must be proclaimed, the spiritual gifts are required to enforce the rule and reign, or Kingdom, of God.

Signs, wonders, and various miracles, and gifts of the Spirit, testified to the message of salvation—not those who communicated it (Heb. 2:3-4). The passage does not say "and only for the first century," as cessationists would like to add. The passage says the two events—proclamation of salvation and miracles—occurred together. The passage more accurately and naturally reads as giving a characteristic of the proclamation of the Kingdom of God, and thus can apply at God's discretion to future proclamations of the gospel.

In conclusion, since none of the spiritual gifts were tied exclusively to the apostles or meant only for them, and signs and wonders and miracles are fundamentally Christo-centric, and the spiritual gifts are meant for the whole Church to edify the Church, then *all* the spiritual gifts were meant to continue until the Lord returns.

Does the Gospel Need the Power of Worldly Reputation?

Some cessationists hold that the miraculous sign gifts were required to start the Church in the first century. The first century was unique with a new, unknown faith, and the Scriptures were being written. The gospel in the first century required miracles, but only in that century. Edgar wrote:

> *The beginning Church was in a different situation from that of the Church after the first century. By the end of the first century,*

the Church was established in the major centers of the known world. Although not officially recognized, it had become a recognized group with some reputation... the message was unusual and astounding. A man executed in a very small country... such facts at least show difficulty faced by early evangelists. Who would accept such a message? However, the miraculous sign gifts put this whole message in a different perspective, since the miracles were evidence that the message was from God. The situation from the first century has never been the same... there can be little doubt, however, that the need for confirmation at the beginning was greater than the need for this today.[17]

This argument is suspect. It appears to substitute God's power with worldly power—as if worldly reputation, size in numbers, can ever replace God's power or any operations of the Holy Spirit.[19] Zechariah wrote "not by might nor by power, but by my Spirit, says the Lord" (Zech. 4:6), thereby underscoring the Spirit's power alone to complete God's purposes. It demeans the inherent power of the gospel,[20] as if miracles were required in the first century due to incredibly overwhelming resistance and disbelief. John the Baptist successfully called people to repentance, and paved the way for the Messiah, without any miracles (John 10:41). Lydia and her household believed simply from hearing Paul speak to a gathering of women—no miracles required (Acts 16:14-15).[21] Paul already knew that the gospel was foolishness and a stumbling block to the world (1 Cor. 1:18-31; 2:6-15). Is this any less true today? Why wouldn't the need for miracles be as important today as then? Is there not the same challenge to present the gospel to an unbelieving world, to a generation who did not see the miracles, and who can only now read about them? This argument falls apart for the evangelization of remote jungle tribes that cannot read or write and have not ever heard of any "recognized group with a reputation."

That would be like a first-century situation. Is not the need to spread the gospel and testify to the name and person of Jesus just as important in any following generation? God performed signs and wonders over many centuries in Israel and also among all mankind (Jer. 32:20), so why stop today? *When* God performs miracles is not the issue, but rather the realization that we worship a God whose *nature* is to perform miracles.

Why cannot every generation since the time of Christ be challenged afresh with the truth and power of God as in the first century? I spent six years in the Islamic world, having heard hundreds of times the Muslim call to prayer from minarets, knowing daily what it feels like to be outnumbered at least one hundred thousand to one. I see absolutely no advantage in God withdrawing any of his spiritual gifts. We can rejoice that 33 per cent of the world's people are Christians, but it is a sobering fact that 33 per cent of the world's people are either Muslims or Hindus[22]—two well-recognized groups with their own reputations.

The most basic problem is that the argument is a non-sequitur ("it does not follow") in the rules of formal logic. The first century is different from today—no one would disagree. But it does not therefore logically follow that miracles need to stop today because of any difference. Because the first century is different from today, would anyone argue that we have any less or no need for cell or home groups (Acts 2:46), or the Lord's Supper (1 Cor. 11:17-34)? Cessationists argue that the miracles, done primarily by the apostles, were thus unique to them and their time in history. Scriptures show that miracles are a characteristic of the Kingdom of God erupting into this world, expressed according to the purposes, plans, and timing of God. A demand by some cessationists that there be an exact duplication of the miracles in Acts, in order to validate any true miracles of God today, amounts to dictating how the Holy Spirit will choose to operate today. Finally and most fundamentally, this view is not supported anywhere in the Scriptures; it's entirely a historical and sociological inference, as no less than Warfield himself argued.[23]

Cessationism is Unscriptural

Cessationism is not biblically based. The supposed "sign" gifts were not unique to the apostles, did not point only to their ministry, had a clearly articulated edification (as opposed to "evidence") role and function, and were characteristic of the gospel and the expression of the Kingdom. Cessationism is incompatible with a theology of the Holy Spirit and a theology of the Kingdom of God. As outlined in chapters one and three, Jesus modeled healing, commissioned the early disciples (the twelve and the seventy-two), and in the Great Commission certainly intended the Church to heal and deliver, as well as preach and do all the other things that he commanded the first disciples (Matt. 28:20). That would be done with the same Spirit of wisdom, knowledge, anointing, power, love, and compassion as seen in Jesus. The gifts of healing were and are meant to operate in the Church as much as preaching and teaching in all eras of the Church. The Holy Spirit of the New Testament era is the same person as the Holy Spirit of today; thus similar manifestations—including all expressions of the spiritual gifts—can occur today. Does it not seem odd that several gifts of the Spirit operated in the Church for less than one hundred years, and then were suddenly revoked or taken back by Father God? Since the spiritual gifts are a manifestation of the presence of the Holy Spirit, then wherever the Holy Spirit is, some of the gifts are now "switched off" due to cessationism. We have no grounds to believe that Satan is any less active today (1 John 5:19); thus, the Church must be strengthened within and fully empowered in its mission of proclaiming and advancing the Kingdom of God.

It is not surprising that cessationism is not biblically based, because a main weakness of cessationism as it relates to the gifts of healing is that there is no verse from Scripture that clearly teaches that gifts of healing would cease after the apostolic era. Cessationism has no clear, direct support from Scripture. Andrew Murray, for one, totally opposed cessationism:

> The Bible does not authorize us, either by the words of the Lord or His apostles, to believe that the gifts of healing were granted only to the early times of the church.[24]

In the context of all of Scripture, cessationism cannot be substantiated. Basing cessationism on Scripture is exegetically difficult. Concerning cessationism, Fee concluded:

> ...there has been a spate of literature whose singular urgency has been to justify the limiting of these gifts to the first-century Church. It is fair to say of this literature that its authors have found what they were looking for and have thereby continued to reject such manifestations in the Church. It can also be fairly said that such rejection is not exegetically based, but results in every case from a prior hermeneutical and theological commitment.[25]

J.I. Packer rejected the cessationism of Warfield. Concerning the signs and wonders as recorded in the New Testament, he concluded:

> There is no clear promise that these manifestations will continue after the apostles' ministry is over. But there is no denial they will either. The New Testament leaves open the possibility.[26]

Some cessationists argue that since the majority of the Christian Church has believed cessationism, it is probably the correct view. But this is not basing the argument on Scripture and is a democratic approach to divine truth. Such an argument goes against the very nature of Protestantism. Should we now believe that Martin Luther and Calvin were totally wrong because their belief was against what the Church at that time believed? Such reasoning undermines the spirit of the Reformation. Arguing from the majority of the Church believing in cessationism becomes weaker each decade, considering that those who reject cessationism—Pentecostals and charismatics—have grown from 2 per cent of all Christians in 1900 to 27.7 per cent in 2000, or 523.7 million believers.[27] Would one not conclude that God is blessing those who reject cessationism?

Ultimately, whose example should we follow? Jesus expected that as the Father sent him into the world, he sends us into the world (John 17:18). The Church must then move in all the gifts of the Spirit, as modeled by Jesus and the apostles, to continue the ministry of Jesus. Paul expects us to imitate him (1 Cor. 4:16-19), and follow his example (Phil. 3:10,17) as he follows the example of Christ (1 Cor. 11:1). Paul admonished the Philippians to put into practice whatever they received, heard, or saw in him (Phil. 4:9). Cessationists are basically saying that we should follow the example of Jesus and the early Church, but minus anything miraculous as they define it.

Witnesses From History

Since cessationists believe and teach that some of the gifts ceased after the first century, then they have a vested a prior interest in maintaining that those gifts have never operated in the Church since. Warfield, for one, in *Counterfeit Miracles* went to great lengths to disqualify and refute miracles and healings in history. Cessationists have a pre-determined interpretive grid of history. More scholars are finding evidence of miraculous healings throughout history, and certainly in the first few centuries since the early Church. Kelsey cites such scholars and writes:

> The sober quality of the writing and the large number of healings recorded by early Christians continues the New Testament record and stands firm against any attempt to turn this body of experience into myth or mere fancy—to say nothing of the fact that spiritual healing has continued into modern times.[28]

A careful study of the writings of the early Church fathers reveals that throughout the first and second centuries, long after the apostles had died, the spiritual gifts were important and exercised in the Church.[29] For example, Ignatius, Bishop of Antioch, writing between A.D. 98 and 117, exercised the gift of prophecy under the guidance of the Holy Spirit.[30] Irenaeus, Bishop of Lyons, sometime after A.D. 177, testified to the miraculous power of Jesus evident among the Church in his day, including the laying on of hands to cure the sick.[31] Martin Luther himself believed in and practiced charismatic healing that relied on the miraculous power of God.[32] As a more contemporary example, Spurgeon had the spiritual gift of word of knowledge which sometimes manifested while he was preaching, although he never formally claimed to have that gift.[33] John Knox, the founder of Scottish Presbyterianism, was among the leaders of the Reformation who exercised the gift of non-revelational prophecy.[34,35]

I don't expect any cessationist to agree with Kelsey or other scholars that present evidence for healings or the operation of other temporary sign gifts in the history of the Church. One could argue that due to the widely believed cessationism down the centuries, there is less evidence for healings than there would have been otherwise. The healings were not absent because God terminated the gift, but because the Church was disobedient by not using it. The Church has not been actively enough cultivating faith in the person and ministry of Jesus in the spiritual soil of belief (John 6:29), teaching people how to forcefully lay hold of the reality and power of the Kingdom of God (Matt. 10:7). Why is the Church warned to not put out the Spirit's fire, nor quench the Spirit (1 Thess. 5:19), nor grieve the Holy Spirit (Eph. 4:30), unless the Church can actually do that? There is sufficient evidence to show that much of the Church has blocked some of the ministry of power and grace of the Holy Spirit. Andrew Murray put it this way:

> ...if the Church has lost these gifts, it is her own fault. It is because she has become worldly that the Spirit acts but feebly in her. It is because she has not remained in a direct and habitual relationship with the full power of the unseen world. But if men and women would spring up in her, living the life of faith and of the Holy Spirit, entirely consecrated to their God, she would see again the manifestation of the same gifts as in former times.[36]

Background Issues of Experience and Methodology

My impression from reading the literature on cessationism, especially concerning healing, is that it is unwittingly experience driven, especially in reaction to negative experiences. This is not surprising, since, if cessationism cannot be supported by Scripture, what is the driving force? Three areas of experience come to mind: one's own, those of others in the past or history, and seemingly negative reactions against others in the present.

One's own personal experience can be a key factor. By definition, cessationists are among those who do not exercise the spiritual gifts which they teach have ceased. Who would teach and argue against that which is real in one's own life? Who would argue with a pilot at 30,000 feet above the Atlantic in a 747 that the laws of aerodynamics have ceased and therefore flight is impossible? Faced with reports of spiritual events or realities foreign to one's own experience, one must either conclude that one has yet to experience more of God, or that those experiences are invalid, unnecessary, or maybe even counterfeit. In other words, if something is not credible to oneself, it must be discredited or invalidated to justify oneself. Not as an accusation but as a call to serious reflection for all Christians in this debate, I suggest that issues of pride, envy, fear, or insecurity can enter the picture. It would take humility to truly evaluate other experiences with an open mind and discerning heart, and admit that one might have much more to learn and experience of God, especially if one is a spiritual leader to whom many look for direction on spiritual matters. The only other option is to deny or discredit other people's experiences. The options are, then, either repudiate the claims of others and thus justify one's own spirituality and theology, or question one's own theology and experience, or perhaps both.

I can understand how cessationists, among others, might be concerned about the emotional "excesses" of those who operate with the gifts of the Spirit. Focus on experience, devaluing the mind, and so forth brings its own problems. Yet some emotions are more inward and subdued, but no less influential and formative than the more outward and demonstrative emotions. It is an illusion to think that emotions operate only with those who passionately advocate and operate in the gifts of the Spirit. Emotions work equally on both sides of the debate, just in different ways. Storms, a former cessationist, wrote:

> *There is one more reason why I remained for years committed to the doctrine of cessationism. This one is not based on any particular text or theological principle; yet it exercised no less an influence on my life and thinking than did the other five. In mentioning this fact, I am in no way suggesting that others are guilty of this error. This is not an accusation; it is a confession. I am talking about **fear**: the fear of emotionalism, the fear of fanaticism, the fear of the unfamiliar, the fear of rejection by those whose respect I cherished and whose friendship I did not want to forfeit, the fear of what might occur were I fully to relinquish control of my life and mind and emotions to the Holy Spirit, the fear of losing what little status in the evangelical community that I had worked so hard to attain* (emphasis by the author).[37]

When David Pytches began to enter into the ministry of healing prayer, he was quite anxious about the issue of reputation. What would others think of him, especially if people were not healed, or God asked him to do something "strange and different"? He was first concerned about God's reputation, and God reassured him that he would look after his own reputation. When he was concerned about the Anglican Church's reputation, God reassured him that he was concerned about that also, and God would look after that. When it then came down to his own reputation, his wife recounts:

> Finally he was forced to admit the truth and he confessed: "Actually, Lord, I am worried about my own reputation." He was humbled by the Lord's reply: "What does that matter? My Son made himself of no reputation."[38]

As Christians we must all examine our hearts and motives, since this is what Jesus will be most concerned about one day (1

Cor. 4:5). Are we more concerned about the fear of man than the fear of God (Isa. 8:13; 51:12-13) or are we unwilling to truly die to self (Matt. 16:24)? In our eagerness to interpret Scripture let us never forget that ultimately the Scriptures will interpret us (Heb. 4:12). This also applies to those who advocate the use of all the spiritual gifts today, yet have any attitudes of superiority or condescension to those who don't. When we lack love we lack what counts most.

While we do not base our theology on experience, no one has a perfect theology and without error knows all the things of God. Theology is never equal to the inspired Word of God, it is always a fallible formulation thereof. Ideas and theological systems in themselves can become idols of the mind and heart. Experiences that do not fit our theology should drive us back into Scripture again, and in the process may well change our imperfect theology. This involves an encounter with both the written Word *and* the living Word, Jesus. Understanding and experiencing the things of God is not the exclusive domain of the wise and learned (Matt. 11:25-26), and requires Jesus to open our minds (Luke 24:45). Jesus challenged the Pharisees for not knowing the Scriptures nor the power of God (Matt. 22:29). We must never use theology as a cover for unbelief. The much-criticized and now deceased John Wimber was among those who initially did not believe in healing, and was convicted by Matthew 9, of which he wrote:

> ...although for years I had refrained from praying for the sick because of a theology that denied God could heal today, my doctoral stand was a facade for the evil of unbelief and skepticism in my heart.[39]

Acts gives us a very clear example of how we must reflect on our experiences, which may well lead to a change in our theology which is never perfect. Peter's theology held that the gospel was only meant for the Jews and not the uncircumcised Gentiles. Did Peter change his mind by studying the Old Testament and using the grammatico-historical method of biblical interpretation? No. God had to break through with a very clear and unforgettable experience that would change his theology. Peter had a vision when he went into a trance (Acts 10:9-17), where he was told three times to arise and eat unclean animals, reptiles, and birds—totally against his theology. He wondered about the meaning of this vision (Acts 10:17), in other words, relating this to his theology. As the Spirit forewarned Peter, three men came looking for him. Peter ended up speaking to Cornelius and his whole house, who all accepted the Lord and received the Holy Spirit (Acts 10:34-48). Peter's imperfect theology was changed by his own admission (Acts 10:34-35), when he said "I now realize how true it is that...." Hence, experience led to a change in theology. The Church in Jerusalem also had to change its theology, going far away from being critical of stepping into uncircumcised peoples' homes (Acts 11:3) and actually eating with them, to knowing that even Gentiles can be saved (Acts 11:18). The idea that by simply applying the rules of biblical interpretation one thereby understands the Scriptures is simplistic.

> In biblical studies it is now commonplace to assume that the truth of faith is procured by hermeneutical method rather than by divine disclosure... We appear to have succumbed to the arrogance of our expertise[40].

Who can claim to study the Scriptures with a completely unbiased, totally objective mind and absolutely no impure motives ever? The inspired Apostle Peter himself didn't, so much more any of us. We cannot interpret the Scriptures apart from experience even if we tried because our personal experiences of culture, family, and faith have already shaped our minds and hearts before we ever come to the biblical text (Rom. 12:1). Hermeneutics is more than method, it's also a matter of the heart. The more we love and obey, the more biblical truth we apprehend.

A deeper question behind this whole debate concerns the ways of knowing, or epistemology. When Adam "knew" Eve (Gen. 4:1) and they had a child, Adam did not just comprehend information about Eve. The Hebrew word *yada*, for knowing, implies an experiential and relational type of knowledge. In the New Testament, there are different kinds of knowledge for different ways of knowing. There is intellectual knowledge from logical thinking (*episteme*, 1 Tim. 6:4), knowledge from logical comprehension (*synesis*), knowledge from observation (*epiginosko*, Luke 23:7), knowledge from "beholding" as in a visionary sense (*horao*, Matthew 2:2), or knowledge from experience or intimacy (*gnosis* or *ginosko*)[41]. Like *yada*, *ginosko* is sometimes used for sexual intercourse—as in Luke 1:34, where Joseph had not yet "known" Mary. The New Testament uses *gnosis* or *ginosko* when referring to our intimate knowledge of God. As Sanford wrote:

> An intimate knowledge of certain things cannot be had by direct observation nor by rational processes but only by an intimate communion with those things. It is faith that opens the soul to such communion. It is also faith that perceives realities that would otherwise not be perceivable. Clement says, "For faith is the ear of the soul."[42]

The Scriptures teach that experiential and relational knowledge is important yet always finally rooted in the Word of God. An analogy, though imperfect, may help here. Imagine going to a flying club for some flying lessons. You can choose between two instructors. The first instructor understands all the laws of aerodynamics cold, has studied all the theory, and can take you up and down safely. The second instructor is aware of the theory and understands it, but has considerably more experience and says he can make the plane do about anything possible. He intimately knows the feel of the plane and what happens in an Immelmann, flying upside down, and more. Who would you choose? Probably the second instructor who has the greater experiential knowledge. The decision here is based on two types of knowledge, not unlike the discussion on types of knowledge in our interaction with the written and living Word.

Thus the experiential knowledge of those who exercise the supposed "temporary" gifts cannot be discounted or marginalized. Cessationists who do not have the experiential knowledge of the temporary gifts are at a disadvantage since they do not have the full spectrum of types of knowledge concerning all the gifts. Cessationists will not seek, develop, and exercise the "temporary" spiritual gifts—why ask for something that is not available? Unbelief will thus prevent the manifestation of the gift, and becomes a self-fulfilling prophecy. Jesus was not able to do many miracles in Nazareth due to their lack of faith, (Matt: 13:58) which amazed him (Mark 6:6).

Cessationists often go to much effort to discredit the spiritual experiences of others, since their theology requires that the miraculous gifts have ceased. This task is difficult and suspect, since immaturity, temptation, impure motives, deception, and counterfeits of Satan can be operating and thus confuse the issue. Of course, there is no justification for falsified claims of healing or prophecy, for example, because this amounts to lying and misrepresentation of the gospel.

Before Jesus began his public ministry and after he was anointed, he underwent temptation in the desert. With spiritual power comes great temptation. Desiring spiritual experiences above holiness or more of Jesus can too easily lead to spiritual lust. Much of the apparent excesses, aberrations, unbalanced teaching, and the like, especially in the healing ministry, can be attributed to yielding to temptation and immaturity. Abuse or improper use of a spiritual gift does not invalidate that spiritual gift. Some preachers and evangelists have used manipulation, methods bordering on abuse, and have fallen to gross sexual temptation—does that mean that we discredit the ministry of preaching or evangelism? Citing such examples proves nothing in itself, since one can be merely criticizing others who are doing the right thing, but the wrong way, while oneself not doing the right thing at all. One must have a true, representative example of other people and ministries, to reach a fair conclusion. As is true in statistics, biased data leads to biased conclusions. Nonetheless, this reasoning in no way justifies sin in ministry, the counterfeit works of Satan, or obviously unbiblical teaching.

Some cessationists argue that since charismatic healers do not heal people at will, like Jesus and the apostles did, the authentic gifts of healing are not operating today. Since charismatic healers have not attempted to go to hospitals and heal everyone[43], it is argued that they do not have the gifts of healing. Yet Jesus didn't heal everyone at will when he walked the face of the earth either. When he visited the pool of Bethesda, Jesus healed only one person, a man who had been an invalid for thirty-eight years, among a great number of disabled people (John 5:2-11). He healed the man only upon asking him whether he wanted to be healed. Jesus did not walk into all the leper colonies, and heal all the lepers. Jesus needed the power of the Lord to heal the sick (Luke 5:17), so it wasn't "automatic" for him, either. It depended on the will and purposes of the Father. Since the apostles continued to heal many people after Jesus ascended, we know for a fact that he did not heal everyone. Jesus did heal all that came or were brought to him (Matt. 8:16), but they came to him. This objection is invalid since healers are now accused of not doing what Jesus himself did not do either. Just as people need to respond to the invitation of salvation, they must also respond to the invitation for healing and come to Jesus, desiring to receive his grace. Just as salvation cannot be forced on anyone, neither can healing be forced on anyone. Spiritual power is not "possessed" by anyone, like packets of energy distributed at will—it's God's power to be used in his service when and how he wills. We don't use God to perform miracles at will and whim. Instead, God uses his humble servants to accomplish his purposes as he sees fit.

Some cessationists argue that since the healing experienced from those in the healing ministry today is not 100 per cent and immediate all the time, and thus not like Jesus and the apostles, it is invalid and thus the gifts of healing are not operating today.[44,45] The argument is faulty since all the spiritual gifts, including the gifts of healing, will vary in their intensity and faith as exercised by Christians. Just like the gift of preaching, for example, the gift of healing is exercised in proportion to one's faith (Rom. 12:6), according to the apportioning of Christ (Eph. 4:7), and by how much one strives to excel in the gift and develop it (1 Cor. 14:12) and collaborates with the Holy Spirit. Just because spiritual healing of today is not exactly like that of the apostles—as instant or dramatic—can it be declared invalid or not a true manifestation of the Spirit. Jesus healed as he did because he was in such close, constant communion with the Father (John 5:19,30; 8:28). Jesus only did and said what the Father instructed him, moving perfectly in the power of the Spirit, which Christians must grow and mature into. It is thus improper to criticize Christians beginning and learning to use, in obedience to the Lord, the gifts of healing. Should we not edify others by encouraging them to greater faith and ministry, instead of discouraging them by declaring that since they have not arrived at the level of Jesus, their ministry or gifting is invalid, or worse yet—not of God? If 100 percent effectiveness is invoked as a criterion for the validity of a spiritual gift, hardly anyone's ministry today would remain valid. Why apply this criterion only to the miraculous gifts? If one were to argue that since much preaching from the time of the early Church has lacked the power and impact of the apostles (1 Cor. 2:4; 4:19-20; 1 Thess. 1:5), would one then conclude that the gift of preaching has ceased upon the death of the apostles, or is exercised very rarely? How much preaching clearly, and without any doubt, comes with a demonstration of the Spirit's power, such that people's faith does not rest on men's wisdom, but only on God's power, as Paul modeled (1 Cor. 2:4)? How many people preach with authority like Jesus did (Mark1:27)? Do we then conclude that the gift of preaching is rarely operating today?

Some cessationists argue that since those in the healing ministry cannot heal themselves, the true gifts are not operating. This is a suspect argument, since Jesus' first temptation was to use his spiritual power for his own needs—turning stones into bread when he was very hungry (Matt. 4:1-4). To insist and expect that those with spiritual gifts of healing must necessarily be able to heal themselves is unbiblical. Epaphroditus was seriously ill and almost died (Phil. 2:25-30), Timothy was not healed by Paul from frequent illnesses (1 Tim. 5:23), Trophimus was left sick by Paul (2 Tim. 4:20), who was ill himself for a while in Galatia (Gal. 4:13-14). The healing power of God is not automatic; we must all submit to God with his mercy, compassion, and purposes.

I expect that arguments from experience will remain confusing and inconclusive. The final appeal as to the spiritual gift of healing must be to the Scriptures. I concur with MacNutt when he cited an old adage, "For the believer no argument is necessary; for the unbeliever no argument will prove sufficient."[46] MacNutt wrote about a visit to Lourdes, where doctors were convinced about God's healing power, with records of some 4,000 "healings" clearly beyond their medical explanations, yet not able to meet the rigid criteria of the Catholic Church as miracles.[47] The doctors were frustrated because the theologians would not believe or accept the evidence of God's healing power. I know of instances of sudden and total healing here in Winnipeg, both physical and emotional. But then, I already believe.

Arguments from silence, where something is omitted in a verse or passage and a teaching is developed from it, is a dangerous methodology. For example, it has been argued that since the "sign" gifts are not mentioned in James 5:14-15, Romans 12:6-8, 1 Peter 4:10-11, or other passages, therefore the "sign" gifts, including healing, were not widely practiced in the early Church or had already ceased.[48] Using this type of methodology, one could well conclude that since communion is mentioned only for the Corinthian church, and omitted in all the other epistles, it was not widely practiced by the early Church and is not intended for today. This is an example of "going beyond what is written" (1 Cor. 4:7) and is dangerous, since there is *no control as to what one chooses as being absent*, and thus support for a supposed inference or teaching. Theology must be based on what is written, not on what is *not written*. Revelation 22:18-19, a serious warning for anyone who adds or subtracts from that book, should make us take this issue very seriously. The challenge is to correctly handle the Word of Truth (2 Tim. 2:15).

Unstated Assumptions About the Word of God

Cessationists place great significance on the Word of God in final written form, especially in the final canonical form with the complete Old and New Testaments. The assumption appears to be that this is essentially what the "Word of God" is all about since so much hinges on it. But what if the "Word of God" is much more than simply what's written? What if it's as much an issue of the Holy Spirit speaking to any of us as our ability to study the written text? What if it's really both the Written Word *and* the Living Word, Jesus? What if the Word is more than just written, but also living and active (Heb. 4:12)? Then the supposed extra significance of the canon diminishes and cessationism with it. If the Word is so much more than what is written, but never in contradiction to it, then any consequence from the Word only being written is lessened.

Cessationism holds that since we now have the written Scriptures in front of us, God no longer speaks to us apart from it, as he did in "Bible times" before. We need the historical grammatical rules of biblical interpretation, maybe some illumination of the Holy Spirit is allowed, and all is sufficient. But if we read Scripture for information rather than for transformation or spiritual formation to become like Jesus, we comprehend little. The informational approach to reading, typical of our age, stresses linear thinking, a desire to master or control the text, analysis, and a problem-solving mentality.[49] Cessationist reasoning, so fixated on the canon and written Scripture along with the rules of hermeneutics, is an example of the consequence of the informational (more rationalistic) mode of reading Scripture. As Mulholland quotes and reflects on Merton:

> In order to read the Bible honestly, we have to avoid entrenching ourselves behind official positions.... That

kind of entrenchment, no matter what it is, is of the informational mode. From within our entrenched position, we seek to read the Bible to find more support for our position or to explain away anything which does not seem to fit our position. This is the analytical, problem-solving dynamic of the information mode. The text is an object to be controlled and manipulated.[50]

Just having the written Scripture is then never enough. We must commune with the Spirit, desire transformation, ask the Spirit to illumine, open our hearts, and know that we learn more as we love and obey more. "To know the full import of what is revealed, we must act in obedience to what we presently ascertain to be the will of God."[51] As Paul argued in 1 Corinthians 1-2, there are certain types of knowledge for which experience is the only key to understanding.[52] There is much more than having the same cognitive understanding as the New Testament Church did. We must enter into the same or similar experiential realities of life as they did to comprehend the Scriptures.[53] Until we fully enter into the life of the Spirit, and the gifts of the Spirit among God's people, there is much we simply will not really know. The task is to relate the cognitive and experiential (affective) types of knowledge. Reflecting on Wesley, Mulholland wrote:

> Wesley clearly saw that the cognitive and the affective dimensions of human existence must be conjoined in mutual interdependence if Christians were not going to fall into the extreme of sterile intellectualism on the one side or mindless enthusiasm on the other.[54]

Cessationism, built on the importance of the Word being written and the canon being closed, then loses significance since the Word is so much more than its written form. My impression of cessationist writing is that the Word and its interpretation revolves almost entirely around the written text.

Assumptions About Spirituality

Another assumption in this debate concerns spirituality, or more specifically, *how one experiences God.* Cessationists accept the spiritual gifts that do not involve miracles or one's direct experience of God. Tongues, prophecy, the gift of miraculous powers, words of knowledge, gifts of healing which are used directly in praying with people, are all gifts that require a more direct involvement with God and are also among the "temporary" sign gifts.

The gifts of preaching, teaching, helps, giving, administration and such are among the clearly accepted "permanent" gifts for today that cessationists affirm. Those gifts can operate with less direct experiences of God and are easier to comprehend in terms of logic, reasoning, study and thinking. But, the "temporary sign gifts" transcend the boundaries of logic and do not come by logic, study or reasoning. They are released in men and women who walk in humility, grace, trust, obedience, and the uncontrollable will of God. While one can study homiletics and preaching in order to preach, one cannot study long or hard enough to start speaking in tongues, or using a gift of healing. Without ever relegating the permanent gifts to a lesser status or devaluing the intellect, one should ask whether this is an unconscious factor behind cessationism.

I know of a pastor who had just completed a D.Min., and was visiting a church's healing prayer service. He noticed a young teenage girl in the sanctuary. He asked her what she was doing, and she replied she healed the sick by laying hands on them and praying for their healing and she cast out demons when necessary. When he asked her how she could do this given he had studied so many years for his D.Min. and hadn't learned this, she simply replied that Jesus had called, empowered, and anointed her, and she simply obeyed. Still somewhat skeptical, he followed her around that evening. To his surprise, this teenage girl who was all of seventeen years certainly was used by Jesus to heal people and cast out demons. It takes humility to realize that the Spirit does indeed distribute the gifts according to his will (Heb. 2:4), which may well include unlikely, relatively untrained, or uneducated Christians. This is not to devalue a D.Min., but rather, to value God's way of doing things.

Another sign that this debate involves one's experience of God and one's personal comfort with spiritual gifts is the disagreement over which gifts are classified as temporary or permanent. MacArthur,[55] for example, has no problem with the gift of discernment as a permanent edifying gift, whereas Dickason is convinced that this gift is only available as a counterfeit gift which opens people up to demonic influence and is really a form of ESP or clairvoyance as occult practitioners use today.[56] Such discrepancies support the view that the distinction between permanent and temporary gifts is subjective, artificial, experience-driven, and not always objectively based on Scripture.

Benner, in his discussion on Christian spirituality describes four main types of spirituality, each with a main emphasis in experiencing God personally. He describes the speculative (the mind), affective (a direct encounter with God in experience), kataphatic (the imagination), and apophatic (meditative) types. Concerning speculative spirituality, Benner wrote:

> Speculative spirituality emphasizes encountering God with the mind and is thus usually associated with a rational and propositional theology. Speculative spirituality is seen in much of Eastern Orthodox Christianity and most Western

Protestant Christianity. It is perhaps seen most clearly in Reformed (Calvinism) Christians who affirm the importance of knowing God through his self-revelation in Scripture. In this tradition, God is not primarily experienced in some nonrational or emotional manner. Rather, he is encountered with the mind and is known through the study of his Word, the Bible. Speculative approaches to spirituality tend to be strong on theology and often somewhat weaker on the direct experience of God.[57]

The above fits well with cessationists, who affirm that since the canon is complete and we have the written Word, some gifts are no longer needed. The debate intensifies when some Christians claim they have direct encounters with God, hear Jesus' voice, see God heal someone directly, and so forth. It appears to me that the whole cessationist debate has more to do with the personal dynamics of experiencing God. The real questions then come from the theology of experiencing God.

Cessationism appears also behind the issue of whether God speaks to Christians today apart from the written Scriptures. White, for one, maintains that "...the Bible gives us no reason to expect that God will speak to his children today apart from the Scriptures."[58] God spoke to his people apart from the Scriptures while the Scriptures were still being written; and now that the Scriptures are complete, the canon is closed, and we have centuries of orthodoxy, God no longer speaks extra-Scripturally to his people.[59] What then could "My sheep will hear my voice" (John 10:27) ever mean for us today? So, for some writers, it's more than just some of the spiritual gifts no longer operating. God has apparently not only ceased some of his spiritual gifts, but has also ceased speaking to his children more directly, also ceased using them directly as agents of healing, and also ceased any more direct experience of himself. This borders on deism.

There is a serious practical problem in believing that once the Scriptures were written, God ceased to speak outside the Scriptures to his people even for encouragement, hope, intimacy in relationship, personal direction, and such. For many centuries, there were very few copies of the Scripture in circulation beyond the ones copied by monks in monasteries. Even if they had a copy, for which the parchment was expensive, many thousands of Christians were illiterate. Of the few Christians who could read and had the Scriptures, it was in Latin. By 382 A.D., the Old Latin had become so corrupt (for example, Luke 24:4-5 had at least twenty-seven variant readings) that Pope Damascus asked Jerome to come up with a new revision, now known as the Latin Vulgate.[60] It was not until the invention of the printing press by Gutenberg that in the sixteenth century the Vulgate was printed and a copy of the Scriptures was even a possibility for all believers. Worse, some Christians were persecuted by the Church itself for the "outrageous" idea of translating and publishing a version of the Bible in English for the average Christian. It is a simple, undisputed fact that over many centuries, hundreds of thousands of Christians did not have ready access to a personal copy of the Scriptures. So, if God really did suddenly cease speaking extra-Scripturally sometime after 100 A.D., they would have been impoverished in their communication with their Lord and Saviour. In my estimation, the supposed spiritual implication of the inscripturation of the Word of God is "cold comfort" for Christians in many centuries as well as illiterate Christians even today.

This view of God not speaking extra-Scripturally is entirely incompatible with the operation of all the gifts of the Spirit today. God does speak through prophetic words, words of knowledge, or the interpretation of tongues, for example. When one rejects cessationism, which I have shown cannot be supported biblically, one must necessarily reject the view that God does not speak to his children apart from the Scriptures. To be sure, he never contradicts what is in Scripture, nor goes beyond what is in Scripture. In healing prayer, as I have seen numerous times, the Lord communicates and applies his truth and compassion right into a person's particular circumstances.

Nancy came to Christ at a very young age. When she was barely twelve years old, her parents took her to an inter-denominational conference where the Lord was moving in power. Soon after arriving in the conference room, Nancy somehow knew that one lady in particular had "something wrong with her," as she put it. It was as if her "spiritual radar" singled out this one person. The lady in question was attractive, well-dressed, and seemed to fit in with all the other believers. It turned out later that Nancy's assessment was totally accurate, since that lady was actually a witch who had come to infiltrate the meeting and pray over people to pass on evil spirits. This was later confirmed by a few pastors. It seemed that Nancy was unknowingly exercising the spiritual gift of discernment of spirits. In effect, she knew by God's direct revelation that the lady had an evil spirit. Over the next few years, Nancy had a number of similar experiences in knowing almost immediately on the first encounter without any prior knowledge of any kind that an individual had a "wrong spirit." If this could ever be construed as a mediumistic counterfeit gift, it is ironic that it helps to expose evil spirits.

On a number of occasions, quite unexpectedly, a fellow brother or sister in Christ has given me a word of prophecy which has encouraged me and given me personal direction. My response has been to write these down in a journal, test them against the written Word of God and wisdom (1 Thess. 5:21), pray over them, and seek counsel from those who know me and also have such a spiritual gift. Discernment is required, because for every true gift of the Holy Spirit, the enemy of our souls has a counterfeit. As the years have gone by, I stand amazed at how often the prophetic words have built upon and complemented one another. They often address precise and specific details and issues totally unknown to the person speaking to me. One lengthy prophecy that I received directly and accurately addressed things on my mind that I had not talked to anyone about. No psychic or deceiving spirit could ever do that. For me, the bottom line here is my faithful Lord using his servants to encourage me in my walk with him.

The Consequences of Cessationism

As concluded above, cessationism is unscriptural. The debate becomes even clearer when one considers the consequences, or "fruits," of this belief.

Nullifying the Word of God. This may sound rather harsh, but I maintain that cessationism nullifies the Word of God. I expect that cessationists truly desire to be faithful in handling and teaching the Scriptures, so I refer here to unintended consequences. In response to the Pharisees, who taught that a man can dedicate something to God as "Corban," and thus not provide for a father or mother (which circumvents the command to honor one's parents), Jesus said (Mark 7:8,13a) "You have let go of the commands of God and are holding on to the traditions of men.... Thus you nullify the Word of God by your tradition that you have handed down." Cessationism is a contemporary example of nullifying the Word of God. Cessationism, as a theological tradition taught and handed down over the centuries by elders (Christian leaders, pastors, teachers, professors), results in the command of Scripture to engage in the healing ministry as modeled by Jesus, being effectively nullified in practice. Among other things, cessationism limits obedience to the healing ministry using the gifts of the Spirit only to the first-century Church. For the contemporary Church, this amounts to subtracting from the commands of God, about which we are warned, as was the nation of Israel in Deuteronomy 4:2—"Do not add to what I command you and do not subtract from it, but keep the commands of the Lord your God that I give you."

Cessationism becomes a tradition applied, or added to, the existing Word of God such that it subtracts from God's commands to us today. It undermines the Word of God by making irrelevant for us today the biblical passages on some of the spiritual gifts, which were supposedly only applicable for less than one hundred years or so in the life of the Church and only now serve to describe what we can no longer experience. This should only be the case when Scripture clearly teaches otherwise that a biblical practice, like offering bulls or goats as sacrifices, must cease.

A weakened Church. Furthermore, the Church is weakened and robbed of power. One can well imagine Satan quite threatened by the early expansion of the Church, fully moving in the power of the Holy Spirit with all the gifts of the Spirit. Despite his plans, he is a defeated foe (1 John 4:4), no match for the gospel quickly spreading by bold apostles and evangelists empowered and anointed by God's Spirit. But what if Satan could convince, or tempt, the Church to forgo, at best, some of the power of the Holy Spirit? What if Satan could seduce the Church into ceasing the use of the "extraordinary" gifts of the Spirit that foil his plans? Better yet, what if he could do so by even making or encouraging the Church to believe it is a biblical teaching? Satan cannot take away any power from the Church, but he certainly would be in favor of the Church simply not using it, or only some of it. A weakened Church would be much less of a threat to Satan. This would be a most diabolically subtle approach—to convince the Church to disarm itself from within wherever possible. Cessationism argument unwittingly serves that very end, for it certainly prevents its followers from seeking the spiritual gifts of healing, miracles or power, prophecy, and the like, which are divinely intended to build up and strengthen the Church. To the degree to which all the spiritual gifts are not sought after, developed, and obediently exercised in maturity and boldness, the Church is weakened, robbed of its power, and more vulnerable to the enemy. This also quenches the Spirit.

The Scriptures warn us to avoid forms of godliness as the appearance of orthodox faith and commitment, which nevertheless deny the inherent power of true godliness that represents the Kingdom of God (2 Tim. 3:5). We must guard against being bewitched into living by human effort or power instead of truly by grace through faith that results in the Spirit's presence working miracles or powerful works (Gal. 3:3-5). This is a supreme irony, given that some cessationists object to desiring the gifts of healing since it apparently makes people vulnerable to evil spirits. In not seeking the spiritual gifts, as taught and commanded in Scripture, cessationists unwittingly give Satan a tactical advantage by weakening the Church. As one small example, De Arteaga reveals how cessationism led to the decline and fall of Protestantism in Northern Europe.[61] Is it really any surprise that there has been such debate, disagreement, and controversy within the Church over the gifts of the Spirit, when Satan himself and his opposing kingdom of darkness has the most to lose when the Kingdom of God is advanced in true Christ-directed spiritual power and truth?

Perhaps an illustration will help. Imagine yourself as the commander of an elite guerrilla unit, given the mission to destroy or at least neutralize an enemy army appearing on the horizon. Your military intelligence informs you that you are outnumbered and the enemy has vastly superior firepower. Without any doubt, head-on attack is suicidal. You and your unit would be totally destroyed. What is your only hope, aside from some carefully-calculated skirmishes to inflict as much damage as possible? Remain hidden and most strategically, convince the large opposing army that they either really do not have, or need not ever use, their vastly superior firepower. If you are able to infiltrate their army and somehow convince them of this, you will have greatly diminished the threat if not effectively neutralizing them. Wouldn't that be diabolically clever?

Temptation to human power. Without all the true power of God, the Church can be tempted to fill any void with human power. Not fully relying on all the gifts of the Spirit, there is always the temptation to use human technique, methods, and organizational power (Ps. 20:7; Jer. 17:5) to advance the Church. Kraft discussed in detail how Evangelicalism has lacked power, looks more like deism, and has emphasized control, information and knowledge, power of reasoning, and many forms of technique over the Spirit's power and God's more immediate presence.[62]

Temptation to idolatry. When the spiritual gifts are not all operating due to unbelief, and there is a real temptation to human power, there is the temptation to engage in idolatry. Quoting Dr. Mackay, Leanne Payne lists the following four major idolatrous substitutions: God's self-disclosure becomes theologism (the idolatry of ideas); the transforming encounter becomes impressionism (the idolatry of feelings); the community of Christ becomes churchism (the idolatry of structure); and Christian obedience becomes ethicism (the idolatry of prescripts).[63] With such Church life, the healing and transforming presence of Jesus is absent. Before any activity at all, a key work of the Church is simply to believe fully in Jesus, the one who has been sent (John 6:26). The church must first believe in the presence, name, saving and transforming power, spiritual gifts, commission, and ministry of Jesus. If not, there will be a temptation to either omit or replace any of the foregoing with other things. This is a key decision, almost a point of departure or crux in ministry and Church life.

Unnecessary suffering and pain. Few cessationists are against prayer for healing as stipulated in James 5:14-16, or intercessory prayer for healing. But prayers from elders, and for one another, will be more effective if the spiritual gifts have been received and cultivated by elders and other believers who have the gifts of healing as appointed by God (1 Cor. 12:28, 30). The prayer of faith offered by the elders could involve the spiritual gift of faith.[64] In churches where the gifts of healing have not been sought, developed, and used for the common good out of love, Christians have needlessly suffered. I for one know, having met many Christians with very deep physical, emotional, and spiritual wounds, for years hoping and praying for God's healing presence. All too often, I am asked why they had to wait so long. There is much pain in the body of Christ. What's more, Jesus feels it also as long as it continues on earth since we are connected to him (Acts 9:5).

Deprivation of spiritual joy. Christians who all along had latent gifts of healing and other "temporary" gifts were not given the joy and encouragement in developing and exercising their spiritual gifts. As a result, they have been denied further experiences of the reality of the Kingdom of God. As Pinnock wrote:

> Sadly, the cessationist mindset becomes self-fulfilling. Failing to take seriously what the Bible sets forth as possibilities, people come under the influence of secular modernity by the back door. It leads to an experiential deficit that prevents people from entering into full Spirit reality.[65]

Default to the world. With the healing gifts not fully operating in the Church, those in the Church and the world, which are in need of healing, will eventually go elsewhere. I know of a church where the ministry of healing prayer has been stifled, while an elder has gone to a psychic for healing, in full knowledge of the church membership. An incredible opportunity for evangelism, for a witness to the world of the power and presence of Jesus' Kingdom is forfeited. When the Church does not exercise the ministry of healing, the void will be filled by "groups that introduce healing through Eastern points of view or through psycho-religious practices."[66] People, often in desperation, are going increasingly to New Age and related healers, where they will encounter very real but deceiving and counterfeit spiritual forces. Where the "sign" gifts are not operating, the Church is at a distinct disadvantage in not being able to offer the true presence and power of God's Kingdom. This is unfortunate considering the postmodern shift away from materialism and rationalism and the growing preoccupation with mediums, psychic healing, near death experiences, angels, and many other forms of supernatural experiences. The Church will also lack discernment in knowing the counterfeit from the real by not having sufficient experience in the real, authentic powers of this coming age (Heb. 6:5).

Accusation of mediumistic powers in ministry. The allegation that all "temporary" gifts only operate as mediumistic or evil counterfeit gifts is a very unfortunate consequence of cessationism. Since those gifts ceased, as argued, it follows necessarily and inescapably that only counterfeits of these gifts operate for Christians as well as non-Christians. This means that Spurgeon, John Knox, some of the early Church fathers, and many more were all using evil power in their ministry. Apparently I also use evil spiritual powers as I pray for the healing of fellow Christians. Was Spurgeon really clairvoyant? This then means that just as Jesus was accused of using demons to cast out demons, Christians today are accused by fellow Christians of ministering by demonic powers. If cessationsim is false, as I have shown above, then such accusations amount to claiming that a true manifestation of the Holy Spirit is actually of Satan. Jesus was not pleased with such notions (Matt. 12:24-32).

Liberal tendencies. It is ironic how cessationism ends up in the same place as liberal theology with respect to the miraculous gifts of the Spirit in the present.[67] Liberal theologians, following the school of Rudolph Bultmann, demythologize the New Testament and claim that miraculous manifestations of the Spirit did not ever occur in the past, as well as notions about angels, demons, and more, and certainly do not today. They believe that the miracles of the Bible must have been myths or legends, but certainly not historical fact. Cessationists would disagree with such an assessment of the past and most would allow for miracles in the present, but not directly through believers. In that respect, liberal theologians and cessationists agree completely. Remarking on the connection between cessationist teaching and the Enlightenment, Kraft writes:

> Such teaching is a product of Enlightenment perspectives applied to theology by those who have not had the kind of spiritual experience that might lead them to question such a belief. I don't mean to belittle those who hold this belief. I have been guilty of it myself for most of my Christian life. Such lack of experience in the area of spiritual power leads even very sincere and committed people to rationalize this lack. They will assert that "Jesus Christ is the same yesterday, today and forever" (Heb. 13:8) but also assert that the constancy of Jesus does not apply to spiritual power—even though he gave his disciples authority and power (Lk 9:1) and told them to teach their followers "to obey everything I have commanded you" (Mt. 28:20).[68]

Conclusion

All things considered, cessationism is an untenable and unscriptural belief. The consequences should alarm us, especially a Church robbed of much power. What possible advantages are there to cessationism? None, as far as I can see. All I see are clear disadvantages for the Kingdom of God and clear advantages for the kingdom of darkness. That alone is a serious indictment. Why not rather believe that the Lord fully empowers the Church he commissions for as long as the commission is in effect? I find it strange that the Lord would give gifts to his Church for less than one hundred years, and then suddenly withdraw them. It is even more strange that while God in his sovereignty terminates some of the spiritual gifts, he allows Satan to operate with his counterfeits. There is a fundamental non-sequitur operating in this debate—just because the Scriptures have been written and the apostles passed away, it does not logically follow that some of the gifts should cease. The Scriptures do not clearly anywhere say that some of the gifts will cease upon completion of the New Testament. That is not an argument from silence, since there is biblical evidence that the spiritual gifts continue until the Lord returns. Wherever the inspiration for cessationism comes from, it's not from the Scriptures. Looking at the long and often involved arguments for cessationism with debatable and often inconclusive inferences from passages of Scripture, it takes exegetical chaos to sustain cessationism hermeneutically.

Cessationism is not the sole reason that the Church has not moved in all the divine power and resources that God has intended, but it certainly has contributed. Many will agree that the Church has largely failed in this respect. Leanne Payne, for one, puts it this way:

> In regard to the matter of spiritual power, the truth is that historically the people of God have seldom comprehended the "divine energy and power," as well as the authority with and in which they are to move. This is in spite of the fact that the truth is plainly spelled out in the Scriptures and in the history of the early church...the Western Church's teachings have become increasingly abstract. Conceptual knowledge about God has almost entirely replaced even the pious attempt to walk with God.[69]

When the dust settles on the cessationist debate, there is one inescapable reality. When we meet Jesus, we will give an account for our actions, beliefs, and motives (1 Cor. 4:5, Heb. 4:13). Can we really imagine Jesus being displeased with anyone for doing, or trying to do, what he did and the disciples after him? Can we not imagine Jesus overlooking those "erring" by following his example too closely? The other error would be to have Jesus' disapproval for not doing what he did by example. Why not err on the side of safety, and seek to develop all the spiritual gifts, including healing? Which error does any of us want to risk?

It's not a matter of being conservative, evangelical, charismatic, third wave, or any other label—it's a matter of being obedient and faithful. Perhaps upon final reflection this whole debate is much less complex than often realized. *In conclusion, it was not that some of the gifts of the Holy Spirit ceased, but rather, belief and obedience within part of the Church ceased. That is true cessationism.*

Endnotes

[1] Jack Deere, *Surprised By The Power Of The Spirit* (Grand Rapids: Zondervan, 1993) p. 104.

[2] C.B Puskas, *An Introduction to the New Testament* (Peabody: Hen-

drickson Publishers, 1992) p. 256.

3 G.W. Barker, W.L. Lane and J.R. Michaels, *The New Testament Speaks* (New York: Harper and Row, 1969) p. 28.

4 Ibid.

5 F.F. Bruce, *The New Testament Documents: Are They Reliable?* (Downers Grove: InterVarsity Press, 1960) p. 27.

6 Barker, p. 30.

7 Puskas, p. 263.

8 Kenneth S. Latourette, *A History of Christianity, Vol.I: to A.D. 1500* (New York: Harper and Row, 1975) p. 135.

9 F.F. Bruce, *The Book of the Acts. Revised Edition. The New International Commentary on the New Testament* (Grand Rapids: Eerdmans, 1988) p. 61.

10 William J. Dumbrell, *The Search for Order. Biblical Eschatology In Focus* (Grand Rapids: Baker Books, 1994) p. 223.

11 Benjamin B. Warfield, *Counterfeit Miracles* (Scribner's, 1918) Republished as *Miracles: Yesterday and Today, True and False* (Grand Rapids: Eerdmans, 1965) p. 5.

12 George E. Ladd, *A Theology Of The New Testament* (Grand Rapids: Eerdmans, 1974) p. 119.

13 Jon Ruthven, *On the Cessation of the Charismata: The Protestant Polemic on Postbiblical Miracles* (Sheffield: Sheffield Academic Press, 1993) p. 116.

14 John F. MacArthur, Jr., *Charismatic Chaos* (Grand Rapids: Zondervan, 1992) p. 243.

15 Gordon D. Fee, *God's Empowering Presence. The Holy Spirit In The Letters Of Paul* (Peabody: Hendrickson Publishers, 1994) pp. 204-205.

16 Clark H. Pinnock, *Flame Of Love. A Theology Of The Holy Spirit* (Downers Grove: InterVarsity Press, 1996) p. 132.

17 Ruthven, p. 80.

18 Thomas R. Edgar, *The Miraculous Gifts: Are They For Today?* (New Jersey: Neptune, Loizeaux Brothers, 1983) p. 264.

[19] Deere, p. 108.

[20] Deere, p. 109.

[21] Deere, p. 110.

[22] K. Rajendran, "The Great Commission Roundtable: One More Step Towards De-fragmentation," Mission Frontiers, Vol. 22:3, June 200, p. 21.

[23] Warfield, pp. 21, 35.

[24] Andrew Murray, *Divine Healing* (New Kensington: Whitaker House, 1982), p. 14.

[25] Gordon D. Fee, *The First Epistle To The Corinthians. The New International Commentary on the New Testament* (Grand Rapids: Eerdmans, 1987) p. 600.

[26] James I. Packer, *Rediscovering Holiness* (Ann Arbor: Vine Books, 1992) p. 205.

[27] L. Bush, "Where Are We Now? Evaluating Progress on the Great Commission," Mission Frontiers, June 200, Vol. 22:3, p. 13.

[28] Morton Kelsey, *Healing and Christianity: A Classic Study* (Minneapolis: Augsburg Press, 1993) pp. 104, 129-199.

[29] Ronald A.N. Kydd, *Charismatic Gifts in the Early Church. An Exploration Into the Gifts of the Spirit During the First Three Centuries of the Christian Church* (Peabody: Hendrickson Publishers, 1984) p. 87.

[30] Kydd, p. 18.

[31] Kydd, p. 44.

[32] Bengt R. Hoffman, *Luther and the Mystics. A re-examination of Luther's spiritual experience and his relationship to the mystics* (Minneapolis: Augsburg Publishing House, 1976) p. 195.

[33] C. Samuel Storms, "A Third Wave View," Wayne A. Grudem (Gen. Ed.), *Are The Miraculous Gifts For Today?* (Grand Rapids: Zondervan, 1996) pp. 201-203.

[34] Don Dunkerley, *Healing Evangelism: Strengthen Your Witnessing with Effective Prayer for the Sick* (Grand Rapids: Chosen Books, 1995) p. 243.

35 Douglas A. Oss, "A Pentecostal/Charismatic Response To Robert L. Saucy," in Wayne A. Grudem (Gen. Ed.) *Are The Miraculous Gifts For Today?* (Grand Rapids: Zondervan, 1996), p. 168.

36 Murray, p. 13.

37 Storms, p. 204.

38 Mary Pytches, *Dying to Change. An Exposure of the Self-Protecting Strategies Which Prevent Us Becoming Like Jesus* (London: Hodder and Stoughton, 1996) p. 133.

39 John Wimber and Ken Springer, *Power Healing* (San Francisco: Harper, 1987) p. 49.

40 Donald G. Bloesch, *A Theology of Word & Spirit. Authority & Method in Theology* (Downers Grove: InterVarsity Press, 1992) p. 22.

41 John A. Sanford, *Healing Body & Soul. The Meaning of Illness in the New Testament and in Psychotherapy* (Louisville: John Knox Press, 1992) p. 65.

42 Sandford, p. 65.

43 MacArthur, pp. 247, 263.

44 MacArthur, p. 162.

45 Edgar, p. 105.

46 Francis MacNutt, *The Power To Heal* (Notre Dame: Ave Maria Press, 1977) p. 67.

47 MacNutt, p. 66.

48 Edgar, p. 104.

49 M. Robert Mulholland, Jr., *Shaped by the Word. The Power of Scripture in Spiritual Formation* (Nashville: Upper Room, 1985) pp. 49-51.

50 Mulholland, p. 51.

51 Bloesch, p.22.

52 Mulholland, p. 62.

53 Mulholland, p. 64.

54 Mulholland, p. 62.

55 MacArthur, p. 243.

⁵⁶ C. Fred Dickason, *Demon Possession & the Christian. A New Perspective* (Wheaton: Crossway Books, 1987) p. 331.

⁵⁷ David G. Benner, *Care of Souls. Revisioning Christian Nurture and Counsel* (Grand Rapids: Paternoster, 1998) pp. 92-93.

⁵⁸ R. Fowler White, "Does God speak today apart from the Bible?," in John. H. Armstrong, (Gen. Ed.), *The Coming Evangelical Crisis: Current Challenges To The Authority of Scripture and the Gospel.* (Chicago: Moody Press, 1996) p. 87.

⁵⁹ White, p. 86.

⁶⁰ George E. Ladd, *The New Testament and Criticism* (Grand Rapids: Eerdmans, 1967) p. 58.

⁶¹ William De Arteaga, *Quenching The Spirit: Discover the REAL Spirit Behind the Charismatic Controversy* (Orlando: Creation House, 1996) pp. 90-95.

⁶² Charles H. Kraft, *Christianity with Power. Your World view and Your Experience of the Supernatural* (Ann Arbor: Servant Books, 1989) pp. 37-49.

⁶³ Leanne Payne, *Listening Prayer. Learning to Hear God's Voice and Keep a Prayer Journal* (Grand Rapids: Hamewith Books, 1994) p. 221-222.

⁶² Storms, p. 214.

⁶³ Pinnock, p. 133.

⁶⁴ Kelsey, p. 201.

⁶⁵ Deere, p. 112.

⁶⁶ Kraft, p. 73.

⁶⁷ Leanne Payne, *The Healing Presence. How God's Grace Can Work In You to Bring Healing in Your Broken Places and the Joy of Living in His Love* (Wheaton: Crossway Books, 1989) pp. 221-222.

Chapter Seven

Spiritual Abuse: When Churches Wound

Bad Church Experiences

I distinctly remember praying with Marlene, a missionary on furlough. Disagreements with her sending church on how the Holy Spirit was using her on the mission field had grown over the last few years. Whatever the differences were, the elders of the church were not justified in shaming her in front of the congregation, grilling her several times and putting her on the defensive to explain herself. It was clear to her that they were looking for an opportunity to accuse her. When she merely questioned how she was treated, the church leadership labeled her as "unteachable." When I asked Jesus to take her to the most painful moments in the interaction with the church leaders, in a few minutes tears began to flow, and I could see that the emotional wounds ran very deep.

Fred belonged to a church with a reputation as being evangelistic. Indeed, no one would dispute that his pastor had an anointing for evangelism, with people continually coming to Christ. Yet as Fred began to grow in the gifts of the Spirit and exercise them in humility, there were more and more conflicts with his pastor. Fred was really confused, since his pastor was "the Lord's anointed," So what was really happening?

As an elder, for over a year David began to wonder about his new pastor. On the surface and certainly in the pulpit, he appeared very godly and trustworthy. Yet when in private with his pastor in his study, his pastor would become accusatory and often volatile even over small things that David had done or said. The more David searched his soul on the issues, the more he realized that there really wasn't any basis for the accusations. Then there was a period of time when things seemed okay, and David felt that the relationship had been restored. David began again to trust his pastor and feel relaxed in his presence. But at an elder's meeting a policy issue came up, and David simply agreed with the church's constitution which meant that his pastor's request, which came suddenly and put the church board under pressure, would be denied. As a last resort to get his way, his pastor suddenly turned red and slandered David's character with verbal venom. In that instant, David's whole world changed, and it was painful. The one person who should be his shepherd and encourager was his direct enemy. The pain was deep because David had opened his heart to his pastor, yet he was now violated and betrayed. David later realized this tactic was an example of character assassination—if you cannot defeat a person's arguments, then defeat the person's character and thus his credibility. David was deeply saddened by the fact that his pastor had opened that very meeting with a devotional, affirming and praising the elders, yet was not above accusing one of them near the end of the meeting.

Charlotte had an obvious growing anointing and calling in the ministry of healing prayer. She shared with me that more and more people came to her for healing in their church, all under direct protocol and in response to leadership and as part of the larger prayer ministry team. The Lord would give her words of knowledge which were directly related to the needs of the person, all a new but welcomed development for her. As she laid hands on people, there was an obvious release of healing from a growing spiritual gift of healing. People were being healed emotionally, spiritually, and in some cases physically. As her anointing grew in this ministry, more and more people started to compare her accomplishments in ministry with her pastor and the elders. At one healing service in particular, a number of people came to the pastor for healing prayer, and little if anything happened. Most of those same people came later to Charlotte, and the Lord revealed the causes quickly to her, and deep healing took place. It seemed that instead of thankfulness that those people experienced more of the healing presence of Jesus there was jealousy. A few days later, she was asked to come to the pastor's office. She was told that she was no longer welcome in the church, and they told her to leave. The reason given was vague, it seemed the minds of the leaders were made up. Charlotte went home stunned and deeply hurt. There were a lot of tears as she shared this with me.

Wanda is a divorced Christian woman who has been attending a church in the hope of receiving encouragement, understanding, and help in getting her life back together after many years of emotional and physical abuse from her former husband. Her former husband had all but totally abandoned the Christian faith. She had the added responsibility of bringing up their children. She was assigned to a cell group that had Christians with similar or equally painful pasts. The unspoken name of this cell group was the one with the "problem people." She was discouraged that her identity from the church seemed to be wrapped up in her past, rather than simply being a child of the living God. The pastor in this church was quite successful and seemed to live well, which included an expensive car. The elders and the leaders in the church were all successful business people. The message that she and others in her group received, which included some Christians coping with long-term depression, was that if they were truly walking with the Lord things would be a lot better. On top of this, Wanda was asked a few times about her tithing. It was stressed that this was a means of obeying the Lord and would in itself bring prosperity. Wanda tried to avoid hard feelings, but was saddened that there was little attempt to help her experience more of the healing love and presence of Jesus. While there was some after service prayer, she was not reassured that the prayer team would have the deep empathy and compassion to minister to the deeply wounded places in her soul. All things considered, there was more burden from their system than grace and freedom in Christ for her.

The above are examples of what some now call "spiritual abuse." Churches are supposed to be communities of blessing, truth, safety, and nurture. Churches should be safe places where wounded people can find healing. Spiritual leaders are supposed to be godly people with integrity and love who can be trusted with the issues of the soul. Fortunately there are many pastors and other spiritual leaders who are indeed caring, trustworthy, and true servants of Jesus. I myself have been blessed by a number of very godly pastors in my life. But sadly, this is not always the case. There are enough unsafe churches and spiritual leaders who will actually wound people or neglect healing for the wounded, instead of bringing healing, that Christians must discern and be aware of such churches and leaders.

The Scriptures warn us not be naive about evil, including its presence in the Church as spiritual abuse. As each year goes by, I encounter more and more Christians who need healing prayer as part of their recovery from bad Church experiences. I also experienced spiritual abuse, and I know full well the emotional pain that can come with it. I needed time and healing prayer to overcome the effects of spiritual abuse. I have been able to redeem those experiences in my life by understanding what others have gone through and become more effective in praying with them for healing. It often takes time to recognize spiritual abuse. This is because most of us are reluctant to believe that any one of our spiritual leaders, who are supposed to model love and holiness, could be consciously or unconsciously violating their spiritual authority and harming us. Sometimes spiritual abusers will make others believe it is "their problem," thus for a long time the victims believe they are at fault.

Norma phoned some years ago, concerned about issues in her church which were terribly upsetting. I suggested she read a book on spiritual abuse, and recommended a title for her. She was able to buy a copy of that book in her local Christian bookstore that day, and read almost the entire book until midnight. She later told me that the moment she heard me use the term, "spiritual abuse" it was as if suddenly lights were turned on, and she knew in her spirit that she had a name for what was happening. What then is spiritual abuse? A recent definition is helpful:

> Abuse of any type occurs when someone has power over another and uses that power to hurt. Physical abuse means that someone exercises physical power over another, causing physical wounds. Sexual abuse means that someone exercises sexual power over another, resulting in sexual wounds. And spiritual abuse happens when a leader with spiritual authority uses that authority to coerce, control or exploit a follower, thus causing spiritual wounds.[1]

Instead of using spiritual authority to bring life, love, healing and thus more of the life of Jesus, people are progressively wounded and their spiritual life is "slowly drained." While spiritual abuse is a modern psychological term like "substance abuse," "sexual abuse," "emotional abuse," or "elder abuse," we must never lose sight of the fact that this is sin. With spirituality comes the possibility of spiritual sin. Jesus had a lot to say about what we now call spiritual abuse.

How do spiritual abusers operate? What are the dynamics? A most instructive place to begin is a close look at a painful drama recorded in the Old Testament.

David and Saul: An Old Testament Story of Spiritual Abuse

Many of us are quite familiar with the incredibly inspiring story of David and Goliath (1 Samuel 17). No doubt you'd be shocked if a Sunday School curriculum didn't include this story. But that is only a very short episode in the long story of David and Saul, which effectively chronicles spiritual abuse among other themes. In the story of David and Saul, God-ordained authority is used for sinful, selfish motives, and many people were hurt.

After Israel had asked for a king and Samuel found Saul hidden among the baggage (1 Sam. 10:22), Samuel prophesied over Saul "The Spirit of the Lord will come upon you in power, and you will prophesy with them; and you will be changed into a different person" (1 Sam. 10:6). As Saul turned to leave, God changed Saul's heart, and all was fulfilled that day (1 Sam. 10:9). The men of Jabesh Gilead were besieged by the Ammonites, who offered a treaty only if all their right eyes would be gouged out, thus disgracing Israel so much that all Israel was demoralized (1 Sam. 11). When Saul heard about it, "... the Spirit of God came upon him in power, and he burned with anger" (1 Sam. 11:6). Saul staged a mighty victory, slaughtering the Ammonites until the next day, and was then confirmed as Israel's king at Gilgal, fully approved by God.

Later, Jonathan attacked a Philistine outpost such that Israel became a "stench to the Philistines" (1 Sam. 13:4), and the Philistines gathered at Micmash for war. The soldiers of Israel hid in fear and started to desert, the troops were "quaking in fear" (1 Sam. 13:7). Saul was supposed to wait for Samuel for seven days and meet at Gilgal, but in the end Saul offered up the burnt offering. Samuel then arrived and rebuked him for not having waited,

You have acted foolishly... you have not kept the command the Lord your God gave you... and now your kingdom will not endure (1 Sam. 13:13-14).

Saul's excuse was that the men were scattering, Samuel was not arriving, the Philistines were closing in, and he really needed the favor of God. Saul gave in to circumstances and fear and then covered it up with an appeal to spirituality—needing God's favor—which he violated by clear disobedience in the very process of presenting the offering. He shifted the blame to the circumstances, saying "I felt compelled," and made the issue appear very complex. Samuel had no pity and saw right through it—disobedience is always disobedience. The circumstances revealed what Saul was really like under stress and exposed the true state of his heart.

Jonathan and his armour-bearer attacked a Philistine outpost (1 Sam. 14:1-15) and routed the Philistines. God sent a panic such that the ground shook and the Philistines killed one another in confusion. Jonathan's desire was to see God win and avenge the honor of his people. Although Saul began to seek the Lord after he discovered that Jonathan and his armour-bearer were missing, he stopped the priest from inquiring further of the Lord and impulsively went to battle when he thought he had a tactical advantage (1 Sam. 14:16-20). Saul made a rash, unwise oath, that no soldier would eat before he had avenged himself on his enemies (1 Sam. 14:24). Saul made it a personal issue, putting his own selfish gratification, the avenging of his honor, ahead of the needs and security of God's people. Jonathan clearly saw that his father's oath made trouble for the country (1 Sam. 14: 29. To overcome the power of the curse, Saul set up an altar to the Lord, the first time he had done this (1 Sam. 14:35). The fact that this was a "first time" reveals Saul's lack of interest in spiritual matters. Saul almost killed Jonathan himself because he came under Saul's curse, having eaten a honeycomb, but others removed him from the presence of Saul (1 Sam. 14:45).

God issued a clear command to Saul through Samuel, to go and totally destroy the Amalekites and everything that belonged to them (1 Sam. 15:1-4). So what did Saul do? He attacked, but Saul and the army spared king Agag and also the best animals which they were unwilling to destroy completely (1 Sam. 15:9). If that wasn't enough, incredibly, he went to Carmel and set up a monument in his own honor (1 Sam. 15:12) as self-glorification. God revealed this all to Samuel (1 Sam. 15:11), saying "I am grieved that I have made Saul king, because he has turned away from me and has not carried out my instructions." God grieves over disobedient leaders. Samuel finally caught up with Saul and confronted him with his disobedience with the undeniable evidence of the animals around him making noise (1 Sam. 15:20-21). Saul actually denied it, claiming he obeyed the Lord and shifting the blame to the soldiers who kept the animals, and then covered it up with false spirituality, saying the animals would be sacrificed to the Lord (1 Sam. 15:9). Saul was trying to rationalize sin.

Saul captured the Amalekite king as his personal trophy to show off to others, as many other kings did in those days.

But Samuel replied: Does the Lord delight in burnt offerings and sacrifices as much as in obeying the voice of the Lord? To obey is better than sacrifice, and to heed is better than the fat of rams. For rebellion is like the sin of divination, and arrogance like the evil of idolatry. Because you have rejected the word of the Lord, he has rejected you as king (1 Sam. 15:22-23).

Saul's confession was not clear. Saul tried indirectly to justify himself by stating that he was afraid of the people and gave in to them. Rather than fear God, he feared people and what they thought of him (1 Sam. 15:24). Saul then asked Samuel to forgive him and come back with him that "I may worship the Lord." This request had a dubious motive covered by false spirituality since Saul was more concerned with his reputation as king. If Samuel didn't leave with him the people would surely notice, and wonder if Saul had the favor of Samuel. Politics and appearance, not spirituality, were at work here. Still insistent, Saul ends up tearing Samuel's robe, upon which Samuel clearly declared that the kingdom was then torn from Saul. The Lord was grieved over his making Saul king of Israel (1 Sam. 15:35). The Lord grieves over leaders he has called but that have not obeyed him. Doing almost all of God's will is never the same as doing all of his will. As I believe C.S. Lewis wrote somewhere, "compromise is the language of the devil."

David was chosen and anointed as king by Samuel and "... from that day on the Spirit of the Lord came upon David in power" (1 Sam. 16:13). Samuel was afraid of Saul, who feared that Saul would kill him if he knew Samuel was going to anoint David (1 Sam. 16:2). Saul ruled by intimidation and fear. God's rejection and now judgment of Saul was clear wherein the Spirit of the Lord departed from Saul and an evil spirit from the Lord tormented Saul (1 Sam. 16:14). God is sovereign and he can use even an evil spirit for his purposes, here for rebuke and judgment. Saul was not yet moved from office as king even though God had rejected him.

David ended up in Saul's court, playing the harp to relieve him of the effects of the evil spirit. The Philistines arrived and declared war on Israel (1 Sam. 17:1). Goliath challenged them such that Saul and all the Israelites were profoundly fearful and intimidated (1 Sam. 17:11). David arrived on the scene and declared "...Who is this uncircumcised Philistine that he should defy the armies of the living God?" (1 Sam. 17:26), and then eventually killed Goliath. Saul soon gave David a high rank in the army (1 Sam. 18:5), and David's success grew since the Lord was with him and all the people and army officers loved him. David returned from a successful campaign against the Philistines and the women sang "Saul has slain his thousands, and David his tens of thousands" (1 Sam. 18:7). What was the reaction of Saul? Was he pleased because victory was in the land and that the enemies of Israel were defeated? Was he pleased because God was truly in their midst, and because David was succeeding in the power of the Spirit? Not at all. Instead of rejoicing and thanking God for David's victories, Saul became angry, was galled by the song, began to feel insecure in that he might lose his kingdom, and from that day onwards was jealous of David (1 Sam. 18:8-9). The next day an evil spirit from God came *forcefully* upon Saul (1 Sam. 18:10). The word *forcefully* is significant, revealing a progressively deepening of spiritual oppression due to continued disobedience with now the added sin of jealousy. Saul was prophesying (Heb. "Uncontrolled ecstatic behavior," cf. 1 Kings 18:29) while David was playing the harp. Saul threw his spear at David, trying to actually kill him. Jealously and insecurity led to violence. Saul was afraid of David because the Lord was with him but had left Saul. When Saul saw how successful David was he feared him (1 Sam. 18:15). Instead of praising God for David's growing success in ministry, Saul becomes David's enemy. Saul was obsessed with his image, his reputation, his popularity, and retaining his position as king of Israel. Saul was becoming increasingly driven by jealousy, anger, and insecurity.

Saul plotted to remove David without actually killing him himself. Saul tried to give David his older daughter Merab in marriage on the condition that he continue to fight the battles (1 Sam. 18:17), hoping that David would be killed in battle. Effectively he set David up for failure, to be wiped out by the enemies, a "clean" solution from Saul's viewpoint. But David wisely declined seeing that on the surface it looked good but discerning that the motives were evil. Then Saul was all too pleased to find out that his daughter Michal loved David (1 Sam. 18:20). Now for round two. Saul attempted to give Michal to David as his daughter-in-law "... so that she may be a snare to him and so that the hand of the Philistines may be against him" (1 Sam. 18:21). Saul ordered others to speak to David and try to convince him with a blatant lie ("the king is pleased with you"), but David declined because of the large bride-price. Shrewdly and still plotting, Saul simply made the bride price one hundred Philistine foreskins under the deceitful pretext of kingly revenge on his enemies, but in reality hoping that David would be killed in the process (1 Sam. 18:25). David and his men killed two hundred Philistines, twice what was required, and then he married Michal. That was basically the last straw for Saul when he realized that the Lord was with David and that his daughter Michal loved David. The result? Saul became even more afraid of him and "remained his enemy the rest of his days" (1 Sam. 18:28-29). Envy of success and insecurity led to hatred. Killing Goliath was easy whereas dealing with Saul was becoming increasingly draining and dangerous for David.

David's popularity and success grew. Saul was still out to kill him, but now in more direct and open ways. Saul actually told his son Jonathan and all the attendants to kill David (1 Sam. 19:1). But Jonathan confronted Saul, demanding, "... why then would you do wrong to an innocent man like David by killing him for no reason?" (1 Sam. 19:5). Saul listened to Jonathan and made an oath: "As surely as the Lord lives, David will not be put to death" (1 Sam. 19:6). The oath was in reality a ploy or cover-up to have people trust him that his hatred of David is now over. David came out of hiding, thinking it was safe, since Saul gave his word as king that he would not be harmed. But all too soon Saul tried to pin David to the wall with his spear, yet David escaped. Saul then sent men to David's house to try to kill him and when he found out he was in Ramah he sent men there to kill him. Saul himself arrived after his men ended up prophesying. But the Spirit of the Lord came even upon Saul and he walked along prophesying until he came to Naioth.

He stripped off his robes and also prophesied in Samuel's presence. He lay that way all day and all night. This is why people say, "Is Saul also among the prophets?" (1 Sam. 19:23b-24).

The passage reveals how alien Saul's spirit was from the true servants of the Lord. So much for Saul keeping his word, he could not be trusted. Saul ended up being humiliated by God—forced to prophesy naked—apparently the last chance from God to repent and turn from his wickedness while being humbled in front of others. It was also a means for God to intervene and foil Saul's attempt to kill David.

David then believed Saul was out to kill him, but didn't know why (1 Sam. 20). David put up a boundary in refusing to come to take his seat at the New Moon Festival, fearing that Saul would try to kill him. David made a test, telling Jonathan what to say, should Saul ask him as to his absence. If Saul replied with a temper, David would be convinced Saul still wants to kill him (1 Sam. 20:8). On the second day of the Festival, Saul asked "why is David absent?" Jonathan explained that he permitted David to go and offer a sacrifice with his family (1 Sam. 20:27-31). Saul's anger exploded at Jonathan and he said to him,

> *You son of a perverse and rebellious woman! Don't I know that you have sided with the son of Jesse to your own shame and to the shame of the mother who bore you?* (1 Sam. 20:30).

Jonathan confronted Saul, and demanded to know what David has done to deserve death. Saul gave no answer, throwing his spear at his own son (1 Sam. 20:32). Saul's tactics here were shame and blame, use of perverse and foul language, character assassination, and anger and violence when confronted with truth—all clear signs of spiritual abuse. Saul embarked on a new tactic in "taking sides" by assessing all people as to whether they are for him or against him, instead of whether they are walking faithfully with the living God.

Saul talked to the men of Benjamin when in pursuit of David, saying, *"None of you is concerned about me or tells me that my son has incited my servant to lie in wait for me, as he does today"* (1 Sam. 22:8). More accusation, false guilt, and selfishness as an expression of "you don't care about me, shame on you!" Saul continued to hunt for David, tracking him like an animal to kill him. He was using his power as a leader for his own personal vengeance. When Saul heard that David was at Keilah (1 Sam. 23:7) he thought God had handed him over to him. Saul was really deluded, convinced that God is with him in the midst of trying to kill an innocent man who is favored by God. He was trying to rationalize his sin and gain support in his sinful campaign against David. David spared Saul's life in a cave in En Gedi where he could have easily killed him (1 Sam. 24). The circumstances of God "delivering" him and his advisers told him to kill Saul, but on principle David declined. David would not kill the Lord's anointed. God would have to remove Saul from the throne and exact his own vengeance. David was not in the business of getting his own vengeance, or promoting himself.

Saul's reaction, upon hearing David's voice and how he had been spared, was to weep, call David "my son," and declare him more righteous than himself (1 Sam. 24:16-22). On the surface, it looks like a genuine change of heart, doesn't it? One would expect that tears, confession, clear evidence of David's true character and innocence of any crime, would lead to a true change of heart. Not so—it was all fake, as the story continues to unfold. Saul was still looking out for himself, but through his descendants, by extracting an oath from David to ensure the continuity of his family line (1 Sam. 24:21). David wisely went with his men up to the stronghold (1 Sam. 24:2), out of Saul's reach, realizing that Saul's words and actions could not be trusted.

When Saul heard from the Ziphites that David was in the hill of Hakilah (1 Sam. 26:7-11), he went with three thousand chosen men to hunt him down. So much for Saul's tears and words (1 Sam. 2416-22). David took Saul's spear and water jug by night from the camp while the Lord brought a deep sleep upon the whole camp. Next day David revealed to Saul how again he spared Saul's life. David again confronted Saul "What have I done? Why am I guilty?" (1 Sam. 26:18). Saul confessed "I have sinned... certainly I have acted like a fool and have erred greatly, and then he blesses David" (1 Sam. 26:21). Round two—perhaps now David can trust him? Apparently not, since David went to the land of the Philistines for safety from Saul. When Saul heard that David was in Gath, he no longer searched for him (1 Sam. 27:4). Until that point Saul was still out to kill David in spite of having been spared twice by David. Saul's words were useless, there was absolutely no change of heart and he could not be trusted.

The Philistines rose up against Israel, Saul was afraid and his heart was filled with terror (1 Sam. 28). He sought the Lord who long ago stopped speaking to him, and then in desperation visited the witch at Endor. Saul dies in battle the next day with Jonathan, and he himself committing suicide—real tragedy!

Lessons on Spiritual Abuse From The Story of David and Saul

As we reflect on the interactions between David and King Saul, we see the following signs of spiritual abuse. Using spiritual authority for one's own ends, to enhance one's reputation, name, and secure one's position of authority and power, instead of for the name and glory of God among his people. Using blame, shame, intimidation, guilt, and accusation to control others. Letting fear and insecurity, especially envy and jealousy, rule one's decisions and actions. Willingly and knowingly attacking an innocent person, when there is no excuse, and none could be given when confronted. Faking change of heart and confession, even with false tears. Covering up disobedience with fake spirituality and rationalizations. Making rash, impulsive decisions that cause problems for others. Self-centred, more concerned about oneself, worried by whether people are on one's side or not, instead of on God's side or not. When confronted, reluctant to confess disobedience, often trying to justify oneself or cover up for sin and making things more complex than they really are. Resorting to sinful motives, scheming and plotting, pretending to repent with tears and confession.

The real problem for Israel was not the Philistines, it was sin within the nation coming from the king himself, that led to disaster and tragedy. It could all have been avoided had Saul been obedient and continually thanked God for the success of others, especially people like David. For David, fighting the Philistines was a piece of cake, but dealing with Saul, that was the major problem when someone right in the nation of Israel opposed him. This is not unlike the Church, when so much time and energy is consumed in dealing with, and confronting, abusive spiritual leaders or congregations, when the real call is to battle Satan. Meantime, more people perish while the Church is embroiled in spiritual civil war.

Saul is an example of "mixture" in that he was anointed and used by God to win many battles. Yet there was progressively more evil in his life. Initially, Saul was an anointed man of God, who started out well, but in time became spiritually abusive, one who was not safe to be around. Jealousy was a main factor in his eventual downfall. By letting envy and jealousy rule in his life, God allowed torment by an evil spirit, causing spiritual bondage. I have heard of a few Christian men, having an apparent anointing for ministry and well thought of by many people, but yet were capable of the most sudden, painful, accusatory outbursts against others. "Anointed," yet not safe, a strange paradox that requires spiritual discernment. Sadly, in a few cases I have seen spiritual leaders progressively engage in the sort of things that Saul did, when others in the Church began to rise up in the gifts of the Spirit and grow in obvious success in ministry due to God's favor.

Listening to the Prophets

Jeremiah bemoaned the moral depravity and disobedience of the nation of Judah. Shockingly, the prophets were prophesying lies and the priests were ruling by their own authority (Jer. 5:30-31). Prophets and priests were no longer functioning in their God-ordained roles. Instead, they were given to greed, deceit, and offering only superficial deceptive help for the spiritual needs of the people (Jer. 6:13-14). It was so bad that these spiritual leaders were no longer ashamed of their actions, and thus abused people with impunity (Jer. 6:15). Jeremiah denounced the spiritual shepherds who actually destroyed and scattered the people, having failed to care for them, all of which is evil (Jer. 23:1-2). Exploitation by leadership was not unknown in Isaiah's day (Isaiah 56:11). Jerusalem fell not because of the power of the opposing armies, but because of the sins of her prophets and priests and their exploitation and devouring of their own people (Lam. 4:12-13). Micah spoke against the leaders who were unjust, distorted what is right, and engaged in bloodshed and evil (Micah 3:9-10). Meanwhile, judges, priests, and prophets were motivated by money instead of truth and righteousness, and all the while declaring that they were walking with the Lord (Micah 3:11).

I include here probably one of the saddest stories of sexual abuse in the Old Testament as an example of how people can be devalued and used. Judges 19 shows an instance of the appalling moral decline of the nation of Israel (Judges 3:11,7,12; 4:1; 6:1; 10:6). A Levite was returning home with his concubine and servant, and spent the night in Gibeah (Judges 19:12-21) in an old man's house. Wicked men from the city demanded that the Levite be brought out so they could have sex with him (Judges 19:22). The owner of the house declined, offering instead his own virgin daughter and the Levite's concubine, saying "you can use them and do whatever you wish. But to this man, do not do such a disgraceful thing" (Judges 19:24). The wicked men disagreed, so the Levite took his concubine (Hebrew: forcibly) and "sent her outside to them, and they raped her and abused her throughout the night, and at dawn they let her go" (Judges 19:25). Somehow the woman survived the absolutely horrid ordeal, and had enough strength left to get back to the house, fell down at the door, and lay there until the morning (Judges 19:26). The Levite was going on his way, apparently without her or not looking for her at all, and noticed her on the threshold of the door. His response was "Get up, let's go," with no apparent regard for her condition (Judges 19:27). When he reached home, he took a knife and cut up his concubine into twelve parts (Judges 19:29). Later in explaining the story the Levite twisted the facts (Judges 20:4-6). Perhaps concubines had a lesser status than some, but this story shows cold and calloused disregard for a woman, who was nevertheless created in the image of God who defends the vulnerable and weak (Exod. 22:22, Deut. 10:18; 24:17,19,20,21; 27:19).

Ezekiel spoke against the princes of the land who would murder their own people for material gain, thus destroying families and leaving women as widows (Ezek. 22:25). The priests, no longer faithful spiritual leaders, dishonor God's law, no longer distinguish holy from unholy, neglect the righteous commands of God, and thus profane God among them (Ezek. 22:26). The officials are like wolves, devouring others for material wealth (Ezek. 22:27). The prophets then "whitewash these deeds for them by false visions and lying divinations" (Ezek. 22:28), claiming that the Lord has truly spoken. They used God's name and pretext of spoken authority to cover their sin. In modern terms, it is like twisting or distorting the Scriptures, or claiming that "The Lord spoke to me ...." in order to silence people's questions or cover up one's actions. The exploitation of spiritual abusers come out clearly in Ezekiel 34:2b-4:

> *...Woe to the shepherds of Israel who only take care of themselves! Should not shepherds take care of the flock? You eat the curds, clothe yourselves with wool and slaughter the choice animals, but you do not take care of the flock. You have not strengthened the weak or healed the sick or bound up the*

injured. You have not brought back the strays or searched for the lost. You have ruled them harshly and brutally.

The leaders or shepherds of the nation—priests, prophets, and officials—exploited people and put their needs above those of the people. Instead of protecting people, they used their authority to harm people.

On top of all this, they neglected the deep needs of people by not ministering to the weak, the sick, and the injured. Blue made some astute observations on this passage in Ezekiel:

> Pastors in the Western world are most often judged on their preaching and administrative skills, but when God reviewed his pastors he did not mention these criteria. He indicted the leaders of Israel for not strengthening the weak or healing the sick ... they had found something more important to do than caring for the people, which was their real job ... Both Ezekiel and Jesus condemned one fundamental error in the shepherds: they used the sheep rather than served them. They acted as if the sheep existed to meet their needs rather than the other way around. When shepherds today look out over their congregations and see their people as church growth statistics, tithing units and workers in their programs, they follow the pastoral style that Jesus and Ezekiel prophesied against.[2]

The consequences for the shepherds as described by Ezekiel are opposition from God himself, being held accountable for their actions, and removal from their positions of authority and influence (Ezek. 34:10). In contrast, God himself as the true shepherd will search for his sheep, rescue them, feed them, give them rest, bind up the injured, strengthen the weak, and rule with justice (Ezek. 34:11-16). Now we turn to the True Shepherd's view of spiritual abuse.

Phariseeism: The Anatomy of Spiritual Abuse

When we study the Gospels, with whom did Jesus have the greatest problems? The horrid Romans who actually nailed him to the cross? The money-greedy tax collectors and others who exploited people? Those who discriminated against women or enslaved people? No. Jesus had his greatest problems with the Pharisees, Sadducees, chief priests, and experts in the law. Ironically, the most theologically trained in the land, the guardians of the law and Moses' teaching were the ones who opposed and harassed Jesus. Numerous encounters between Jesus and the Pharisees and Sadducees are recorded in the Gospels, as well as Jesus' rather pointed and blunt teaching about or to them. While the Pharisees and Sadducees are no longer with us, their spirits still operate today in the Church.

Why was Jesus' teaching so harsh and direct concerning the Pharisees and Sadducees? How could Jesus have been so blunt by calling them "broods of vipers" (Matt. 12:34; 23:33)? Why did Jesus tell us to be on guard for such leaders (Matt. 16:6; Luke 12:1), or watch out for false prophets that are like ferocious wolves in sheep's clothing (Matt. 7:15), or deceivers who claim to be Christ (Matt. 24:4)? Was Paul paranoid when he told the Ephesians to beware of savage wolves that will come after them, even from among the Ephesians themselves (Acts 20:29)? I believe it is because Jesus entrusts the Church with proclaiming the gospel, and therefore whenever the Church becomes spiritually abusive it becomes a "spiritual bottleneck." It's as if the channel of love and grace from God the Father gets plugged. It becomes a counter-witness and hindrance to the gospel (1 Cor. 9:12).

Part of our commitment as disciples of Jesus (Matt. 28:20) includes being aware and alert to spiritual abuse as a modern form of Phariseeism. When we are not alert and spiritual abuse occurs, our heavenly Father's name is dishonored in the eyes of the world, his gospel discredited, and it is more difficult for people to experience the love and grace of God. If we understand the essence of Jesus' teaching, we realize that spiritual abuse is a matter of degree, and that we must all guard against any critical or Pharisaical tendencies in our hearts. In fact, ministry and the use of spiritual power have an occupational hazard given the temptations and seductions from Satan. Commenting on Jesus' identifications of the Pharisees as belonging to Satan in John 8:44, Page wrote:

> ... it is especially those who pride themselves on their religious and moral superiority who are candidates for membership in Satan's family. John 8:44 is a solemn reminder that the devil is especially active among those who appear to be respectable and upright.[3]

Sometimes spiritual leaders are loving and godly, but it is the followers who abuse their leaders. From the Gospels and Acts, we see the following symptoms and dynamics of spiritual abuse.

Fixation on Authority. Authority is very important to spiritual abusers, since it's required to exert control and influence. When Jesus entered the temple courts and taught, the chief priests and elders asked by what authority did he teach (Matt. 21:21-27; Mark 11:27-33). There is no indication that they marveled at what he taught, allowed their hearts to be touched by the truth, or considered whether the teaching glorified God or was fruitful. They asked these questions because they cherished their authority and felt threatened when someone else moved in godly authority. The more Jesus amazed and captivated people by his authoritative teaching and obvious spiritual power (Luke 4:32-36), even evoking awe by raising from the dead (Luke 7:16), the more irritated and defensive the Pharisees became. Matthew noted a comparison between Jesus' authoritative teaching and that of the teachers of the law (Matt. 7:29). They questioned Jesus on his authority to forgive sin (Mark 2:8-12, Luke 5:17-24). Authority was more important than love and grace. A current example would be a leader who would remind people, especially when he wants control in a situation, that he is "the leader," therefore he must be followed, or he is the "Lord's anointed," so no one should question. This is power posturing:

> Power-posturing simply means that leaders spend a lot of time focused on their own authority and reminding others of it as well. This is necessary because their spiritual authority isn't real—based on genuine godly character—it is postured.[4]

True spiritual authority is grounded in one's ability to love and one's faithfulness to Jesus, one's own example and life, one's fear of God, not the position or title in and of itself. When leaders remind their followers of their authority, there usually is a problem. That is like asking people to follow beyond their leader's ability to love them. While obedience and submission to leaders in the Church are important (Rom. 13:1; Heb. 13:17; 1 Pet. 5:5), we also submit to *one another* out of reverence to Christ (Eph. 5:21), we all are priests (1 Pet. 2:9), and in the end always obey God rather than men (Acts 5:29). The Apostle Paul did not "lord it over" the Corinthians, but worked for their joy (2 Cor. 1:24).

Authority issues can appear in leaders who are "control freaks" and need to know as much as possible about people and the affairs of the church. In order to control, you need to know. I know of one spiritual leader who actually kept attendance, unknown to his congregation, after the people left from worship on Sunday morning.

Rather than being preoccupied with feeding the sheep, he spent time counting the sheep.

Diotrephes (3 John 9-10) was a Church leader who had such control from his authority that he rejected the Apostle John and his co-workers, gossiped maliciously about them, and rejected fellowship with those who knew John. His control over the congregation is seen in his preventing those who wanted to fellowship with people he disapproved of, and expelling them from the Church if they did so. He used his authority to control and intimidate the flock.

Desire for recognition and title (Matt. 23:5-12). Since they operate from authority and control instead of from love and humble servanthood they want people to notice them and be reminded of their position (Luke 11:43). They love importance and honor in the eyes of others (Luke 20:46). In effect, they learn how to exalt themselves, instead of being exalted by the Lord because they love much, forgive many, and bless all. The height of their title is more important to them than the depth of their compassion and the size of their heart.

Emphasis on theological pedigree. Instead of clear evidence of fruit in their lives coming from true repentance, there is a reliance on theological training and tradition. When John the Baptist saw the Pharisees and Sadducees coming to where he was baptizing, he admonished them to produce fruit in keeping with repentance (Matt. 3:8-9) and not rely on claiming Abraham as their father. Modern day examples might be emphasizing one's theological training or denominational school or seminary of origin over spending time with Jesus (Acts 4:13). This also comes from a fixation on authority.

Using Scripture to control people. This is incredibly subtle. Since spiritual leaders are often trained theologically, there is then the temptation to use their knowledge of the Bible to control others. Johnson and VanVonderen give but one example:

> We have counseled far too many Christian women who were being brutalized, emotionally crushed, even bloodied by Christian husbands. And we have listened, appalled, to the "counsel" given by pastors and other spiritual leaders to these wounded daughters of God all too often: "Wives, submit to your husbands ..." This mishandling of Scripture is, sadly, widespread, and used to press abused women into staying in destructive situations.[5]

Marcie was a Christian woman not long married to an elder who became quite abusive, especially verbally. There came a point when she needed to leave for a while for her own emotional and spiritual safety. She was so emotionally distraught that she almost didn't make it safely to the women's shelter as she drove her car. Her subsequent counsel from the church was that she should go back to her husband and submit. Shockingly, the spiritual leader who oversaw several churches advised her also to return to her husband and simply tell him that if he hits her, he is actually hitting Jesus.

A Christian clinical psychologist recounts the true story of a Christian woman whose Christian husband explained to the church that he "beat their oldest child, punched and brutalized his wife, and forced her to engage in sadomasochistic sexual rituals" because she was not "submissive enough."[6] The horrid fact is that the college-educated pastor and elders believed him and saw no problem. This is a million light years away from loving others as Christ loved us! Due to denial, codes of silence, rationalization, lack of understanding, and other reasons, much of the misogyny (hatred of women), which does occur in the Church is typically undetected.[7] This type of abuse is found in all types of churches, from conservative to charismatic, and becomes spiritual abuse when Christian leaders use the Bible, doctrine, theological arguments, or church authority to control, manipulate, shame, exploit, or dominate women. Spiritual manipulation is the most insidious and least expected. Of the women that I have prayed with for healing from spiritual abuse, almost all had no knowledge of misogyny. Rinck identified the behavior and signs of Type I through Type IV misogynists.[8] What is more subtle still is that some women are misogynists.

What happened to challenging a husband to love his wife as Christ loved the Church (Eph. 5:25,28) or as his own body, and especially if he is a leader in the church? What does it mean for a wife to submit to her husband as to the Lord (Eph. 5:22)? What happened to Paul's command that husbands should love their wives and not be harsh to them (Col. 3:19)? How can a man claim to love God and his neighbour if he abuses his wife and remains unchallenged by spiritual leaders? Jesus said "As I have loved you, so you must love one another" (John 13:34). Does that simple and direct command of Jesus not also speak directly and profoundly to spousal abuse? Why not question if a Christian really is a disciple of Jesus if he does not love his own spouse (John 13:35)? Does not a Christian man who forces his Christian wife to engage in sadomasochistic sexual rituals hate his own body (Eph. 5:29)? *How Scripture is applied, in what spirit, and what other parts of Scripture are not quoted can be even more important than the Scripture that is quoted.* Is there a "pretext for the proof-text"?

Demanding trust. Those in authority cannot really function if no one will trust them. Trust is the "glue" that holds it all together. Thus, Jesus takes issue with those who will have people trust them, or believe their word, by oath or swearing on another authority (Matt. 23:16-22) instead of simply telling the truth with clear, direct integrity. One's words should stand on one's integrity alone, and not on one's position or anything else, since that becomes manipulation of relationships, which is evil (Matt. 5:33-37). A spiritual leader today saying "Trust me, I'm your leader" is no different than saying "Trust me, I speak by the gold in the temple" in Jesus' time. Trust is earned and when it's demanded there is cause to wonder.

Legalism. The Pharisees were pre-occupied with their rules, regulations, and appearances. The Pharisees had a problem with Jesus and his disciples eating with sinners (Matt. 9:10-13; Mark 2:15-17), upon which Jesus challenged them about the importance of mercy over sacrifice. Similarly, Jesus was questioned by the Pharisees regarding eating on the Sabbath (Matt. 12:1-8; Mark 2:23-27; Luke 6:1-5), wherein they condemned the innocent disciples (Matt. 12:8). Jesus again pointed out how they did not understand mercy over sacrifice. They were quick to condemn, slow to show mercy.

Legalism becomes the means by which people are controlled by authority. Conformity to the rules and performance measured by them now becomes the essence of the spiritual system. *You can't control if you can't measure.* Yet it was freedom for which Christ set us free (Gal. 5:1), and since we were bought by the precious blood of Jesus we should not become slaves of men whether in the church or outside (1 Cor. 7:23). Legalism is totally incompatible with grace and love. Spiritual abusers want to succeed on their terms at the expense of the freedom of their followers. Legalism leads to bondage and slowly suffocates the spiritual life.

When the Pharisees and teachers of the law challenged Jesus about his disciples breaking their rules by not washing before they eat, Jesus challenged them how they actually nullified the word of God by following the tradition of their elders, or their theology, over the Scriptures (Matt. 15:1-6; Mark 7:1-14).

Modern day examples are forcing total abstinence as a requirement for church membership or banning all musical instruments from worship. Veronica wanted simply to raise her hands in worship, and thus express in her own way her joy and thankfulness to Jesus. She didn't even expect or require anyone else to do likewise. However, the looks she received from others and the comments that came later from some of the leaders in the church sent a powerful negative message. Her "sin" was that she had encountered an unspoken rule in the church, which was "Thou shalt not raise thine hands in worship," in spite of Ps. 63:4. Inevitably, legalism challenges the word of God.

Majoring on the minors (Matt. 23:23-24). A direct consequence of legalism is the focus on rules that are typically petty, instead of majoring on mercy, justice, and faithfulness (Luke 11:42). The whole intent and purpose of legalism is so different from grace, that this should be no surprise. Straining out gnats while swallowing a camel. I was told of a church that lost members due to a debate on ceiling fans, another to arguments over the choice of hymns, and a church that split over a gravel pit. Never mind that Jesus commanded us to love one another. Meantime, more people perish without Jesus. Hearts become hardened and blinded to spiritual truth, a consequence of legalism when rules are cherished more than people.

Mark returned from an evening of healing prayer ministry where a Christian woman had been finally freed from over thirty years of the fear of death, fear of loneliness, inability to bond with others, and rejection from her parents. He told me he would never forget that evening, it was as if he walked on holy ground. All he could think of was rejoicing in the healing and freedom this dear sister in Christ had finally experienced. The very next day, his pastor who had accompanied him that evening began to berate him for the fact that this lady had initially contacted Mark for healing prayer, and not him as pastor. Mark reminded him that there was nothing wrong in the ministry protocol, and the most important fact was that this lady had experience more of the love of Jesus, and that is the only thing that mattered. Mark added that he didn't really care whether it was through him or someone else (a minor issue); the major issue was that this lady experienced more of Jesus.

Jealousy and indignation. This is often a by-product of legalism. After Jesus overturned the moneychanger's tables in the temple, he healed the blind and the lame in the temple. But when the chief priests and teachers of the law saw the wonderful things Jesus did, and even the children shouting "Hosanna to the Son of David," they were indignant. (Matt. 21:12-17). Rather than praising God for the healing of a poor man with a shriveled hand or healing a crippled woman, they were furious and indignant because Jesus healed on the Sabbath (Luke 6:6-11; 13:14).

As a ministry, movement, or church grows, there are sometimes those who are jealous, which comes from pride and insecurity. After the apostles performed many miracles and many people were healed, the high priests and associates who were Sadducees were filled with jealousy (Acts 5:17). Instead of praising God for the people healed, and the obvious mercy and love of God in action, they were jealous of the attention, ministry success, and rising popularity of the apostles.

Obsession with image (Matt. 23:3-5; 23:25-28). Much effort goes into externals, but their own inner life is a contradiction and they do not do what they preach. This is hypocrisy, which follows from a focus on authority and legalism at the expense of issues of the heart and soul. *You cannot grow on the inside if you live for the outside.* So once the rules are applied and appearance is everything, spiritual abusers want to "make a good impression outwardly" and "boast about your flesh," like a successful ministry (Gal. 6:12-13). I know of a pastor who preached a series on the love of God, all the while unknown to the congregation he was sexually and emotionally abusing his wife. I once believed that such things simply were not possible. Jesus was not exaggerating when he said that hypocrisy means being full of wickedness on the inside (Matt. 23:28) while appearing quite righteous on the outside. No wonder he commanded us to be on guard against hypocrisy, which is the yeast of the Pharisees (Luke 12:1), which in small amounts slowly permeates and corrupts relationships and spirituality.

Recruits as converts. Jesus spoke against the teachers of the law and Pharisees in their attempts to win converts (Matt. 23:15) from traveling over land and sea. They were interested in converts to their system, more workers who would become like them instead of like Jesus, who would maintain their religious system instead of proclaim and extend the Kingdom of God. They sought "proselytes of righteousness" who would go beyond simple love for God to loyalty to their religious system.[9] This occurs today, where there is more effort in promoting a church or denomination than spreading the gospel, or more emphasis on being a "good" Baptist, Lutheran, Pentecostal, Presbyterian (etc.) than loving Jesus and fearing the living God.

Contempt. The chief priests and Pharisees referred to the people as "a mob that knows nothing of the law" and that was cursed (John 7:49). In reality, the chief priests and Pharisees knew nothing of grace and mercy and were thus blinded to spiritual truth while "simple" people merely praised God for the miracles of Jesus. Rather than rejoicing with a man born blind who could now see, the Pharisees hurled insults at the man, declared that he was "steeped in sin at birth," and then threw him out of the synagogue (John 9:24-34). Notice the irony and massive contradiction in accusing someone of being sinful in the very midst of treating them sinfully. In effect, the man was devalued and dishonoured. A litmus test of a church's true spirituality is how poorly educated, disadvantaged, or vulnerable people are treated and valued.

Intimidation. If legalism or authority is questioned or challenged, tactics soon appear from spiritual abusers to maintain their authority and their system. Even though some of the leaders believed in Jesus, they were afraid to confess their faith, since the Pharisees would put them out of the synagogue (John 12:42; 9:22). This is like threatening members of a church with excommunication or being shunned for not obeying or believing as required. I remember talking to one Christian couple, increasingly concerned about the control and hypocrisy in their church, yet afraid of leaving since they knew they would be publicly shamed and then banned from the church. It was not my place to tell them whether they should stay or leave, but I did say that it did not seem very loving for a church to do such a thing. They acknowledged that many people go there because they are afraid of leaving. Instead of being drawn to the church by the love of Jesus they are kept there by fear. Statements of guilt and shame like "if you leave our church, God will never bless you" are forms of spiritual blackmail. Another couple felt they could never leave their church because they were reminded by the leaders that they became Christians through them and thus in a subtle way they "owed it" to them to stay in their church. I reminded them that they were purchased by the blood of Jesus, not the leader's, and their salvation rested on the finished work of Christ and nothing or no one else. I encouraged them to pray and listen to the Lord, and then decide.

Accusation. This is another major tactic spiritual abusers might use to defend themselves or attack others. When Jesus healed a mute demonized man so he could speak, the people were amazed and joyous, whereas the Pharisees accused Jesus of healing via the prince of demons (Matt. 9:32-34; Mark 3:23-30). The Pharisees were envious and insecure in the face of Jesus who was now doing things never done before in Israel. Obviously, Jesus was doing something that the Pharisees had not done, and could not do. Rather than be thankful that the mute could now speak, incredulously, they accused Jesus of ministering by evil powers. The same happened when Jesus healed a demon-possessed man who was blind and mute (Matt. 12:22-29). The crowds were astonished and said "Could this be the Son of David?" Faced again with Jesus' obvious success in ministry and rising popularity, the Pharisees accused and discredited Jesus of ministering by Beelzebub. Rather than say anything good about Jesus, they defamed him.

When Jesus was faced with a man with a shriveled hand in a synagogue on the Sabbath, the Pharisees were looking for a reason to accuse Jesus, so they asked him if it was lawful to heal on the Sabbath (Matt. 12:9-14; Mark 3:1-6). They were *not* interested in learning theology. The goal was to find a reason to accuse Jesus—clearly false motives. Jesus answered their question so that there would be no ground to accuse him if he healed the man, which he did. Rather than being thankful that they had learned more theology and also that a man's hand was healed, they left and plotted how to kill Jesus. Their hearts were so incredibly hard that Jesus was angry and deeply distressed at their stubborn hearts (Mark 3:5). Just after Jesus healed many people and *many* crowds were following him, the Pharisees came to test him on the issue of divorce (Matt. 19:1-12: Mark 10:2-12). They were not seeking theological answers, they were seeking a way to discredit Jesus as his ministry and popularity steadily grew. In fact, such a clear example of God's grace and love in healing a man caused the Pharisees to leave and plot Jesus' death (Mark 3:6).

Laying intentional traps. As competition for authority heats up, comparisons become more obvious, and the system of the spiritual abusers is threatened. Hence, more desperate measures beyond accusation or intimidation are employed. For example, the Pharisees "went out and laid plans to trap him in his words" (Matt. 22:15-22; Mark 12:13-17). The Pharisees and teachers of the law "began to oppose him fiercely and besiege him with questions, waiting to catch him in something he might say" (Luke 11:53), and later actually sent out spies to trap him (Luke 20:20) while pretending to be honest. The spies deceitfully complimented and affirmed Jesus (Luke 20:21-22), then posed a question on paying taxes to Caesar designed to trap him, forcing him into an impossible situation where he would have to side either with the Herodians or the Romans. Such actions are evil intents of the heart (Matt. 22:18). Then the Sadducees questioned Jesus on the resurrection, hoping to put him in an impossible situation (Matt. 22:23-33; Luke 20:27-39). This was obviously a trap since the Sadducees didn't even believe in the resurrection. Undaunted, an expert of the law, a Pharisee, tested Jesus on the greatest commandment (Matt. 22:34-40). Concerning the woman caught in adultery the Pharisees asked Jesus whether she should be stoned (John 8:3). They were clearly using the question as a trap in order to accuse Jesus (John 8:6). Worse still, they were using the woman for their own evil plans. Modern examples are testing a person to see what they believe about charismatics, gifts of the Spirit, dispensations, end times theology, Catholicism, for example, not to learn, but to "brand" or label the person. Ps. 55:21 provides further insight: "His speech is smooth as butter, yet war is in his heart; his words are more soothing than oil, yet they are drawn swords." True discernment is required where words appear positive and edifying, yet the reality is the just the opposite. I have learned the truth of this verse the hard way.

The Consequences of Spiritual Abuse

Spiritual blindness. The story of the man born blind shows how the Pharisees as spiritual leaders were completely blind to spiritual reality (John 9:39-41). Their hardness of heart, in spite of their theological proficiency (John 9:28), blinded them to the obvious mercy, goodness, and love of God as shown in the miracles of Jesus. In contrast, the man no longer blind believed in Jesus and worshiped him (John 9:38-40). Likewise, the Pharisees who had physical eyes and saw the miracles of Jesus repeatedly right in front of them were spiritually blind, while the blind beggar Bartimaeus who never saw Jesus or his miracles could see spiritually enough to call out to Jesus and be healed (Mark 10:46-52). Spiritual reality is seen through our hearts (Eph. 1:18) and not just apprehended by our minds.

Burden and exploitation (Matt. 23:4,14). Instead of bringing freedom, life, joy, and more, one result of spiritual abuse is burdens—their rules, requirements, and ministry expectations—all the while not really willing to help (Luke 11:46). This is the exact opposite of being servants, and at times sacrificing for others in the body of Christ. This is unlike Jesus who invites us to give our burdens and heavy yokes to him (Matt. 11:29-30). As Christians we should bear one another's burdens and so fulfill the law of Christ (Gal. 6:2). Jesus castigated the spiritual abusers of his day for exploitation in devouring widow's homes (Matt. 23:14). One of the worst examples today is sexual abuse by spiritual leaders who thus use people for their sexual gratification.

Closing the door on grace. Jesus was against those who "shut the Kingdom of heaven in men's faces" (Matt. 23:13-14). This is an unfortunate result of Phariseeism, since the life and example of Pharisees prevents people from experiencing God's love and grace. Not only that, they will prevent people from entering Kingdom reality. Jesus accused them of "taking away the keys of knowledge," not entering truth and spirituality themselves, and hindering others in doing so (Luke 11:52). Experiencing more of the Holy Spirit and Jesus' presence is virtually impossible under their leadership.

Such spiritual leaders cannot take others where they themselves have never been, nor can they preach or teach beyond what they have experienced. It comes down to less of God and more for them at the expense of the followers. It was so bad in Jesus' day that the last place to meet God was in the Temple itself (Matt. 21:12-13).

Opposition to the Holy Spirit. When Christians excel in using their spiritual gifts, especially with the more public gifts (prophecy, preaching, teaching, or healing), they are sometimes attacked or squelched by insecure, envious spiritual leaders. David obviously moved in the power of the Spirit, his only "crime" was that God used him mightily. Jesus obviously moved in the power of the Holy Spirit and began a renewal movement centered on his Father's Kingdom, and all without sin. I know of cases where the motive to keep "unity in the church" or "prevent confusion" has been used by spiritual leaders to prevent or remove a believer from using his/her spiritual gifts. This is an extremely dangerous thing for church leaders to do. The gifts of the Holy Spirit are distributed according to God's will (Heb. 2:4) and are a manifestation of God's presence. If a Christian with a growing spiritual gift is attacked, *the attackers are really taking aim at the Holy Spirit!* This is apart from the ungodly or immature use of a spiritual gift that requires wise and loving church discipline and spiritual direction.

Removal from ministry. Much responsibility comes with spiritual leadership, since the spiritual well being of many people will be affected. The story of Saul versus David reveals how the Lord grieved over Saul who turned away from him and disobeyed his clear instructions (1 Sam. 15:11,35), and finally rejected him as king. Eli's two sons, Hophni and Phinehas, were priests (1 Sam. 1:3) who treated God's offering with contempt by taking the best part of the offerings by force (1 Sam. 2:16-17,23) and also sexually abused women who served at the entrance to the Tent of Meeting

(1 Sam. 2:22). They did not listen to their father's rebuke, because they had sinned too much for so long such that God's judgment was upon them (1 Sam. 2:22-25). The Lord rebuked Eli for honoring his sons more than God and his offering (1 Sam. 2:29), with the result that the life and strength of his whole family line would be cut short, his sons would die the same day, and his family would be removed in their priestly role. Since the privilege of priesthood was abused, it was eventually removed (1 Sam. 12:31-36) from the family line. It seems as if Eli thought that he was basically immune from such judgment since God promised beforehand that his father's house and thus family line would minister before the Lord forever (1 Sam. 2:30). But this was still dependent upon honoring God, "Those who honor me I will honor, but those who despise me will be disdained" (1 Sam. 2:30). Finally, God held Eli fully accountable for not correcting and restraining his sons (1 Sam. 3:12-14). Eli knew about the sin, but failed to act, and was thus eventually judged by God. This applies to the Church today, wherein Church leaders know of sin or spiritual or sexual abuse in the Church, but they fail to act to protect the flock. *In so doing, they honor or value the abusers more than God himself.*

A related issue is spiritual bondage as clearly seen in the life of King Saul who was oppressed by an evil spirit because of his disobedience. Marla is the wife of a spiritual leader in her church, and one day she phoned me, quite alarmed. That morning, when her pastor came out of his study just before the worship service, she saw a dark cloud or presence above his head for a minute or so. She thought she was seeing things, since this was a new thing for her. After prayer and counsel, she reluctantly suspected that this was a sign of a demonic influence upon him. She interceded for him, talked to a spiritual leader in the church she could trust, and exercised caution and wisdom. Later developments gave more evidence to demonic influence from spiritual abuse, which included the loss of ministry credentials upon abusing the church and most sadly, his family. She was consistently amazed at how her former pastor could not ever clearly admit doing wrong and how impossible he had become in all discussions and attempts to resolve some very clear and painful issues.

Deep wounds. Obviously, years spent living and trying to perform in a legalistic and abusive system, or under such leaders, has a toll on the human spirit. Memories of painful encounters may linger for a long time. The psychological weapons of shame, accusation, fear, and false guilt cause wounds that require healing. Most sobering is the realization that *to hurt and wound Christians is the same as hurting and wounding Jesus himself* (Acts 9:4-5).

Discerning Spiritual Abuse

Jesus commands us to beware of the spirit of the Pharisees, and spiritual abusers in general. Sadly, the issue is as real today as it was in Jesus' time:

> The stories of hundreds of Christians confirm that spiritual abuse is as alive today as it ever was. The means by which it happens now is the same as always: First, there is the neglect of real needs in favor of the "needs" of authority; then legalism replaces rest in God with demands for spiritual performance. Abuse is perpetrated by people in positions of power.[10]

Charles Swindoll quoted Lewis Johnson's paper, *The Paralysis of Legalism,* where he wrote "one of the most serious problems facing the orthodox Christian church today is the problem of legalism."[11] Legalism is all too common in the evangelical church today and "strict legalistic people in leadership drain the very life out of a church."¹² Would one not think that after all the Biblical teaching, countless expository sermons, mountains of Sunday School materials and hundreds of Christian books, that the church would understand the most fundamental concept—how to live by grace? This shows the power, deception, and subtlety of legalism, which is so much a part of spiritual abuse. Legalism actually has a "bewitching" effect (Gal. 3:1).

We need to be careful but not paranoid about who will minister to us. Trust must be earned, and comes easily to those who do minister in the authentic servant love of Jesus. The Scriptures admonish us to receive ministry based on righteousness and character, not on position or authority:

> *My eyes will be on the faithful in the land, that they may dwell with me; he whose walk is blameless will minister to me. No one who practices deceit will dwell in my house; no one who speaks falsely will stand in my presence.* (Ps. 101:6-7)

Jesus has given us symptoms and signs of spiritual abuse, especially in Matt. 23 and Luke 11:37-53. But he also said we will "recognize them by their fruit" (Matt. 7:16-23; 12:33). Jesus emphasized fruit (results) over theological pedigree or authority (origin) as emphasized by the Pharisees and others. The Pharisees exercised flawed discernment by looking at origins. In contrast to Jesus, they were looking at the *wrong end of reality*. The reasons Jesus emphasized good fruit is because it is a sign of repentance (Matt. 3:8; Luke 3:8; 7:30), and most fundamentally, can only come from relationship with him (John 15:5). In the final analysis, we recognize trustworthy and true spiritual leaders by how much they are like Jesus and how much time they spend with him. The Lord is our shepherd (Ps. 23:1), he gathers his lambs (us) in his arms and carries us close to his heart (Isaiah 40:11). Jesus is indeed the good shepherd (John 10:11), the great Shepherd (Heb. 13:20), and the chief shepherd (1 Pet. 2:25). Like learning the look and feel of true money to recognize counterfeit bills, we most readily recognize false spiritual leaders by spending time with Jesus, the one true authentic presence.

But what about situations where there is no personal knowledge, like when a new pastor is being called? Adrienne clearly remembers the first time she met a pastoral candidate who would become their new pastor. She took an instant dislike to him, which bothered her because she thought she was being critical, yet that was so unlike her. As a few years went by, the basic feeling persisted, and there were other instances when she had the similar feeling. Was it just woman's intuition, or was it a character clash? On the surface, the new senior pastor appeared highly evangelical, spiritual, and aggressive for the Kingdom of God. But eventually the church leadership and congregation understood clearly that hidden underneath was a spiritual abuser who was eventually asked to resign and leave. Among all this, it was discovered that another woman in the congregation also had a similar dislike for the man, right from the first encounter, and again for no real apparent reason. What was happening here? This is an example of discernment of spirits, or perhaps a word of knowledge coming as a strong sense, where the Lord was revealing to these women that there was a problem with this candidate. The women did not realize that the Lord could have been speaking to them in such a way. Had they known, they could have shared this with the leadership and asked the leaders and search committee to check the references much more thoroughly. Had this been done, a lot of pain could have been avoided. While there are certainly many very godly and spiritual men being called as pastors, church search committees should exercise all the spiritual gifts of discernment.

Like Jesus, we need to judge beyond mere appearances (Isaiah 11:3, John 7:24).

Hope For Abusers and the Abused

Spiritual abusers are often very wounded people themselves. While this does not justify anything they have done, nor lessen any pain inflicted on others, it helps in being merciful and understanding. Godly confrontation and even church discipline may be called for, but hopefully healing and restoration of the abuser is sought after. Some abusers were abused themselves, or have deep-seated unresolved anger, or are looking for acceptance and affirmation. Where there is true repentance, grace should be extended. If this is not readily grasped, remember that one of the greatest spiritual abusers of all time, Saul of Tarsus, was shown the grace of God. Saul approved of the death of Christians (Acts 8:1), tried to destroy the church (Acts 8:3) and uttered murderous threats against the disciples (Acts 9:4). If there was grace and healing for such an obvious spiritual abuser, there is grace for abusers today! The chief of sinners (1 Tim. 1:15) was transformed by the grace of God (1 Cor. 15:10). We should all be aware of any spiritual abuse tendencies in our lives as part of our humility before the Lord (Matt. 7:3).

We must not forget faithful pastors with true servant hearts, yet have been abused by their congregation. I have known of a number of pastors who experienced deep pain and hurt from their own flock, sometimes to the extent that they have quit the ministry entirely. North America has all too many such wounded warriors. I remember being at a conference where a pastor testified to wanting to commit suicide due to the pain and abuse from his own congregation. Pastors should be encouraged, honored, and covered in prayer. All too often, a factious group within the church brings dissension and forces the pastor to resign. Unseen needs mixed with pride and resistance, leading to blame shifting or transference, can wreak havoc in church fellowships.[13]

Finally, for those who have been abused, there is healing. This often starts with forgiveness and confessing any bitterness and sinful reactions. Reconciliation may not always be possible. Trust will often need to be slowly rebuilt, most easily around safe and caring spiritual leaders. Distorted views of God may have to be dealt with, as well as the pain and shock that comes with painful memories. Guilt, shame, and fear often need to be ministered to in healing prayer and through caring relationships. From my experience, these are the deepest of wounds since they come from a violation of trust and vulnerability. Johnson and VanVonderen offer counsel on either contending with, or leaving, abusive spiritual systems.[14]

Endnotes

[1] Ken Blue, *Healing Spiritual Abuse. How To Break Free from Bad Church Experiences* (Downers Grove: InterVarsity Press, 1993) p. 12.

[2] Blue, 41.

[3] Sydney H.T. Page, *Powers of Evil. A Biblical Study of Satan & Demons* (Grand Rapids: Baker Books, 1995) p. 126.

[4] David Johnson and Jeff VanVonderen, *The Subtle Power of Spiritual Abuse* (Minneapolis: Bethany House Publishers, 1991) p. 63

[5] Johnson, p. 98.

[6] Margaret J. Rinck, *Christian Men Who Hate Women* (Grand Rapids: Zondervan, 1990) p. 139.

[7] Rinck, p. 27.

[8] Rinck, p. 22.

[9] Johnson, pp. 163-164.

[10] Johnson, p. 32.

[11] Charles Swindoll, *The Grace Awakening*. (Dallas: Word Publishing, 1990) p. 79.

[12] Ibid.

[13] Valerie J. McIntyre, *Sheep in Wolves' Clothing. How Unseen Need Destroys Friendship & Community And What to Do About It.* (c/o P.C.M., Box 720, Warrenville, IL 60555: Hamewith Books, 1996). Pp. 1-76.

[14] Johnson, pp. 213-232.

 Chapter Eight

Deliverance Ministry: Myth or Mandate?

Overcoming Personal Skepticism

The topic of "deliverance ministry" has caused confusion, misunderstanding, and disagreement within the Church. Committed Christians claiming to be equally rooted and grounded in the Scriptures have some of the most divergent opinions on this topic.

For many years as a young Christian, I was skeptical of the teaching and practice of this ministry. Stories of the most bizarre types of practices and phenomena associated with this type of ministry made me especially wary. I really didn't encounter any situations where I saw the need for it, yet logically I realized that did not disprove or disqualify it. While I believed the gospel accounts where Jesus encountered and rebuked evil spirits, it was just not part of my world. I met a few Christians who claimed they could actually see demons, and others who had seen angels. That was not my experience either, but again, that did not logically rule out the reality and truthfulness of their experiences. When I was told how absolutely horrid and hideous demons look, I was glad that I was spared any such "spiritual ability."

As the Lord brought me more and more into the ministry of healing prayer, I began to encounter phenomena and situations that directly pointed to the presence of evil spirits. Some years ago I was asked to take the lead in praying through the house of Mark and Wilma, a Christian couple, where there was a very obvious demonic presence. A suddenly occurring and repeated bizarre disturbance caused terror for Wilma most nights. Not having much time to think through this new and unfamiliar ministry challenge, I just decided to believe the Scriptures that "greater is he who is in you than he who is in the world" (1 John 4:4), and to simply follow the example of Jesus and the early apostles in rebuking any evil spirits. I asked a few Christians in our church to intercede for this couple and me. I noticed within me a real anger in the evil one harassing Wilma, who was my sister in Christ. Upon arrival, I asked them to re-affirm the complete Lordship of Jesus in their lives and their desire to have their home wholly dedicated to Christ. With Mark and Wilma and a ministry associate, I then walked through each room in their house blessing it in the name of Jesus and expressly commanding any evil spirit to leave. The focus was always upwards, looking to Jesus and the Father and His full presence and glory in the entire home. As we prayed, Wilma could sense the darkness and oppression gradually leave their house, which was confirmation from the Lord of his presence and power. Since that time, there have been no more bizarre and terrifying disturbances in their home. That incident has always encouraged me in the true power of Jesus' name over evil spiritual forces when spoken in faith and acted upon in simple obedience.

For some time I avoided deliverance ministry as I prayed for healing with people, mostly due to a fear of the unknown or unfamiliar. I also wondered if only those with a special anointing were called into this ministry. But I also wondered about the biblical basis, since I wanted a conscious theological grid through which I would minister to others. I did not want to base my own theological understanding on feelings, manifestations, or other experiences. I could begin to see how an evil spirit might harass externally someone in his or her home or some other place. But are we sure that, in fact, demons can oppress or inhabit or demonize Christians in any way? And if so, how does one achieve freedom from their presence and influence? Are Christians expected to engage in deliverance ministry and follow the example of Jesus and the apostles by casting out demons? To these fundamental and important questions we now turn our attention.

Possessed or Demonized: A Semantic Shell Game?

Deliverance ministry writers maintain that people, including Christians, can in certain circumstances be demonized, but Christians are never "possessed" by demons. There is much controversy among churches and theologians on this point. Many Christians would prefer to believe that they could not ever be demonized. Some scholars disagree that there is a real distinction between being demonized or demon possessed, seeing no real difference between the two and unconvinced that demons can have degrees of control.[1] Pride might stand in the way of ever wanting to admit that this could be a possibility in one's Christian life. After all, it is not a terribly comforting thought. Yet this distinction is important, biblically based, and must be appreciated in order to correctly understand deliverance ministry.

The term "demon-possession" originated with the King James version as a translation for the Greek *daimonizomai*. That translation was most likely a reflection of the church's use of the Latin *possessio* to describe people under demonic influence. "Possess" as an English word in those days meant occupancy or control as much as ownership.[2] Thus, "demon-controlled" or "demon-occupied" could have been meant instead of "demon-possessed" necessarily implying ownership. The meanings of words change over time, like in the King James where "charity" is now often translated as "love." Since the English word "demon' is a transliteration of the Greek *daimon* or *daimonion*, then a likewise transliteration of *daimonizomai* into "demonized" would be more consistent rather than reading a meaning into the translation.[3]

Unfortunately, the legacy of the early King James translation continues to influence current translations with the "possession" rendering. For example, the Greek translated directly as "having a spirit of an unclean demon" in the NIV reads "possessed by a demon, an evil spirit." The Greek *echei daimonion*, literally "to have a demon" is translated by the NIV in Luke 7:33 as "has a demon" but in John 7:20 as "demon-possessed." Another term for demons in the New Testament is "unclean spirit" (*pneuma akathartos*), such as for the man in the synagogue (Mark 1:23) who simply had an unclean spirit, not "possessed by an evil spirit" as the NIV reads. Mark 3:30 correctly translates the same Greek words as "has an evil spirit," and Mark 5:2 correctly translates it as "with an evil spirit" for the man who lived in the tombs. The Greek in Mark 7:25 simply states that the Syrophoenician woman's daughter had an unclean spirit, yet the NIV here reads "whose little daughter was possessed by an evil spirit." The Greek in Luke 4:33 literally reads "having a demon, an evil spirit" yet the NIV reads "possessed by a demon, an evil spirit." A careful study of the Greek reveals that "possession" has been read into the translations, and thus the question of "possession" as opposed to "having a demon" or "being oppressed" is real and valid.

When the same Greek words are translated as "having a demon" or "demon-possessed," where there is no contextual, textual, or linguistic reason for the difference, we see again that this is a valid issue. Many people brought to Jesus for healing were "troubled by evil spirits" (Luke 6:25), and the apostles saw many that were "tormented by evil spirits" (Acts 5:16). The crippled woman was not possessed but bound by an evil spirit for eighteen years (Luke 13:16) and still belonged to the nation of Israel as a daughter of Abraham. Luke refers to the ministry of Jesus as "healing all who were under the power of the devil," not possessed by the devil (Acts 10:38). Being under the power of the devil was the general statement for being tormented, troubled, or bound, or simply "having" an evil or unclean spirit. Luke emphasized the power, not the possession, of the enemy in the context of the ministry of Jesus. That power had different degrees and influences on people. This distinction is real, and is not a semantic shell game.

The term "demonized" allows for degrees of demonization and reflects the biblical accounts and language. Another argument against true and full demon possession is that this would end one's moral accountability before God and they would no longer be responsible for their actions.[4] How could God ultimately judge anyone for their actions (Rev. 20:12) if in fact they were possessed by the devil or demons? There is no doubt about cases of severe demonic manifestation and strong control by demons, like the man under the power of a Legion of demons (Mark 5). I expect the closest one can come to this is those who willingly commit and give themselves over to Satan in clear and overt rituals. Yet even such people are not beyond ever coming to Christ.

A Christian is the full property and ownership of the Lord. All Christians have been transferred from the kingdom of darkness to the Kingdom of light (Col. 1:13), adopted as sons (and daughters) of God (Eph. 1:5), sealed by the Holy Spirit (Eph. 1:13), purchased by the precious blood of Jesus (1 Pet. 1:19), been born again (1 Pet. 1:23), and fully accepted as the very children of God (Rom. 8:16-17). Nothing can separate Christians from the love of God—neither death nor life nor angels nor *demons*, nor any powers—hence nothing can ever own or totally control a Christian. Jesus himself has given each Christian eternal life, and no one, not even Satan, can snatch any Christian away from the Saviour (John 10:28-29). Since our position and identity in Christ is secure, the real debate is not ever about possession but about being "oppressed," "influenced," or "inhabited" or "obsessed."[5] Others refer to *demonization* versus *infestation*.[6]

It is often reasoned that since Christians belong to Jesus and are indwelt by the Holy Spirit, then they simply cannot "have a demon." Masters, for one, wrote:

> It is utterly impossible for any demon to co-occupy with the Holy Spirit the body or soul of a genuine believer. Says Paul, What? Know ye not that your body is the temple of the Holy Ghost which is in you? (1 Corinthians 6.19). Once truly converted, the indwelling Holy Spirit will never leave us, for we have the Saviour's promise to this effect ... John 14,16.[7]

The basic logic is: A Christian is indwelt by the Holy Spirit, and the Holy Spirit cannot co-habit with a demon, therefore a Christian cannot have a demon. Murphy shows that this is a syllogism. The major premise, that the Holy Spirit indwells every Christian is surely correct (Rom. 8:9; Gal. 4:6). The minor or second premise, that the Holy Spirit cannot dwell with demons, is unsupported from the Scriptures hence the syllogism is incorrect. Murphy gives the following parallel syllogism: the Holy Spirit indwells

Every Christian; the Holy Spirit cannot dwell with sin; therefore Christians cannot sin.[8] We know that this is simply not true, thus it casts serious doubt on the first syllogism regarding the presence of demons in Christians.

From my first-hand experience in deliverance ministry I know that the distinctions are real. Different types and degrees of manifestation were recorded in the Gospels—from the bent-over and probably unassuming and discouraged woman who nevertheless had an evil spirit, to the demoniac living by the tombs who could not be chained down and wanted to kill himself. Those are real recorded differences of degree of control. There simply are different degrees and forms of bondage, harassment, torment, and the like. Considering the Greek and the gospel accounts,

> ...it seems quite clear that we may define demonization as demon caused passivity or control due to a demon's residing within a person, which manifests its effects in various physical and mental disorders and in varying degrees.[9]

Can Christians Be Demonized?

Since the question is one of degree of control or influence from evil spirits rather than outright possession, as those involved in deliverance ministry maintain, we might ask if this is a possibility for Christians.

At first, one might think this should not be possible since not only are we possessed by Jesus and indwelt by His Spirit, but we have also been regenerated and made into a new creation (1 Cor. 5:17). We are permanently indwelt by the Holy Spirit (John 14:16, Rom. 8:16) who unites with our spirit, and demons cannot dwell therein.[10] But demons can live in a Christian's mind, emotions, will, and body.[11]

Nevertheless, one potential means of demonization in this life comes when we let sin reign in our lives. Consider Rom. 6:12,

> *...do not let sin reign in your mortal body so that you obey its evil desires. Do not offer the parts of your body to sin, as instruments of wickedness, but rather offer yourselves to God.'*

Rom. 6:16 reads,

> *Don't you know that when you offer yourselves to someone to obey him as slaves, you are slaves to the one whom you obey—whether you are slaves to sin which leads to death, or to obedience which leads to righteousness?*

Those are commands that require a decision on our part to live out in daily experience the reality of our new position in Christ, who is our righteousness. Otherwise we can end up under the power of other spiritual forces in our life. Arnold wrote:

> ... if the power of sin can inhabit a Christian's body and exert such a significant influence that Paul could say it "reigns" (Rom. 6:12-13), why do we suppose that another form of evil influence cannot dwell there? After conversion the "flesh"—the evil inclination (the *yetser harah*), a structure of the present evil age—continues to be present with the believer. This is the locus of much of the struggle for the believer. It is an evil, a part of us and within us, resident in the same body as the Holy Spirit of God.[12]

But can the presence of sin in our life lead to demonization? The story of Saul is a clear example of how moral sin can lead to direct influence from an evil spirit. Due to disobedience and rebellion from the Lord the Spirit left Saul, and then the Lord sent an evil spirit to torment him (1 Sam. 16:14-15). Then later Saul became angry at the rising popularity of David (1 Sam. 18:8), with the result that an evil spirit came *forcefully* upon him the next day (1 Sam. 18:10). The final and worst stage of demonization was resorting to the occult for direction after inquiring of the Lord (1 Sam. 28:5-19). Saul's growing disobedience, pride, self-centredness, envy, jealousy, anger, and rage led to progressively stronger stages of demonization. Saul was still part of the nation of Israel, was still visited by the Spirit of the Lord in the midst of all this (1 Sam. 19:20-24), and even though he was rejected as king he was still the Lord's anointed (1 Sam. 24:6,10; 26:9,11,16,23; 2 Sam. 1:14,16). Even if Saul was not a believer any more as some allege, the fact that an evil spirit may come as judgment for sin is the lesson here. When Saul turned away from the Lord, he made himself vulnerable to evil forces. We see in this story that sinful disobedience can lead to demonization, which then can manifest as behavioral change.

John Bunyan, a Puritan, in his great work entitled "The Holy War," wrote about how sin in the life of Christians can give ground in their inner being (Mansoul) to demons (Diabolonians) under Satan's (Diabolus) direction.[13] Since there are enemies from without and within, the soul must be purified, cleansed, with no "carnal security" as one pursues holiness in the Lord.

Just because we are Christians, we cannot presume that we could not come under the power of Satan. Achan had hidden in his tent some devoted things from battle, and then when the Israelites were defeated at Ai Joshua was facedown on the ground, asking God what had happened. The Lord spoke to Joshua,

> *Israel has sinned; they have violated my covenant... they have taken some of the devoted things, they have stolen, they have lied... that is why the Israelites cannot stand against their ene-*

> *mies... they have been made liable to destruction. I will not be with you anymore unless you destroy whatever among you is devoted to destruction* (Josh. 7:11-12).

They have been made liable to destruction... the protection, presence, and blessing of God required their obedience to God, it was not automatic or presumed because they were God's chosen people. As Achan confessed later, it was his coveting, his falling to temptation, that was the sin.

Judges shows repeatedly that when the nation of Israel, God's own covenant people, disobeyed, they came under defeat, bondage, and oppression to enemy nations. The phrase "did evil in the eyes of the Lord" is frequent, often preceded by "again" or "once again" for emphasis by the writer so that we don't miss the point. This is seen very clearly in Judges 2:11-13 with 2:14-15, Judges 3:7 with 3:8, Judges 3:12 with 3:13-14, Judges 4:1 with 4:2-3, Judges 6:1 with 6:2-3, Judges 10:6 with 10:7-8, Judges 13:1 with 13:1. Whenever the nation of Israel had a hole in their spiritual armour (Eph. 6:10-20), they were defeated. When the nation of Israel did not drive out all the inhabitants of the promised land, those remaining became barbs or thorns to the Israelites (Num. 33:55). Israel was not to dialog, intermarry, or associate with the pagans of the promised land (Josh. 23:7, 12-13). These passages clearly show that protection from the Lord and the ability to withstand the enemy requires our obedience to the Lord and our desire for his uncompromising holiness. Like the nation of Israel, we as believers are not immune from spiritual bondage if we do not live under the Lordship of Christ. We also must expel all intruders and evil in our lives in Christ, the "new promised land."

We can unwittingly give turf in our lives to Satan, like the Israelites did. Paul wrote "In your anger do not sin; Do not let the sun go down while you are still angry, and do not give the devil a foothold" (Eph. 4:27). The Greek word for "foothold" is topos, meaning place or area. Jesus was born in a manager because there was no topos in the inn (Luke 2:7). When Jesus refers to his Father's house having many rooms (John 14:3), John uses topos. There is a clear idea of space, room, a sphere of influence in spiritual terms. While this verse does not explicitly talk of believers being demonized like Saul was, it does not rule it out either. Anger can affect the Christian community as a whole, but it also pertains directly to the believer who sins in his anger. In the context of extending forgiveness, Paul writes,

> *I have forgiven in the sight of Christ for your sake, in order that Satan might not outwit us. For we are not unaware of his schemes* (2 Cor. 2:11).

Again, Satan must not be given any opportunities and we must be aware of his schemes.

But some writers argue that since Satan is defeated, we don't have much to fear. Heb. 2:14-15, for example, apparently states that for believers Satan has been rendered powerless.[14] Hence, we need not fear ancestral demons or ever have to worry about breaking a hold from demonization. But this passage only states that Satan's legal hold and his power through the fear of death has been broken, and the Greek word used does not mean reduction to no power at all.[15] Satan has been defeated at the cross, but not yet rounded up and banished to hell. There is still opposition since not everything is yet subject to Jesus (Heb. 2:8). Satan is still the god of this world. If he has been rendered totally powerless to us, then why do we need spiritual armour (Eph. 6:10-18) and how did Satan stop the apostle Paul (1 Thess. 2:18)? Satan is *not yet* crushed under the church's feet (Rom. 16:20; Gen. 3:15). The very fact that in the name of Christ we can cast out demons demonstrates how Satan has lost much power and is defeated. This is not about any spiritual paranoia concerning Satan but all about knowing our position in Christ and exercising the spiritual power and authority he has given to us.

Given the remaining power of Satan, bondage for Christians can, in fact, be severe (1 Tim. 4:1). "The Spirit clearly says that in later times some will abandon the faith and follow deceiving spirits and things taught by demons," so we must be on guard in what we believe and are taught. In reference to Christians who do not submit to godly teaching, Paul instructs Timothy,

> *Those who oppose him he must gently instruct, in the hope that God will grant them repentance leading them to a knowledge of the truth, and that they will come to their senses and escape from the trap of the devil, who has taken them captive to do his will* (2 Tim. 2: 25-26).

Is it not serious when a Christian can become captive to do Satan's will? Satan set a trap, and they fell into it. We are to be alert for the devil who "... prowls around like a roaring lion looking for someone to devour" (1 Pet. 5:8). This is strong language meant to signify the real possibility of strong control in our lives, if we allow the devil to intimidate us when we waver in our faith. Paul went so far as to state that severe affliction can result for those excluded from Christian fellowship and "handed over to Satan" (1 Cor. 11:30-31; 1 Tim. 1:20). This is strong language.

In the story of Ananias Peter said to Ananias:

> *...how is it that Satan has so filled your heart that you have lied to the Holy Spirit and have kept for your self some of the money you received for the land? (Acts 5:3).*

This shows the extent to which Satan can have control in our lives, if we let him. Though we might not count Judas as a believer, the fact that Satan *entered his heart* (John 13:27) again shows the extent to which Satan can wield his influence.

When we look at the encounters between Jesus and those oppressed with demons, we must remember that those he encountered in the synagogues were believers, true members of the nation of Israel.[16] Jesus often preached in the synagogue where he rebuked demons from the believers who were present (Mark 1:39). The crippled woman in the synagogue was afflicted with a spirit of infirmity, yet she was a believer, a daughter of Abraham (Luke 13:10-15). One cannot argue from the Scriptures that believers were not oppressed by evil spirits.

Evil spirits really want to live in a "host." As disembodied spirits, they might be content to live in the wilderness for a while, but they want to live in or at least oppress people (Matt. 12:43; Luke 11:24). One would expect that they would prefer to live inside or oppress Christians, who by definition stand opposed to Satan. By their very nature they seek any means to inhabit a person and thus influence their body, will, emotions, behavior, feelings, and belief. We should not be completely surprised when they are detected and expelled from Christians.

Likewise, we can expect God's protection and blessing when we obey Him and walk in his ways, pursuing holiness so there is no opportunity for the enemy to invade our life. When we continue to indulge in sinful anger, say, we are turning our backs on God and rebelling against the Lordship of Jesus in that area in our life. For some Christians, there comes a point where an evil spirit comes and begins to "encourage" the anger. Satan, then, has legal right of access. God in his sovereignty then allows it. The anger becomes the "breach" in one's spiritual wall, a hole in one's spiritual armor (Eph. 6:10-20). We no longer enjoy God's full protection because by our actions we have come into agreement with Satan who promotes and agrees with anger, among other sins and evils. In that area of life, one has given in to sin which was crouching at the door (Gen. 4:7) and wanted to master. Protection from God is conditional on not giving the flesh opportunity (Rom. 13:14), submitting to God and resisting the devil (Jas. 4:7) and standing in the armor of God (Eph. 6:10-20).

There is no "demonization of sin," as some authors critical of deliverance ministry allege. One's sin is one's own responsibility before God and must be dealt with through repentance and the power of the cross. When a demon is involved, it must be expelled. This is totally different from identifying, say, a demon of anger, and once it is expelled, the problem is solved. This is not the case in true, mature, balanced deliverance ministry. Any notion of blaming demons for one's sin misrepresents true deliverance ministry and trivializes the biblical doctrine of sanctification.

We agree that Christ who is in us is greater than Satan who is in the world (1 John 4:4). The question is: can we presume upon Christ's complete protection if we *turn our back on him* in some area in our life? Yes, we are the temple of the Holy Spirit (1 Cor. 3:16; 6:19). The question is: what are we bringing into the temple and what are we allowing to remain there?[17] The Holy Spirit will never leave a Christian, but rather will remain and be grieved (Eph. 4:30) and continue to convict when sin is present and regrettably, any evil spirit.

As Christians, Satan has no authority over us, since Jesus has given us authority (Col. 2:15; Eph. 2:6; Matt. 28:20) to advance His Kingdom at the expense of Satan's kingdom. Satan's tactic is therefore to have us give him authority or permission to wreak havoc in our lives. He does this through deceit, temptation, fear, intimidation, false teaching, exploiting our weaknesses, using our past against us, and also authority lines around us. Satan is a legalist, so he will use anything from our life and our past to gain a foothold or entry point. It is helpful to think of indwelling demons as trespassers that must be confronted, challenged, and expelled.[18] Satan absolutely hates our relationship with God (that he once had), so that he attempts to steal our intimacy with Jesus. I can't help but wonder if he is so incensed at the Holy Spirit dwelling in Christians that he wants to counter with inhabitation or control of Christians by his evil spirits. Satan is angry when people do not worship him, therefore he wants us to worship him through idolatry. He despises our freedom in Christ so he schemes to put us into bondage with his lies. Since he lost us upon our coming to Christ and leaving his kingdom, he switches his tactics, to make us as miserable and ineffective as possible and thus the least threat to his kingdom. Satan has no right or place in our lives unless we give it to him. We must be on guard for anything from the world, the flesh, or the devil and his demons, that lures us away from the Lordship of Jesus.

This can include sins committed against the Lord before coming to Christ, especially true for any occult involvement. The clearest example from the New Testament is Acts 19:13-20, where the sons of Sceva, a Jewish priest, attempted to drive out evil spirits. They failed and were utterly and publicly humiliated. The result was fear with the name of Jesus being honored such that

Many of those who believed now came openly and confessed their evil deeds. A number who had practiced sorcery brought their scrolls together and burned them publicly (Acts 19:18-19).

Considering the pagan beliefs and practices of the day, it is quite likely that those new Christians who had practiced sorcery would have had the type of deliverance ministry that Paul practiced before and after coming to Christ.[19]

Apart from sin issues as discussed above, Christians might come under the influence of evil spirits due to situational evil. In other words, involuntary on their part as opposed to voluntary from wrong choices or willful disobedience to the Lord. The enemy will seek to exploit weakness, vulnerability, the sin of others against us, or the bondage that comes with sin in our family line. Here, the enemy exploits the corporate nature of sin and the built-in authority structures in human relationships. Children are especially vulnerable.[20] The young boy with seizures and convulsions was under the power of an evil spirit from birth (Mark 9:12-18). The SyroPheonician woman asked Jesus to heal her daughter that had a demon, and because of her faith, the daughter was healed that very hour (Matt. 15:22,28; Mark 7:30). Since the mother had spiritual authority and responsibility over her daughter, she could ask for freedom and healing on her behalf and it was granted. If a parent asks evil powers to come upon a child, Satan will not see this as "unfair" and refuse. Satan will always act upon any invitation by anyone to enter into their life, family, or family line. Since demonic influence can come with sin, and sin is corporate, then demonic influence can extend beyond just the person immediately involved. When Achan sinned by keeping a devoted object, the result was that thirty-six Israelites died in battle and God declared that Israel had sinned (Josh. 7:1-10). It was a corporate issue, not just Achan and his family alone.

The final argument for the demonization of Christians is that this is known from experience in deliverance ministry. Dickason, for example, refers to many well documented and attested cases of demonization of Christians.[21] Friesen recounts the detection and removal of demons from Christians with multiple personality disorders.[22] I know of many examples over the years as well. Of course, one would expect that those who are critical of deliverance ministry would try to explain away or discredit the experiences of those who are involved in this ministry. Those who are involved in this ministry will of course put forth their experiences as valid. From the above, I have shown that there are no theological reasons from Scripture that precludes the demonization of Christians. Arnold concludes that

> "there is sufficient biblical, theological, and historical evidence to assert that a Christian can be inhabited or controlled by a demonic spirit."[23]

Should Christians Ever Cast Demons Out?

If we accept that a Christian could be demonized—whether oppressed, inhabited, influenced—what does one do about it? This of course assumes that one would want to do something about it. How does one engage in spiritual warfare in such a situation? What does Jesus expect us as his disciples today to do when encountering demons?

Janine, a Christian woman, can clearly and vividly remember her first encounter with a spiritual presence. She was eleven years old, and one day happened to be in the living room in her parent's home for some time. While she was in the room, a consistent voice was invading her mind, like a continual oppressive and distracting conversation coming from outside of her. The invading words were full of mockery and negative thoughts. She realized that this "nattering" voice had come and gone over the previous few years. She then remembered reading a few days before, in the Gospels, how Jesus rebuked an evil spirit by just commanding it to leave. Convinced that this voice was from an evil spirit, and not wanting to endure its presence any longer, she did what Jesus did and spoke out loud saying "In the name Jesus, I command you to leave." Instantly there was silence, and the voice never came back. Her parents were godly Christians, both given to prayer, but not very vocal or demonstrative of their faith and had never taught her how to confront an evil presence. Looking back now, she is convinced that the Holy Spirit brought the passage from the Gospels to her mind, and encouraged her to follow the straightforward and simple teaching of the Scriptures.

Many years later, on the day of her mother's funeral, Janine clearly remembers waking up early in the morning and hearing someone playing the piano, but completely off key and with an impression of mockery. She thought this was completely strange, for who on earth would be playing the piano so early in the morning, let alone in such a manner? Maybe she was hearing things? She woke her husband up, and asked him if he could "hear it'"? He said "no", and was annoyed at being woken up. As she lay there pondering the situation, she prayed quietly and clearly in her mind that only God's presence would fill the piano room downstairs. Instantly the playing stopped. She remains convinced that an evil presence had been expelled from the house, since the turning point was when she invoked the presence of God, effectively rebuking any evil presence. Was Janine right in doing this? Was she becoming paranoid, superstitious, or practicing magic? Should we as Christians ever cast out demons like Jesus did?

If we first look at the Old Testament, we see that demons were never cast out even though they certainly were prevalent (Deut. 32:17; Ps. 106:37; Jude 9:23; 1 Sam. 16:14-16, 1 Kings 22:21-23, etc). God is sovereign and demons are constrained, humans are responsible for their sin and evil, and yet no demons are cast out.[24] In the face of evil and the occult, repentance and calling out for the mercy of God was the response. Sin was not seen as an issue of evicting demons, as we saw in Joshua and Judges above. From the full context of the books of the Old Testament and this absence of casting out demons, it has been argued that this "decisively undercuts" the modern type of deliverance ministry involving the casting out of demons.[25] But when we understand the Old Testament in the context of all of Scripture, the answer is simply that since no one walked the face of the earth in Old Testament times with the direct authority to command demons to leave, it never happened. The closest was David playing his harp to give Saul temporary relief (1 Sam. 16:23). That's the simple reason there is no example in the Old Testament. Only since the coming of Jesus the Messiah could demons be rebuked. Unlike the first Adam, Jesus did not give in to temptation, and thus had the moral authority to rebuke Satan. So rather than the Old Testament decisively undercutting the practice of casting out demons on command, it anticipated the need for it as part of God's salvation and fulfillment in Christ. That's why there's a new covenant with new ways under Jesus. We no longer sacrifice bulls and goats because Jesus is the perfect sacrifice once and for all. Likewise, we no longer back down from evil spirits because Jesus has given us the authority and power to rebuke them. The coming of the Messiah has simply and clearly made all the difference. At the same time, as was true in the Old Testament there is still the need to repent, confess, and obey the living God and avoid all evil.

Looking into the New Testament we clearly see many examples of Jesus and the apostles and others casting out demons by words of command. These were examples of situational evil, or circumstances where the person with the evil spirit needed deliverance for their healing and freedom. Should we ever follow the example of Jesus and the apostles whenever evil spirits are uncovered, including cases of situational evil or simple circumstance? Some authors would argue that we should not ever follow the example of Jesus and the disciples.

Masters argued for that view, reasoning that the New Testament did not give us any instructions on how to do it and that this was not a part of Paul's instructions on spiritual warfare in Rom. 6-8, Gal. 5-6, and Eph. 6:11-18.[26] But this is a suspect argument from silence. First, the New Testament nowhere prohibits the casting out of demons by Christians. Second, the Apostle Paul for one practiced casting out demons as we know from Acts, and all his readers would have known this was part of his ministry. Everyone knew Jesus did this as well, and the disciples and the seventy-two, so there was ample knowledge and instruction on this topic. Why would Paul, Peter, or James have to remind their readers about what was clearly demonstrated in their time? The epistles give much counsel about sanctification and spiritual warfare that among other things would help avoid and prevent demonic influence.

Others argue that Jesus ministered in a *different way* that we are not expected to today. Powlison has argued that Jesus used both the classical mode (faith, confession, prayer, repentance, belief in God's sovereignty, etc.) and the command-control mode (cast out demons, calm the wind and water, feed the thousands, etc.) in his ministry. Today, we are then only to minister in the classical mode. Powlison wrote about EMM (Ekballistic, *ek balleo*—to throw out—Mode of Ministry):

> There is no direct command in Scripture to do EMM, even to relieve suffering. And—to repeat—contrary to EMM teaching, moral evil is not in view either in demonization or ekballistics. But what about demonic torments that need healing? Is there reason to expect a mode shift to the classic way of facing and addressing situational evil? Do any passages from Scripture give possible warrant for

an ongoing ekballistic method for relieving demon-induced sufferings?[27]

Many authors consider Mark 16:17-18 as the closest passage that might possibly support a mandate to cast out demons. However, they then challenge the passage by suggesting it is relevant only to the apostles due to their unbelief (Mark 16:14), signs accompanied only Jesus and the apostles, the apparent confusion over tongues, the apparent problem of handling snakes and drinking poison, and the doubt about those verses even being part of Scripture. As already discussed in the section *Getting Beyond Snake Handling* in the chapter *Re-Thinking The Great Commission*, there are absolutely no valid objections at all to seeing Mark 16:17 as a clear command for believers to engage in the casting out of demons like Jesus did when obeying His Father. When Scripture is used to interpret Scripture, a good Reformation hermeneutical principle, the problems vanish. Further, from the chapter *Re-Thinking the Great Commission*, an inescapable and totally biblical view is that casting out demons is something that the Church is expected to do today as part of the Great Commission. It is an "unavoidable commission" expected of the church in all ages.[28] I totally concur with Horrobin, when he wrote:

> There is far more teaching about deliverance ministry implicit in the Gospels than is normally appreciated. Clearly, Jesus considered it to be a primary ministry for the emergent church, and there is no indication anywhere in the scriptures that at any time this ministry would be discontinued in favour of any other practice or that there would be any other dispensation (before Jesus comes again) in which it will no longer be required.[29]

Authors who argue against deliverance ministry typically confuse the debate with cessationist reasoning. Powlison argued that the power encounters of Jesus performed in his "command-mode" were meant to bring people to repentance, show who Jesus was, and identify his apostles as the authoritative messengers of the gospel.[30] This is true, but is that the whole story? Are those the only reasons for his command-control mode in all cases? Are all command-control mode examples of Jesus ruled out for us? Powlison wrote that the casting out of demons was temporary,[31] which can only mean that it has supposedly ceased since the New Testament era. That is evidentialist reasoning of cessationsim. I refer the reader to the chapter *Unmasking Cessationism* which deals with cessationism at length, concluding that it is unbiblical and untenable.

Sometimes the sovereignty of God is made an issue, as if God in his sovereignty will deal with the spirits assuming we practice classical spiritual warfare or he perhaps would not allow them in our life in the first place. This is no problem for deliverance ministry, since it's fundamentally a question of following the clear commands of Jesus. What if we apply the very same reasoning to evangelism? It was once argued that we need not send missionaries since those who have been elected unto salvation will be saved. Carey thought otherwise, set sail for India, and the rest is history. Perhaps such reasoning avoids responsibility or supports a spiritualized form of fatalism? The other angle is that God is in his sovereignty would not allow demonic control of his children in the first place. But as we have seen, that does not hold since God's protection comes with some assumptions and requirements on our part.

It has been suggested that modern deliverance ministry teachers have failed to consider that even if demons are a factor in the suffering or torment of a Christian (including a child, I expect) that the casting out mode of ministry is still not expected by

Jesus.[32] The reason this has not been seriously considered is simply that obedience to Jesus would not allow it. Just as Jesus had compassion for the hurting and those in bondage, and delivered them with his authority and power, we do likewise today. One might wonder if withholding deliverance ministry is an example of "spiritual malpractice" as Pearson has used the term for withholding healing prayer.[33] I suspect that those who argue against casting out demons realize that if this is allowed for "involuntary" cases, one is then faced with discerning when this is the case. At that point, one is basically endorsing deliverance ministry, so it comes down to "all or nothing." Imagine a Christian couple in some desperation coming to the church for relief for their child who is obviously being tormented by evil spirits. Imagine even further trying to explain to them the idea of "mode shifts" and why no Christian can cast out a demon today. What would that couple think? What if it was your child?

There is indeed much emphasis in the New Testament on the "classical mode" of spiritual warfare with repentance, faith, perseverance, resisting the devil, desiring holiness, knowing the Scriptures, and more. Those who faithfully practice deliverance ministry have no problems with this at all. As in the Old Testament, this still applies. It is not a case of simply and only casting out demons associated with sin or a situation or circumstance without sin. Rather, one begins with classical spiritual warfare in confession, repentance, and so forth, and then where required, casts out a demon. It is never classical mode *versus* command-control mode, as if they oppose one another. It is sometimes *both*.

Given the clear commands of Jesus, I advocate the *obedience mode*. The concept of Jesus having a different mode of ministry than ours appears to be a re-packaging of cessationist thinking. As far as casting out demons is concerned, the command-control mode was inaugurated by Jesus and has never yet ceased. I disagree with any claim that a fundamental error of modern demon-deliverance ministries is that it fails to account for the change in mode shift from command-control to the classical mode.[34] The reverse is true in that it would be an error if the deliverance ministries did take this into account. I maintain that in deliverance ministry the correct "equation" for us is: *classical mode + command-control mode = obedience mode.*

So did Janine do the right thing? Yes, absolutely. Thankfully, she had no knowledge of ministry modes or cessationism. With simple childlike faith, she just followed the example of Jesus.

We shouldn't necessarily rule out the "command-control mode" in other areas that Jesus modeled beyond casting out demons. For example, Pytches wrote how not unlike Jesus rebuking the wind, a Christian rebuked the rain:

> The Rev. Eric Townson (formerly with the Church Missionary Society) tells of an experience which he had as a fairly new missionary. He attended an open-air meeting in East Africa when the rain began to fall. This was going to ruin plans for an open-air conference. Eric felt an urge to rebuke the rain, which he did loudly in Christ's name. The rain stopped instantly![35]

The "urge" was God's prompting encouraged by the spiritual gift of faith, leading to the obedience mode which involved uttering a control command in the name of Jesus against the rain. A missionary in Tanzania, seeing a lion that had just killed a woman and child now approaching the congregation gathered for Easter worship, cursed the lion in the name of Jesus, whereupon the lion was immediately struck dead by a bolt of lightening from the sky.[36] The key is obedience coupled with faith in each situation.

Is modern deliverance ministry a "radical and recent innovation" as some writers claim?[37] Not at all. In fact, the early church was fully involved in the ministry of deliverance, as is well attested by the early church fathers. Harris recounts the clear testimony of Justin Martyr, St. Ambrose, Tertullian, Cyril of Jerusalem, St. Augustine, Origen, Bishop Cornelius of Rome, and more as cited in many of the writings of the early church on the casting out of demons.[38] Arnold reviews some of the literature of the early church, showing clearly how the casting out demons was practiced for new believers in particular and was covered in the Apostolic Tradition as preserved by Hippolytus of Rome.[39] The casting out of demons was clearly practiced in the early church, and often for new Christians, and is thus actually part of the Church's "classical spiritual warfare." Since the early church was so close to the apostolic era, we must take their example seriously. The church today is recovering what was once more commonly practiced. The term "classical spiritual warfare" begs the question: *whose classics you are referring to?*

Answering Some Objections To Deliverance Ministry

Aside from the basic theological issues in deliverance ministry, there are secondary objections frequently made against this ministry. For some of the more common objections an answer is given below. At times, objections are made against immature or non-representative examples of deliverance ministry. That is a reaction to negative experiences and only serves to confuse the issue.

Using the name of Jesus in engaging evil spirits. It has been argued that when Deut. 18:10-12 prohibits involvement with evil spirits (divination, sorcery, witchcraft, omens, spells, mediums, spiritists, conjuring), that "God has forever forbidden verbal interactions between His people and demons."[40] The obvious exception, though, is casting out demons as practiced by Christ and the apostles. In no case should we have any verbal interaction with demons or evil spirits. This argument is clearly untenable. First, Deut. 18:10-12 only says that no one should engage in those evil activities and nothing at all about speaking to an evil spirit, hence this is an example of reading into the text (eisegesis). Second, the goal of casting out an evil spirit is to expel it from people since it is evil and detestable, thus to prohibit deliverance ministry actually goes against the very intent of passages like Deut. 18:10-12. Third, if the passage really does prohibit talking with evil spirits and if that in itself really is detestable, then Jesus and the apostles sinned and broke the law, which Jesus himself said he would never do since he came to fulfill the law to the smallest part (Matt. 5:17). This is an impossible view to hold because exempting Jesus and the apostles puts them in a category above the law.

Magic. When authors of deliverance ministry refer to using the name of Jesus or the blood of Jesus, this is seen by some as magic.[41] Commenting on Paul's command in the name of Jesus to cast out a demon, Masters wrote:

> Should we not use the name of Jesus to cast out demons today? The very definite answer is—no; under no circumstances must we abuse the name of Jesus and use it like a lucky charm or superstitious formula for waving at evil spirits ... As far as we are concerned, we must never use the name of Jesus as a magic key for something which He has not commanded us to do.[42]

Granted, some Christians might use the name of Jesus in this way, but that is not ever the intention of deliverance ministry. First, it is done out of obedience, as we have seen. Second, using the name of someone was clearly understood in Hebrew thought as standing for the entire person, as if he were there and in total accord with his will, purposes, and character.[43] Using the name of Jesus in deliverance is thus done in accord with his will, as if he were physically there. His name does bring power, which is why Jesus prayed that God would protect his followers by the power of his name (John 17:11). When Peter healed a lame man, he was later asked by what power or name did he do it (Acts 4:7), thus it was understood that real power comes with a name. Healing and miracles were performed through the name of Jesus (Acts 4:30). If using the name of Jesus is "magic," then is it "magic" to ask for anything in the name of Jesus (John 14:13,14; 15:16; 16:23)? Is it "magic" to believe you have life in the name of Jesus (John 20:31)?

Using the name of Jesus comes directly out of our personal relationship with Jesus. One must be convinced of the power of Jesus' name (John 17:11). On occasion I have prayed with Christians wanting deliverance from spirits of witchcraft. Sometimes reference to the blood of Jesus has been crucial to finally remove those spirits. Why? In part, because witchcraft involves rituals that specifically mock the blood of Jesus.

Misinterpretation or even production of the experiences.[44] Having ministered healing prayer and deliverance at conferences and on several healing prayer teams, I dispute this allegation. While there might be some expectations for demonic manifestations in some meetings and circles due to the power suggestion,[45] this has not been my experience or that of others I know that minister deliverance. In fact, the demonic has appeared many times to people that had no previous idea on the topic in meetings where this was not the emphasis or expectation at all. More than once I have seen people receiving this ministry surprised, especially from denominations where it has been taught that the demonization of Christians is just not possible. While some may abuse this ministry by overlooking sin issues, again, that is not representative at all of those who minister with wisdom and maturity.

At an intense weekend in deliverance ministry training, we all read through a prayer on intergenerational sin. The Lordship of Jesus was first proclaimed and then confession and renunciation of a series of sins which may or may not apply to one's forebearers (Dan. 9:2). The prayer was not unlike the apostles' Creed in its affirmations of biblical truth. As we prayed, several people experienced sudden and rather dramatic manifestations. There was no prior knowledge and expectation, and in a few cases it involved clergy who were more surprised than anyone else. One person's voice changed and started speaking about defiance to the Lord and how "he will not come out." A man who had a less dramatic experience went home that night and found out that his son, who was not at the training conference, was suddenly attacked with major fear and anxiety the exact moment he was. The trainees were all mature and biblically astute Christians, some leaders in their churches, and they were not searching after drama or manifestations. How does one explain this? Production of experiences by the trainers or the atmosphere? Certainly not! It had all to do with encountering evil spiritual forces in a desire to gain more freedom in Christ.

I have personally encountered evil and unclean spirits many times in healing prayer ministry with committed Christians. There have been occasions when the person receiving ministry would suddenly choke, feel a pain in the stomach, cough, shake, or even (thankfully rare!) suddenly scream violently and sprawl on the sanctuary floor in front of me. Those people were not "faking it," it was not expected at all. Other times a demon would speak through the person with statements like "you can't get me out." Typically, these things happen the very instant the name and authority of Jesus is called upon, because in that instant the Kingdom of God comes right against the kingdom of darkness.

A young man heard me speak at a conference, and actually ran out of the sanctuary in fear, but was brought back by a friend. He came later for prayer, telling me he was full of fear, but did not know why. The fear was instigated by the demon that was trying to prevent the deliverance, which occurred after issues of repentance and forgiveness were deeply dealt with. He had no idea this could be the case, and I said nothing until almost the moment of deliverance, which he experienced with a minor manifestation of sudden choking and coughing. Imagination? Expectation? This is not the case. Again, the goal in prayer ministry is not seeking or hunting for demons, demon chasing, or imagining them. The goal is wholeness in Christ, sanctification, and experiencing more of the love and freedom of Jesus.

Pre-occupation with technique. Some will allege that this is the main emphasis in deliverance ministry and that a specific technique or method is required to gain freedom.[46] Although some Christians in this ministry may focus on technique not unlike much of ministry in general—evangelism, preaching, "church growth" have all been criticized for reliance on techniques which are well known—that is a misrepresentation of deliverance ministry. The so-called techniques reflect biblical principles in prayer ministry and engaging evil spirits as well as strategies and approaches learned experientially. There is no place for technique or magic in this ministry which so heavily relies on the presence of Jesus and the empowering of his Spirit. There is no place at all for any idolatry of method since deliverance ministry must be under the direction of the Holy Spirit.[47] Anyone truly engaged in this ministry knows that unless one abides in Christ and really believes in the power of his name one's effectiveness is seriously compromised.

Satan himself produces these manifestations on purpose to support errors in theology.[48] One can easily argue the opposite that Satan would rather remain hidden and eminently deceptive and deceitful in order to keep Christians in bondage and a measure of defeat. Causing manifestations brings up the issue to those who are not convinced there is any erroneous teaching involved, then Satan risks being exposed. But Satan is no fool. We know that Satan is a deceiver, a liar, and will even masquerade as an angel of light. Hence, causing manifestations in deliverance goes against his schemes. Those who minister deliverance first-hand are aware of many other valid reasons for such manifestations, like causing fear for those being delivered, trying to prevent deliverance, intimidating or distracting those ministering, and sometimes causing pain on the "way out."

I remember praying with Anne, a young Christian who had many bad church experiences. Just when the ministry session began to unfold as we came to the deeper root issues, she apparently suddenly received several verses from the Lord. As she reflected on them, she felt we should terminate the session and meet again some day. When I looked up the verses in context, her interpretation didn't fit well with her reasons for terminating. I knew something was wrong, but couldn't prevent her from leaving since that would violate her personhood. As I reflected later, I suspected that an evil spirit had given her those verses, not unlike Satan tempting Jesus with verses, as a subtle way of stopping ministry just as we were approaching some deeper issues. This is another example of the enemy's extreme subtlety and desire to remain hidden.

Deliverance ministry could invoke demonic activity due to hypnotic or other techniques.[49] This may have some relevance where ministers are controlling or using mediumistic techniques. However, this is simply not the practice of mainstream deliverance ministry where people being ministered to are expected to be alert, involved, desiring control of the Holy Spirit, and in complete understanding and agreement with the ministry session. Anything else violates personhood and devalues people. Deliverance ministry sometimes involves release from demonic influences caused by such hypnotic and other techniques in other contexts.

Occult theology in deliverance ministry, especially when there is mention of familiar spirits or intergenerational sin. Deliverance ministry will not "stand or fall" on this issue. This is an attempt to explain the presence of evil spirits which are more or less involuntary for the person receiving ministry. The person ministered to will often ask where or how these evil spirits came into the person's life. Jesus did not give an explanation of the cause of the evil spirit for the boy in that condition from childhood (Mark 9:21), but how would one explain that? On the one hand, some accuse deliverance ministers of not considering involuntary demonization, yet when attempts are made to explain this, it is labeled as occult thinking. A fuller awareness of the corporate dimension of sin and how Satan exploits lines of authority helps to explain these cases.

The apparent subjective nature of diagnosis is leveled against deliverance ministry.[50] For those critical of this ministry, the apparent difficulty of knowing if there is a demon in one's life is a major problem. My reply is that this is an obvious reflection of Satan and his demon's subtlety and deception rather than the failings of this ministry. Quite simply, demons want to remain hidden and will resist any attempts to be exposed. They are extremely subtle and crafty, and have had thousands of years of practice. Like any ministry, this requires training and wisdom. In addition to practical knowledge about the many symptoms of demonization and possible points,[51] there is the spiritual gift of discernment of spirits which helps immensely in this ministry. This spiritual gift of discerning spirits is valid and very necessary in our day and age.[52] Finally, this objection is no more a problem with deliverance ministry than it is of modern medicine. Just consider the fact that around forty per cent of people diagnosed with a treatable physical illness have been misdiagnosed with a supposed psychiatric "disorder,"[53] a symptom of "diagnostic tunnel vision."[54] The serious mental and physical costs to people, sometimes leading to long term brain damage and even death, is far more prevalent and serious than apparent misdiagnosis in deliverance ministry. Why single out deliverance ministry on this issue?

A deficient view of salvation. I can readily see how some writers might believe that deliverance ministry poses serious questions for salvation.[55] Although we are saved, it seems disconcerting that an evil spirit may influence us, or even the possibility of ancestral or familiar spirits. But Christians are not immune from accidents, illness, and persecution (Matt. 5:44; Luke 11:49; Luke 21:12), all allowed by God. Christians, even though saved, can be beheaded for their loyalty to Christ—is that not a greater issue than identifying and rebuking a demon? So why necessarily exclude the influence of evil spirits in one's life? The presence of an evil spirit in a Christian's life to whatever degree and from whatever source does not at all in the least effect one's name being written in the Lamb's book of life (Rev. 20:11-15), salvation from the coming wrath of God, forgiveness from past sin and its present power, one's indwelling of the Spirit, and one's connection to the love of Christ and his eternal life (John 10:10). The challenge is to enforce the victory of Christ over Satan in one's life and appropriate the power of the cross and the name of Jesus in one's life. Perhaps some views of salvation border on magic as if in coming to Christ much of the pain and bondage suddenly vanishes.

Demonization of sin. This has been discussed above, but merits emphasis. Whenever practitioners of deliverance ministry readily name demons of emotions, for example, and suggest their eviction solves the problem, there must be a correction. The Sandfords admonished others in deliverance ministry when they wrote, "Such things as anger, lust, greed, hate, fear, envy and jealousy are not demons; they are flesh. And flesh is not to be cast out; it is to be put to death on the cross by repentance."[56] There can be demons attached to sinful emotions, but they are not the root and primary problem.

A "Pelagian" or simplified view of sin. Some will offer this criticism, wherein sin is seen in actions or decisions only and does not address addictions, compulsions, and issues of the will.[57] There is a critical view of listing off occult involvements for example, followed by confession and renunciation. My reply is that those ministering deliverance firmly believe that one's heart and mind must be fully engaged in the confession and prayer, and that the Scriptures definitely teach the incredible importance of confession (Ps. 32:5; 38:18), and God's promise of cleansing from sin upon confession (1 John 1:9). For past occult involvement, it's not a question of a compulsion or addiction but rather of confession and closing any opportunity to the enemy with an intact breastplate of righteousness (Eph. 6:14). Issues of the will, addictions, and more involve the direction of the Holy Spirit and the healing presence of Jesus to transform the human soul and spirit. The power of the cross becomes key in sanctification as part of the ministry of healing prayer.

I can distinctly remember praying with Ted and Alice regarding their marriage. Ted had committed adultery, and Alice was trying to rebuild trust. In my opinion, Ted conveyed a "cavalier" attitude to his sin, saying simply he was sorry and that it will never happen again and that Alice should be able to trust him again. It was clear to me that Ted was just not willing to deal with the deeper background issues in his life. The prayer time ended somewhat inconclusive, and that evening I spent some time interceding for Ted, that he would submit to whatever the Holy Spirit wanted to reveal. About a month later Ted went to a men's conference on sexuality where he was so convicted of his sin that he wept at the altar for almost an hour. It was a major turning point for seriously confronting the deeper issues in his life, and bringing his will more fully under the direction of the Holy Spirit. The elements of deliverance ministry must never be confused with the issues of personal transformation and sanctification and in no way involves a simplistic view of sin or of the human spirit. We must always be on guard for the seductions and rationalizations of sin and never underestimate the power of sin. One of the best realizations to put sin and temptation into stark perspective comes from Lundgaard:

> Let the sorrows of your Saviour on the cross move you. Imagine his cries and groans in your behalf, till your heart breaks. Daydream about how much love he showed you as he hung naked in your place. And see if the baits and lures of the flesh don't grow ugly and repulsive. Will you give your hours to fantasizing about the dwelling on and longing for the vile things that nailed the Lover of your soul to the cursed tree?[58]

The Need for Both Healing and Deliverance

A basic aspect of the ministry of Jesus and his commissioning of the disciples is often overlooked, perhaps because it is so obvious and familiar. Jesus commanded his disciples to *both* heal *and* deliver whenever and wherever required. He did not command some to go and do only healing, and others to go and do only deliverance. He apparently expected the disciples to have the wisdom, anointing, and empowering to do *both together when required*. Notice how Jesus sends out the Seventy-Two and commands them to heal and preach (Luke 10:9), yet upon their return they emphasize how even the demons submit to them in the name of Jesus (Luke 10:17-19).

I began to see all too often that deliverance ministry without healing prayer can lead to minimal fruit in people's lives, or at times, near disastrous results. Conversely, healing prayer without deliverance ministry where required lacks full effectiveness.

Beth was making great progress through healing prayer. Jesus was dealing with much of the pain of her past, and her friends agreed that she was finally experiencing more wholeness. Then a Christian speaker well known in "deliverance ministry" circles came to town. An excited friend of Beth invited her to come. Beth went to the meetings, expecting another touch from the Lord and more wholeness. After a ministry session with Beth wherein the speaker was unable to expel any demons that he was convinced were there, he told her that it was due to her "being rebellious," and until that was dealt with, there would be no more freedom or healing. Beth went home devastated, and after a horrid night, attempted suicide. Fortunately, she ended up in a hospital and was soon stabilized, surrounded by caring friends.

Robert was diagnosed with Bipolar Disorder I and had coped with depression for many years in his life. He had received considerable counseling and psychiatric care, but to no great avail. His ability to remember and discuss things was slowed down due to the impact of many years of psychotropic drugs. As I ministered healing prayer with an assistant, the Lord quickly revealed the roots of his depression and he experienced deep healing from many emotional and spiritual wounds. A few issues of forgiveness and resentment were dealt with along the way. Through the spiritual gift of discernment, I knew there were a numbers of demons that had been operating in his life for at least thirty years. In the name of Jesus, I simply and quietly commanded them to leave this dear brother in Christ. He immediately coughed and felt some pain in his stomach, from where one very strong demon in particular was expelled. Just when this was over, he looked at me and said that no one had ever prayed like this with him. This all took about one hour, and the core of all that happened was experiencing the healing and transforming power of Jesus. The key is to minister healing prayer and deliverance whenever required for the wholeness of the whole person. Just expelling demons, or just healing prayer, or just counsel, or just professional psychiatric intervention is not enough, as was the case for Robert for all those long years. Robert clearly needed both healing prayer and deliverance ministry under the direction of the Holy Spirit. The goal is wholeness or more *shalom* in one's whole being, involving healing and freedom. This made all the difference and was therefore effective in a very short period of time. Sadly, Robert believed and was taught that he was a failure for most of his Christian life. I disagreed with Robert, and said that he was simply a precious child of Jesus that needed more of the love of Jesus. If anything, the church had failed Robert by not offering the ministry of deliverance clearly modeled by Jesus as well as the healing presence of Jesus as demonstrated in the Gospels. How lamentable when one's Christian faith adds condemnation rather than bringing joy and hope! This ministry to Robert was a turning point with lasting results and good fruit in his life. As an added blessing, Robert has been able to stop taking his psychiatric medication under the direction of his psychiatrist, and his mind is beginning to restore itself.

Kraft's analogy of rats and garbage is helpful in relating healing and deliverance where there is a sin issue. Remove the rats alone, and eventually the rats will appear again. Remove the garbage and expel the rats, then the rats will be gone for good, assuming no "new" garbage appears.[59] The garbage stands for any emotional or spiritual wounds, sin, rebellion, and other causes that give authority or permission for the demons. Once that is dealt with according to the healing presence of Jesus and "classical warfare," then one can expel the demons since they no longer have a legal right in the person's life.

Proper ministry then recognizes the need for healing, confession, repentance, deliverance, and all the issues of the soul and spirit. Focusing on deliverance to the exclusion or minimization of other issues must be avoided. Otherwise, people will be short-changed in their journey into wholeness, freedom, and renewal of the mind.

Avoiding Temptation and Pitfalls in Deliverance Ministry

Any ministry can be abused and is subject to temptation. Every ministry must be done in obedience to God the Father and with maturity and wisdom. Having taught deliverance ministry courses in the church, these are some of the more common temptations, excesses, imbalances, and pitfalls that come to mind.

Fascination with evil spirits and powers. When the Seventy-Two came back from their first mission in healing and deliverance, Jesus replied to their excitement with "*... do not rejoice that the evil spirits submit to you, but rejoice that your names are written in heaven*" (Luke 10:20). We must always focus on Jesus and our relationship with *him*. Jesus is the source of our life, authority, and power, all purchased by his blood, and our first fascination should always be with him. When our eyes are taken off Jesus, problems begin. A great temptation is to become more excited or enamored about what we can do for Jesus than what he has done for us. One of the reasons for the rise of the occult is people's fascination with spiritual power, even if it's evil. Our fascination is first and foremost for Jesus and his incredible love for us.

Pride. Once when I was ministering deliverance, it suddenly and unexpectedly became very noisy with the person letting out a loud blood-curdling scream in the church sanctuary and wanting to claw the carpet and me. As I subdued the spirits in the name of Jesus, I looked around to see how many people noticed that I was "so competently" handling the situation. Indeed, I might soon have a reputation as one heavily anointed in this ministry. About a tenth of a second later, the Lord convicted me of my pride. As in all ministries, there is the potential for sin. Pride is the worst sin, being the chief sin of Satan himself.

Focus on power encounters. Deliverance ministry requires encounters as directed by Jesus and his Spirit. Sometimes it is more direct in commanding an evil spirit to leave. On numerous occasions I have seen people suddenly experience sharp pain, massive headaches, numbing of the mind, or difficulty in speaking. In Jesus' name I have directly commanded any evil spirit to stop such effects, and invariably there is sudden relief. But truth and love are also powerful.

John was telling me how powerful he thought Satan was. I agreed that we should never underestimate Satan's power or tactics, but as a created being he is not anything like God. But such statements kept coming during the ministry session. I sensed the Lord wanted me to simply speak forth his powerful names from Scripture, and in a posture of worship declare his utterly powerful and magnificent names and deeds. I did so for about five minutes, right after he confessed and agreed that the Lord alone is mighty and powerful. When I was done, he said that as I spoke he could feel demons leave his mind and his mind began to clear up. Truth can also be a power encounter. Acts of love and compassion can also conquer evil. The goal is the *type of encounter that Jesus expects* for each situation, not our idea of what will happen. We are called to obedience without any "power trip," we must focus on Jesus-directed encounters.

Spiritual technique, formulae, or any hint of magic. I was really concerned when I read in one deliverance ministry training manual the phrase "these prayers always work." That borders on magic. We must never ever divorce our ministry from Jesus (John 6:29). The basis of all we do is faith, hope, obedience, and integrity. Ministry comes out of relationship and belief in Him (Mark 9:29). *Deliverance prayers are models only, built around sound theology not unlike the creeds of the church.* The Holy Spirit way well require at times an addition or elaboration of some part of a deliverance prayer. The basis always is faith and belief. Anyone in deliverance ministry can tell you that demons catch on if you really don't believe. Mockery comes quickly from the enemy. Any hint of using deliverance prayers as some formula apart from abiding in Jesus leads into witchcraft. The essence of witchcraft is non-relational and impersonal spiritual power. Deliverance ministry is not ever spiritual technology.

Seeing demons everywhere. Satan does not have such power, though he has many hordes of demons. When beginning such a ministry there is a tendency to think that demons are causing just about every problem around. This is not the case. When they are encountered they must be dealt with, they do not lurk everywhere. Some people lose sight of the sovereignty of God and almost begin to live in some fear, superstition, or paranoia about Satan. We live in the light and glory of the presence of the living God, Maker of heaven and earth, not in any fear of evil spirits who know their ultimate fate.

Tendency to blame demons. This is the "The devil made me do it" syndrome. On a few occasions I have prayed with people who really wanted a demon to manifest, since if it did, that would then be the source of their problem. It would then be a quick fix since upon casting out a demon their problems would instantly vanish. However, this bypasses the larger issues of sanctification and discipleship.

Focus on the dramatic. There is never any real need for obvious, outward manifestations. The real goal is fruit in the life of a believer, and there is nothing wrong if the Spirit chooses to achieve freedom in a rather quiet but still powerful way. Any desire for "drama" has more to do with Hollywood than Jerusalem. Sometimes a manifestation will occur so that the person will know there really was a demonic presence and thus the need for deliverance. Some deliverance ministers probably want the dramatic encounter to "build their reputation." That is clear spiritual exploitation in using the experience of others for one's own personal gain. I wonder if Jesus walked away from the crowds with some people who were healed or delivered because he wanted it to be personal. As a rule, one should avoid all dramatic manifestations as much as possible so the person being ministered to is not embarrassed or uncomfortable. Even so, Jesus had some very dramatic encounters and they sometimes occur today as well.

Praying against Satan. This is not asking demons for their name and "how they got in" as an aid in ministry. I prefer not to do that, relying on the Spirit to reveal the information and knowing that evil spirits are consistent liars (John 8:44). What I mean here is the temptation to pray against Satan rather than to God.[60] We must focus on the Lord and call upon his power and presence, such that he is invited in his fullness and the powers of darkness must then "scream and run." Praying against demons, principalities, powers, and such diverts us from focusing on any issues of sin and the need for God's presence. We focus on praying in the "positive" such that the "negative" is pushed out and away. The unscriptural practice of the presence of the powers of darkness [61] can actually bring attention from those very powers and invite chaos and harm from them. The very calling upon them invokes their presence, something the people of the Lord should never do. We must never let Satan chose the battleground and be drawn into his evil ways and dialog. As Leanne Payne astutely writes in her chapter entitled *Wrong Ways to Do Battle*:

> One of the strong temptations we must eschew is the enemy's attempt to get us to leave the positive work of the Kingdom. He works toward luring Christians from their creative, proper, redemptive work, and down into battle on his own turf, one charged with his negatives: his accusations, rationale, deceptions, and lies.[62]

Conclusion

Deliverance ministry is a mandate for the church at large. It is an integral part of the Great Commission, alongside the ministry of healing. Many within the Church have challenged and even at times ridiculed those who have practiced the ministry of deliverance. It is well known that the writers of deliverance ministry have been often accused of erroneous or dubious theology. There is one obvious and simple reason for this. The theologians of the Church, to a large degree, have not sufficiently dealt with this topic, especially the practical ministry. As a result, the development of the practical theology was often left up to those "on the front lines." One can very well ask: where were the theologians when those in this ministry needed them? Theology should be for the whole Church, theologians should be servants of the Church.

The Church should be grateful for those who embarked on this ministry in spite of ridicule, misunderstanding, and sometimes scorn and almost slander. I know that those who have finally received their freedom through deliverance are grateful.

This ministry, though abundantly practiced by Jesus and commanded for his church, has been largely overlooked by the church. As Dickason wrote:

> I know of no school of psychiatry or psychology, even of Christian orientation, that gives serious place in the curriculum or training or counseling the demonically oppressed or demonized. I know of only one Christian postgraduate school that recognizes this possibility and has faced it to some degree. Why is this so? First, it is not considered reality or, if recognized at all, a proper domain for their studies. Such education suggests no way to recognize the possibility, to diagnose with certainty, and to treat with any confidence or expertise a case of demonization. If they did, they would be the laughingstock of the professional community, just as evolutionists laugh at creationists. [63]

This is a clear omission. What is more important, professional recognition or obedience to Jesus, the very Lord of Lords and King of Kings? Is this a case of the Church being ashamed of Jesus and his words (Mark 8:38; Luke 9:26)? Has the Church here let go of the commands of God in order to embrace the traditions of men (Mark 7:8)? Jesus admonished the Pharisees concerning their valuing of money with the statement "what is highly valued among men is detestable in God's sight" (Luke 16:15). Might this apply here, where professional reputation and acceptance in the larger academic community is highly valued *at the expense of following Jesus?* I remember asking the president of an evangelical Christian graduate school why deliverance ministry was generally not taught or addressed by theologians. His immediate reply was that they were afraid of the whole topic.

I have not addressed all the issues surrounding the ministry of deliverance. The goal of this chapter is to establish the essential integrity of, and necessity for it. The ministry of deliverance will not stand or fall on what one believes about binding spirits, or familiar spirits, whether one needs to talk to demons, and so forth. Those are details to be worked out by others. This debate has been complicated by critics who have little or no first-hand experience of deliverance ministry or who have focused on its less representative examples.

Some books critical of deliverance ministry give stories of people who were not helped by deliverance ministry, but were helped by classical spiritual warfare or counseling or both, for example. There is an attempt to dispute stories about the "tough cases" where deliverance ministry would be called for. Rather than offer true stories of my own, I will simply say that I have met many Christians who were finally healed and set free, involving deliverance, after many years of *everything but deliverance and healing*. I have prayed with a few Christian men who have had sex with women who turned out to be witches, and came in understandable desperation for release from very real and powerful spiritual forces. I have also prayed with Christians who have survived the horrors of Satanic ritual abuse, the evil of which is virtually beyond comprehension. I simply cannot imagine helping such brothers and sisters in Christ without the healing presence of Jesus, the active gifts of the Spirit, and a clear sense of the place and power of deliverance ministry. I remember a lady testifying at a Deeper Love conference that she had traveled the world for just about every therapy, psychological technique, and all forms of counseling, and in the process spent thousands of dollars, but all to no avail. She knew her spirit needed deep healing and release. Several hours of concentrated healing prayer with some deliverance at the conference proved far more effective with lasting results.

There are all too many Christians who are either deeply wounded, or in bondage, or both. I know, because I have met them and have often heard sad and heartbreaking stories. Christians are meant to be soldiers of the cross with full allegiance to the Lamb. In final response to those who claim that the ministry of deliverance does not take classical spiritual warfare seriously, I reply that Christians are commanded to "be strong in the Lord and in his might power" and be able to "put on the full armor of God" (Eph. 6:10-18). But more Christians are in bondage than we care to admit, and they cannot fully stand as soldiers of the cross. The combined ministry of healing prayer and deliverance seeks to build up Christians so that they can in fact stand and function as strong soldiers of Jesus. I see each church as a local battalion of the body of Christ, with Jesus as the chief commanding officer. Doesn't Jesus expect each church to operate at full battalion strength? This is part of the larger call to wage a war of love to defeat the enemy of death.

I remember a worship service where I was blessed by the worship team as they led in worship. I was almost brought to tears when I realized that almost all the team members had received deep healing and deliverance, and I had the awesome privilege to have a small little part. Considering their stories of deep pain and bondage, they should still be living quiet lives of hidden desperation. Of such are my treasures in heaven.

Endnotes

[1] John H. Armstrong (Gen. Ed.), *The Coming Evangelical Crisis. Current Challenges to the Authority of Scripture and the Gospel* (Chicago: Moody Press, 1996) p.233

[2] Clinton E. Arnold, *3 Crucial Questions About Spiritual Warfare* (Grand Rapids: Baker Books, 1997) p. 80.

[3] Edward F. Murphy, *The Handbook For Spiritual Warfare. Revised and Updated Edition.* (Nashville: Thomas Nelson Publishers, 1996) p. 50.

[4] Murphy, p. 51.

[5] John Loren Sandford and Mark Sandford. *A Comprehensive Guide to Deliverance and Inner Healing* (Grand Rapids, Michigan: Chosen Books, 1992) pp. 28-39.

[6] Francis MacNutt, *Deliverance from Evil Spirits. A Practical Manual* (Grand Rapids: Chosen Books, 1995) p. 73

[7] Peter Masters, *The Healing Epidemic* (London: The Wakeman Trust, Elephant and Castle, 1988) p. 93.

[8] Murphy, p. 431.

[9] C. Fred Dickason, *Demon Possession & the Christian. A New Perspective* (Wheaton: Crossway Books, 1987) p. 40.

[10] Charles H. Kraft, *Defeating Dark Angels. Breaking Demonic Oppression in the Believer's Life.* (Ann Arbor: Vine Books, 1992) p. 66.

[11] Kraft, p. 67.

[12] Arnold, p. 82.

[13] John Bunyan, The Holy War (1678) in G. Offor, (ed.) The Whole Works of John Bunyan, (Grand Rapids: Baker Book House, 1977 reprint) Vol. III, Chapter 13, pp. 330-333.

[14] Armstrong, p. 234.

[15] Dickason, p. 85.

[16] Murphy, p. 271.

[17] Arnold, p. 82.

[18] Frank and Ida Mae Hammond. *Pigs in The Parlor. A Practical Guide To Deliverance* (Kirkwood: Impact Christian Books, 1973) p. 1.

[19] Arnold, p. 91.

[20] Noel and Phyl Gibson, *Deliver Our Children From the Evil One* (Kent: Sovereign World Ltd, 1992) pp. 49-72.

[21] Dickason, p. 169-213.

22 James G. Friesen, *Uncovering the Mystery of MPD* (Eugene, Wipf and Stock Publishers, 1991) pp. 205-287.

23 Arnold, p. 114.

24 Powlison, p. 60.

25 Powlison, p. 61.

26 Masters, p. 109.

27 Powlison, p. 95.

28 Noel and Phyl Gibson, *Evicting Demonic Intruders. Guidelines for Pastors and Counsellors on Ministering Freedom to Oppressed Christians* (Chichester: New Wine Press, 1993) p. 45.

29 Peter J. Horrobin, *Healing Through Deliverance: The Biblical Basis* (Kent: Sovereign World Ltd., 2nd edition,1994) p. 270.

30 Powlison, pp. 94-96.

31 Powlison, p. 91.

32 Powlison, p. 95.

33 Mark A. Pearson, *Christian Healing. A Practical and Comprehensive Guide* (Grand Rapids: Chosen Books, 1995) p. 61.

34 Powlison, p. 91.

35 David Pytches, *Come Holy Spirit. Learning How To Minister In Power* (London: Hodder and Stoughton, 1985) p. 108.

36 Ibid.

37 Powlison, p. 34

38 C.W. Harris, *Resist the Devil. A Pastoral Guide to Deliverance Prayer* (South Bend: Greenlawn Press, 1988) pp. 13-27.

39 Arnold, pp. 107-108.

40 Masters, p. 94.

41 Powlison, p. 148.

42 Masters, pp. 110-111.

43 Francis MacNutt, *Healing* (Notre Dame: Ave Maria Press, 1974) p. 127.

44 Powlison, p. 134.

45 Ibid. p. 134

46 Armstrong, pp. 228, 237-238.

47 Sandford, p. 139.

48 Powlison, p. 135.

49 Powlison, pp. 135-136.

50 Sydney Walker III, A Dose of Sanity. Mind, Medicine, and Misdiagnosis (New York: John Wiley and Sons, 1996) pp. 90-91.

51 Peter J. Horrobin, Healing Through Deliverance. The Practical Ministry (Kent: Sovereign World Ltd., 1995) pp. 57-202.

52 John P. Newport, *Satan and Demons: A Theological Perspective. In John* Warwick Montgomery (ed.), *Demon Possession. A Medical, Historical, Anthropological and Theological Symposium* (Minneapolis: Bethany Fellowship, 1975) pp. 329-330, 343.

53 Walker, p. 13.

54 Walker, p. 38.

55 Armstrong, pp. 233-234.

56 Sandfords, p. 40.

57 Powlison, pp. 122-123.

58 Kris Lundgaard, *The Enemy Within. Straight Talk About The Power And Defeat of Sin* (Phillipsburg: P&R Publishing, 1998) p. 97.

59 Charles H. Kraft, Deep *Wounds Deep Healing: Discovering the Vital Link Between Spiritual Warfare and Inner Healing* (Ann Arbor: Vine Books, 1993) p. 45.

60 Leanne Payne, Restoring *The Christian Soul Through Healing Prayer. Overcoming the Three Great Barriers to Personal and Spiritual Completion in Christ* (Wheaton: Crossway Books, 1991) p. 208.

61 Payne, p. 208.

62 Payne, p. 202.

63 Dickason, p. 312.

Chapter Nine

Conclusion

Theological Schizophrenia

The ministry of wholeness as healing and deliverance is an integral and inescapable part of the Great Commission. A simple reading of the Gospels shows that Jesus devoted much of his time to healing and deliverance, alongside preaching and teaching. Just as the disciples patterned their ministry after Jesus, so must the Church today. This requires, among other things, the empowering of the Holy Spirit. The Church should use God's spiritual resources to accomplish God's commission and commands. Specifically, this will include the full use of all the spiritual gifts. As I have shown, none of the spiritual gifts ever ceased or vanished from the apostolic era. God in his sovereignty has not allowed any of his authentic gifts to cease while allowing Satan to deceive the world with counterfeit gifts. This is especially important in a postmodern world strongly embracing New Age beliefs and practices.

While healing and deliverance was clearly and obviously important to Jesus, it hasn't been terribly important to much of the

Church and most theologians. In a comprehensive survey of 150 recent theologians, *not one* took seriously the theology of healing prayer.[1] Except for Pentecostal seminaries, less than six of the hundreds of Christian seminaries offer courses in spiritual healing and in most seminaries the subject is *dismissed with scorn*.[2] The practical theology of deliverance ministry has been given even less attention than healing. As a result, many pastors are not trained in the theology and practice of healing and deliverance due to the obvious fact that it is not emphasized in seminary or Bible colleges because theologians have not been terribly interested. While thankfully this is beginning to change, much must be done to reflect the priorities of Jesus. While one might argue that counseling responds to these needs, it must be realized that *counseling is not the same as healing prayer*. Strictly speaking, Jesus did not say "Go and counsel," but he did say "Go and heal and deliver." There is a vital difference, with all due respects to the benefits of good and godly counsel. Healing prayer is different from both counseling and spiritual direction. Payne stated it well:

> Healing prayer is not the "instant fix," nor the bypassing of slow and steady growth. It is that which clears the path and makes such progress possible. It is the appropriation of the power given us at Pentecost—power having to do with God's Presence with us, issuing forth through us quietly, unobtrusively, or, at times, dramatically, to the healing of persons.[3]

It is disconcerting that so much is done in Church life and practice from little if any direct biblical basis yet when the issue of healing prayer and deliverance comes up, many will suddenly argue that we should do only what has a clear biblical basis. For example, Armstrong wrote concerning deliverance ministry "If we cannot be theologically precise and if the text is not conclusive at all, why build so much practice on what we have so little explicit biblical basis for in the first place?"[4] This is a good question, putting aside issues of excesses and imbalances in ministry. But why then stop at deliverance ministry? Why not apply this uniformly to all of church life and practice?

To me this is a double standard, sort of like a theological schizophrenia, given that much occurs in Church life without clear and direct biblical basis. Consider the following. The order of worship came from Pope Gregory around A.D. 500 and has evolved ever since in both Protestant and Catholic churches, yet it is not based on Scripture and may even contradict it (1 Cor. 14:26).[5] Sermons tend to follow the tradition of Chrysostom who introduced Christian oratory based on Graeco-Roman rhetoric, but which is not ever the same as how the prophets and apostles spoke.[6] Paul came to Corinth in weakness, fear, and spoke not with wise or persuasive words (1 Cor. 2:3). Apparently the 11th hour for worship is attributed to Martin Luther who in later years preferred more time to recover from visiting the pub the night before.[7] Church buildings were not a part of the Christian faith until after the time of Constantine in A.D. 323.[8] The early church for the first three hundred years was a house church movement with explosive growth amidst persecution. Having led a house group for several years, I know the blessings and strategic importance of house groups. The Christian faith was the first religion that did not use temples for worship; rather the believers are the church and temples of the Holy Spirit—a totally revolutionary development! While apart from the "edifice complex" we can agree to some advantages of church buildings, no one can disagree that this is not even a minor interest of the New Testament. Although Sunday School has been a blessing to many and the church survived without it for many centuries, it is not a Scriptural mandate given that parents are to instruct their children in the faith. In brief, all the following have little or no basis in Scripture and came after Constantine: church buildings, church names, pews, the 11 a.m. starting time, stained glass windows, high vaulted ceilings, liturgies and rituals in church worship, costumed clergy, seminaries, children named after "saints," denominations, funerals, the modern pastoral concept.[9] If all the foregoing is allowed, with such little biblical basis, then why omit the ministry of healing and deliverance which has such a strong biblical basis and Jesus himself modeled? If the types of arguments used against healing, deliverance, and the full use of spiritual gifts were also applied consistently against the foregoing, none of the foregoing would be allowed today.

I am not arguing that unless something is clearly indicated in the Scriptures it is not done, for that would lead to a rather barren, closed, and negative view of life. The goal is to develop the mind of Christ in each situation and apply biblical principles to modern life since the Scriptures do not intend to address all situations and concerns directly. I do argue, though, that different thinking should not be suddenly applied to the ministry of healing and deliverance.

It is ironic that *opposition* to the ministry of healing and deliverance and the use of all the spiritual gifts has come from within the Church itself. More ironic still is the fact that the opposition often comes in the name of biblical orthodoxy and commitment to the Word of God. The issues have been both confused and confounded with personal motives and feelings, examples of immature or unbalanced ministry in healing and deliverance and the use of spiritual gifts, cultural and denominational bias, inconsistent hermeneutics, flawed reasoning, and many critical but unstated background assumptions. When all the foregoing has been accounted for, the simple and clear commands of Jesus still stand for today: preach, heal, and deliver.

The commands of Jesus to preach, heal and deliver are incredibly and increasingly relevant today. Healing, wholeness, and spirituality are on people's minds like never before. New Age healing practices proliferate and their books are rapidly filling up bookstores. The void and need for healing the whole person is being addressed by practices like Reiki, chakra healing, pranic healing, angelic healing, Chi Gong, Therapeutic Touch, energy healing, crystal work, aura cleansing, and much more. While some might argue that this is a sign of the "end times," the church cannot escape responsibility for not sufficiently demonstrating the saving and healing power of Jesus. There are many wounded and lost people who would consider darkening the doors of a church (or better, a neighborhood house church) if they knew they would have a real spiritual experience and possibly spiritual healing. A key criticism that un-churched Americans have of the church is that spiritual depth and experience is lacking.[10] In the UK from 1978 to 1989, the Anglican Church lost 10 percent of its membership, the Methodist 11 percent, Roman Catholic 14 percent, and United Reformed 18 percent, with similar trends in North America.[11] Why? A failure to meet the deepest spiritual needs of people, including healing.[12]

Desperate Searches For Inner Peace and Spiritual Reality

Some years ago I happened to meet Laura, a very enthusiastic and joyful lady. I decided to ask Laura the basis of her joy, wondering if she might be a Christian. She immediately replied that ever since she got her spirit guide, she has been happy and secure in life. That gave me an instant chill. I asked her how this came about. She explained that when she was young, her parents were totally turned off by their church experiences—too much politics, too little relevance, and little spiritual reality. As a family, they simply stopped going to church and eventually developed a fascination for the New Age. She began a search for spiritual meaning and fulfillment, and ended up inviting a spirit guide into her life. She told me that this spirit guide had given her so much direction and inner peace. She shared with me a number of "miracles" that she attributed to her spirit guide. The details and events were quite astounding in themselves. Yes, it was she and her parent's decisions to leave the church, but is the church really blameless in all this?

Elinor Ellsworth was a longtime lieutenant of the famous New Age teacher and author, Marianne Williamson. Elinor went through EST, Nichiren-chanting, aura cleansing, crystal workshops, gurus, and A Course In Miracles in order to fill a spiritual void in her life and healing from pain, guilt, despair, anger, shame, and a series of broken relationships.[13] Notably, Elinor comes from a New England family directly descended from the famous Puritan preacher and revivalist, Johnathan Edwards. But by her generation, the family's loss of the true presence of God led her to agnosticism and cynicism towards the Christian faith.[14] Fortunately, through a faithful church and a Bible study on Romans, Ellie experienced the power of the gospel and the transforming presence of Jesus.

I have met other people like Laura with "miraculous" stories and experiences of spiritual realities. What alarms me more are professed Christians who once were part of conservative and evangelical churches and have left the church and are now involved in New Age practices. Christian youth are not immune from this either. This is in addition to Christians who seek out

New Age healing in some desperation. I concur with Pearson when he wrote:

> I have met many people who have gotten involved in dubious or even dangerous groups because their own churches have left them spiritually starving. I have met many who have gone to occultic healing services because their churches neglect or even refuse to have services of Christian healing.[15]

The Great Substitution

There are at least four major consequences of the Great Omission. First is the needless suffering, pain and bondage of many in the body of Christ. As I and others in this ministry pray with fellow Christians, we are continually reminded that there is much deep pain and woundedness among Christians. Whatever we do to the least in our midst, we do as unto Christ (Matt. 25:40), and I see no reason why that would not include healing. Secondly, there will be a whole new set of problems as Christians seek healing from New Age practices due to the disinterest and void in their church. Thirdly, many outside of the Church will never come to the Church, or won't stay long if they do, due to the spiritual vacuum. Fourthly, there is the disfavor of Jesus by not having obeyed his commands in this part of the Great Commission.

Due to the Great Omission, much of the Church is now not equipped to offer the true healing and delivering presence of Jesus. Thankfully, this is changing. Could it be that the Church has been out-maneuvered by Satan? What is Satan's next strategy? The Great Omission and its consequences is only part of the story. What's even more critical will be addressed in my forthcoming book, *The Great Substitution*.

Endnotes

[1] Morton Kelsey, *Healing and Christianity: A Classic Study* (Minneapolis: Augsburg Press, 1993) p. 265.

[2] Kelsey, p. 3.

[3] Leanne Payne, *The Healing Presence. How God's Grace Can Work in You to Bring Healing in Your Broken Places and the Joy of Living in His Love* (Wheaton: Crossway Books, 1989) p. 55.

[4] John H. Armstrong (Gen. Ed.), *The Coming Evangelical Crisis. Current Challenges to the Authority of Scripture and the Gospel* (Chicago: Moody Press, 1996) p.233

[5] James H. Rutz, *The Open Church. How to Bring Back the Exciting Life of the First Century Church.* (Beaumont: Texas, 1992) p. 49.

[6] Rutz, p. 50.

[7] Rutz, p. 60.

[8] Rutz, p. 55.

[9] Rutz, p. 3

[10] Rutz, p. 73.

[11] Tom Harpur, *The Uncommon Touch: An Investigation of Spiritual Healing* (Toronto: McClelland & Stewart, 1994) p. 217.

[12] Harpur, p. 217-218.

[13] Tony Carnes, *"Leaving Marianne Williamson & A Course In Miracles. An Insider Converts,"* Spiritual Counterfeits Project Journal 1998, 22:2-22:3, pp. 18-33.

[14] Carnes, p. 20.

[15] Mark A. Pearson, *Christian Healing. A Practical and Comprehensive Guide* (Grand Rapids: Chosen Books, 1995) p. 184.

 Bibliography

Armstrong, John. H., editor. *The Coming Evangelical Crisis: Current Challenges To The Authority of Scripture and the Gospel.* Chicago: Moody Press, 1996.

Arnold, Clinton E. *3 Crucial Questions About Spiritual Warfare.* Grand Rapids: Baker Books, 1997.

Barker, G.W., Lane, W.L., and J.R. Michaels, *The New Testament Speaks.* New York: Harper and Row, 1969.

Benner, David G. *Care of Souls. Revisioning Christian Nurture and Counsel.* Grand Rapids: Baker Books, 1998.

Berkhof, Louis. *Systematic Theology.* Grand Rapids: Eerdmans, 1939, Fifteenth printing, 1977.

Bloesch, Donald G. A *Theology of Word & Spirit. Authority & Method in Theology.* Downers Grove: InterVarsity Press, 1992.

Blue, Ken. *Authority to Heal.* Downer's Grove: InterVarsity Press, 1987.

Blue, Ken. *Healing Spiritual Abuse. How To Break Free from Bad Church Experiences.* Downers Grove: InterVarsity Press, 1993.

Bockmuehl, Klaus. *Listening to the God Who Speaks.* Colorado Springs: Helmers & Howard, 1990.

Breggin, Peter R., and D. Cohen. *Your Drug May Be Your Problem. How And Why To Stop Taking Psychiatric Medications.* Cambridge: Perseus Publishing, 1999.

Brown, Colin. *The New International Dictionary of New Testament Theology.* Grand Rapids: Zondervan, 1978.

Bruce, F.F. *The New Testament Documents: Are They Reliable?* Downers Grove: InterVarsity Press, 1960.

Bruce, F.F. *The Book of the Acts. Revised Edition.* The New International Commentary on the New Testament. Grand Rapids: Eerdmans, 1988.

Bush, L. *"Where Are We Now?" Evaluating Progress on the Great Commission,* Mission Frontiers, June 200, Vol. 22:3.

Carnes, Tony. *"Leaving Marianne Williamson & A Course In Miracles. An Insider Converts,"* Spiritual Counterfeits Project Journal 1998, 22:2-22:3.

Cherry, Reginald. *Healing Prayer. God's Divine Intervention In Medicine, Faith, and Prayer.* Nashville: Thomas Nelson, 1999.

Dalby, Gordon. *Healing The Masculine Soul.* Milton Keynes: Word Publishing, 1988.

De Arteaga, William. *Quenching The Spirit: Discover the REAL Spirit Behind the Charismatic Controversy.* Orlando: Creation House, 1996.

Deere, Jack. *Surprised By The Power Of The Spirit.* Grand Rapids: Zondervan Publishing House, 1993.

Dickason, C. Fred. *Demon Possession & the Christian.* A New Perspective. Wheaton: Crossway Books, 1987.

Dumbrell, William J. *The Search for Order. Biblical Eschatology In Focus.* Grand Rapids: Baker Books, 1994.

Dunkerley, Don. *Healing Evangelism: Strengthen Your Witnessing with Effective Prayer for the Sick.* Grand Rapids: Chosen Books, 1995.

Edgar, Thomas R. *The Miraculous Gifts: Are They For Today?* (New Jersey: Neptune, Loizeaux Brothers, 1983.

Edwards, Brian H. *Revival! A People Saturated With God.* Darlington: Evangelical Press, 1990.

Fee, Gordon D. *The First Epistle To The Corinthians.* The New International Commentary on the New Testament. Grand Rapids: Eerdmans, 1987.

Fee, Gordon D. *God's Empowering Presence. The Holy Spirit In The Letters Of Paul.* Peabody: Hendrickson Publishers, 1994.

Ferder, Fran. *Words Made Flesh. Scripture, Psychology and Human Communication.* Notre Dame: Ave Maria Press, 1986.

Foster, Richard J. *Prayer: Finding The Heart's True Home.* San Francisco, Harper, 1992.

Friesen, James G. *Uncovering the Mystery of MPD.* Eugene, Wipf and Stock Publishers, 1991.

Geldenhuys, Norval. *The Gospel of Luke. The New International Commentary on the New Testament.* Grand Rapids: Eerdmans, 1951.

Gibson, Noel and Phyl. *Deliver Our Children From the Evil One.* Kent: Sovereign World Ltd, 1992.

Gibson, Noel and Phyl. *Evicting Demonic Intruders. Guidelines for Pastors and Counsellors on Ministering Freedom to Oppressed Christians.* Chichester: New Wine Press, 1993.

Grudem, Wayne A., editor. *Are The Miraculous Gifts For Today?* Grand Rapids: Zondervan, 1996.

Gumprecht, Jane. *Abusing Memory: The Healing Theology of Agnes Sanford.* Moscow: Canon Press, 1997.

Hammond, Frank and Ida Mae. *Pigs in The Parlor. A Practical Guide To Deliverance.* Kirkwood: Impact Christian Books, 1973.

Harpur, Tom. *The Uncommon Touch: An Investigation of Spiritual Healing.* Toronto: McClelland & Stewart, 1994.

Harris, C.W. *Resist the Devil. A Pastoral Guide to Deliverance Prayer.* South Bend: Greenlawn Press, 1988.

Hoffman, Bengt R. *Luther and the Mystics. A re-examination of Luther's spiritual experience and his relationship to the mystics.* Minneapolis: Augsburg Publishing House, 1976.

Horrobin, Peter J. *Healing Through Deliverance: The Biblical Basis.* Kent: Sovereign World Ltd., 2nd edition, 1994.

Horrobin, Peter J. *Healing Through Deliverance. The Practical Ministry.* Kent: Sovereign World Ltd., 1995.

Houston, James. *The Transforming Friendship. A Guide to Prayer. Batavia*: Lion Publishing, 1989.

Hart, Thomas N. *The Art of Christian Listening.* New York: Paulist Press, 1980.

Jekel, James F. "Biblical Foundations for Health and Healing," Journal of the American Scientific Affiliation, Vol. 47(3), 1995.

Johnson, David and Jeff VanVonderen. *The Subtle Power of Spiritual Abuse.* Minneapolis: Bethany House Publishers, 1991.

Kelsey, Morton. *Encounter With God. A Theology of Christian Experience.* Minnesota: Bethany Fellowship, 1972.

Kelsey, Morton. *Healing and Christianity: A Classic Study.* Minneapolis: Augsburg Press, 1993.

Koch, Kurt E. *Christian Counseling and Occultism. A Complete Guidebook to Occult Oppression and Deliverance.* 21st edition. Grand Rapids: Kregel Resources, 1994.

Kraft, Charles H. *Christianity with Power. Your World view and Your Experience of the Supernatural.* Ann Arbor: Servant Books, 1989.

Kraft, Charles H. *Defeating Dark Angels. Breaking Demonic Oppression in the Believer's Life.* Ann Arbor: Vine Books, 1992.

Kraft, Charles H. *Deep Wounds Deep Healing: Discovering the Vital Link Between Spiritual Warfare and Inner Healing.* Ann Arbor: Vine Books, 1993.

Kydd, Ronald A.N. *Healing through the Centuries. Models for Understanding.* Peabody: Hendrickson Publishers, 1998.

Ladd, George E. *The New Testament and Criticism.* Grand Rapids: Eerdmans, 1967.

Ladd, George E. A *Theology Of The New Testament.* Grand Rapids: Eerdmans, 1974.

Latourette, Kenneth S. *A History of Christianity. Vol.I: to A.D. 1500.* New York: Harper and Row, 1975.

Lundgaard, Kris. *The Enemy Within. Straight Talk About The Power And Defeat of Sin.* Phillipsburg: P&R Publishing, 1998.

MacArthur, John F., Jr. *Charismatic Chaos.* Grand Rapids: Zondervan, 1992.

MacNutt, Francis. *Healing.* Notre Dame: Ave Maria Press, 1974.

MacNutt, Francis. *The Power To Heal.* Notre Dame: Ave Maria Press, 1977.

MacNutt, Francis. *Deliverance from Evil Spirits. A Practical Manual.* Grand Rapids: Chosen Books, 1995.

Martinez, Julia C. *"Owens signs faith-healing bill,"* Denver Post Capital Bureau, www.denverpost.com, 17 April 2001.

Masters, Peter. *The Healing Epidemic.* London: The Wakeman Trust, 1988.

Matthews, Dale A., with Connie Clark. *The Faith Factor. Proof of the Healing Power of Prayer.* New York: Viking, 1998.

McGrath, Alister. *Suffering & God.* Grand Rapids: Zondervan, 1992.

McIntyre, Valerie J. *Sheep in Wolves' Clothing. How Unseen Need Destroys Friendship & Community And What to Do About It.* c/o P.C.M., Box 720, Warrenville, IL 60555: Hamewith Books, 1996.

McNeil, J.T. (ed.) *Calvin: Institutes of the Christian Religion. The Library of Christian Classics, Volume XXI, Book IV.* Philadelphia: Westminster Press, 1975.

Milne, Bruce. *The Message of John. Here is your King!* Downer's Grove: InterVarsity Press, 1993.

Moberg, David O. *"The Great Commission and Research,"* The Journal of the American Scientific Affiliation. Vol. 51(1), 1999.

Montgomery, John Warwick, editor. *Demon Possession. A Medical, Historical, Anthropological and Theological Symposium.* Minneapolis: Bethany Fellowship, 1975.

Morris, Leon. *The Gospel According to John. Revised edition. The New International Commentary on the New Testament.* Grand Rapids: Eerdmans, 1995.

Mulholland, M. Robert, Jr. *Shaped by the Word. The Power of Scripture in Spiritual Formation.* Nashville: Upper Room, 1985.

Murphy, Edward F. *The Handbook For Spiritual Warfare*. Revised and Updated Edition. Nashville: Thomas Nelson Publishers, 1996.

Murray, Andrew. *Divine Healing*. New Kensington: Whitaker House, 1982.

Musselman, Lytton John. "*Solomon's Plant Life: Plant Lore and Image in the Solomonic Writings,*" Journal of the American Scientific Affiliation, Vol. 51, 1999.

Noll, Mark A. *The Scandal of the Evangelical Mind*. Grand Rapids:Eerdmans, 1994.

Offor, G. (ed.) *The Whole Works of John Bunyan*. Grand Rapids: Baker Book House, 1977 reprint.

Ogden, G. *The New Reformation. Returning The Ministry To The People Of God*. Grand Rapids: Zondervan, 1990.

Oswalt, John N. *The Book of Isaiah Chapters 1-39. The New International Commentary on the Old Testament*. Grand Rapids: Eerdmans, 1986.

Packer, James I. *Rediscovering Holiness*. Ann Arbor: Vine Books, 1992.

Page, Sydney H.T. *Powers of Evil. A Biblical Study of Satan & Demons*. Grand Rapids: Baker Books, 1995.

Payne, Leanne. *The Healing Presence. How God's Grace Can Work In You to Bring Healing in Your Broken Places and the Joy of Living in His Love*. Wheaton: Crossway Books, 1989.

Payne, Leanne. *Restoring The Christian Soul Through Healing Prayer. Overcoming the Three Great Barriers to Personal and Spiritual Completion in Christ*. Wheaton: Crossway Books, 1991.

Payne, Leanne. *Listening Prayer. Learning to Hear God's Voice and Keep a Prayer Journal*. Grand Rapids: Hamewith Books, 1994.

Pearson, Mark A. *Christian Healing. A Practical and Comprehensive Guide.* Grand Rapids: Chosen Books, 1995.

Pink, Arthur W. *The Holy Spirit.* Grand Rapids: Baker Book House, 1970.

Pinnock, Clark H. *Flame Of Love. A Theology Of The Holy Spirit.* Downers Grove: InterVarsity Press, 1996.

Posterski, Don and G. Nelson, *Future Faith Churches: Reconnecting With The Power Of The Gospel For The 21st Century.* Winfield: Wood Lake Books, 1995.

Powlison, David. *Power Encounters. Reclaiming Spiritual Warfare.* Grand Rapids: Baker Books, 1995.

Puskas, C.B. *An Introduction to the New Testament.* Peabody: Hendrickson Publishers, 1992.

Pytches, David . *Come Holy Spirit: Learning How To Minister In Power,* 2nd ed. London: Hodder & Stoughton, 1995.

Pytches, Mary. *Dying to Change. An Exposure of the Self-Protecting Strategies Which Prevent Us Becoming Like Jesus.* London: Hodder and Stoughton, 1996.

Rajendran, K. *"The Great Commission Roundtable: One More Step Towards De-fragmentation,"* Mission Frontiers, Vol. 22:3, June 200.

Rinck, Margaret J. *Christian Men Who Hate Women.* Grand Rapids: Zondervan, 1990.

Ruthven, Jon. *On the Cessation of the Charismata: The Protestant Polemic on Postbiblical Miracles.* Sheffield: Sheffield Academic Press. 1993.

Rutz, James H. *The Open Church. How to Bring Back the Exciting Life of the First Century Church.* Beaumont: Texas, 1992.

Sandford, John Loren and Mark Sandford. *A Comprehensive Guide to Deliverance and Inner Healing.* Grand Rapids, Michigan: Chosen Books, 1992.

Sanford, John A. *Healing Body & Soul. The Meaning of Illness in the New Testament and in Psychotherapy.* Louisville: John Knox Press, 1992.

Smail, Thomas A. *The Forgotten Father.* Vancouver: Regent College Bookstore, 1995, reprint and first printing. First published by Hodder and Stoughton, 1980.

Stott, John R. W. *Christian Mission in the Modern World.* Downer's Grove: InterVarsity Press.

Swindoll, Charles. *The Grace Awakening.* Dallas: Word Publishing, 1990.

Van Gemeren, Willem A., editor. *The New International Dictionary of Old Testament Theology & Exegesis.* Grand Rapids: Zondervan, 1995.

Walker, Sydney, III. *A Dose of Sanity. Mind, Medicine, and Misdiagnosis.* New York: John Wiley and Sons, 1996.

Warfield, Benjamin B. *Counterfeit Miracles.* Scribner's, 1918, republished as *Miracles: Yesterday and Today, True and False.* Grand Rapids: Eerdmans, 1965.

Wilkinson, John. *The Bible and Healing. A Medical and Theological Commentary.* Grand Rapids: Eerdmans, 1998.

Willard, Dallas. *The Spirit of the Disciplines. Understanding How God Changes Lives.* New York: New York, 1991.

Williams, Redmond and Virginia. *Anger Kills.* New York: Harper Paperbacks, 1993.

Wimber, John and Ken Springer, *Power Healing.* San Francisco: Harper, 1987.

About the Author

Dieter K. Mulitze, Ph.D., completed graduate theological studies at Regent College, British Columbia, and a doctorate in quantitative genetics from the University of Saskatchewan. Dieter worked as a scientist at an international agricultural research center (ICARDA) in Syria and then was an assistant/associate professor of agronomy with the University of Nebraska while working in Morocco. Upon returning to Canada, Dieter founded a computer software company.

Responding to God's call, Dieter has become increasingly involved in the ministry of healing prayer and deliverance. He serves on a healing prayer team in the local church and has conducted training courses and seminars on healing prayer and deliverance. In 1998, with Rev. Carsten Pellmann and Rev. Dietrich Desmarais and their wives, Dieter co-founded Deeper Love Ministries, Inc., a ministry for advancing spiritual wholeness, healing and growth in individuals, based on the model and ministry of Jesus Christ. Dieter is the president of Deeper Love Ministries, and he and his wife, Ellen, are the Spiritual Directors of Ministry Development. Deeper Love Ministries conducts healing prayer conferences in the local church. To contact the author, e-mail dieter@deeperlove.ca, or visit the ministry web site at www.deeperlove.ca. Dieter and his wife Ellen, and daughter Karissa, live in Winnipeg, Manitoba.